RED GENES, BLUE GENES

EXPOSING
POLITICAL
IRRATIONALITY

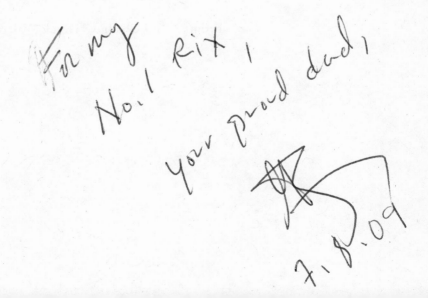

With a change in government no change in the cricket's chirrup,
the low, comical bellow of the bull, or
the astonishing symmetry of tossing horses.
With a change in government the haze of wide rain
which you begin to hear as the ruler hears the crowd
gathering under the balcony, the leader who has promised
the permanent cobalt of a change in government
with the lilac and violet of his cabinet change.

From "A Sea Change," Derek Walcott

RED GENES, BLUE GENES

EXPOSING
POLITICAL
IRRATIONALITY

GUILLERMO C. JIMÉNEZ

AUTONOMEDIA

Autonomedia
POB 568 Williamsburgh Station
Brooklyn, New York 11211-0568 USA

info@autonomedia.org
www.autonomedia.org

Printed in Canada

TABLE OF CONTENTS

PREFACE AND ACKNOWLEDGEMENTS

This book started out as a guide for the politically perplexed — specifically, me. I wanted to understand why the realm of politics is so full of sound and fury and why political conflict is so often intractable.

I was somewhat amazed to find answers to my questions. Over the past 50 years, modern science has made huge progress in understanding human social and political interaction. Sadly, these insights are not widely discussed outside of universities, and they seem to have made no impact whatever on our popular political discourse, which remains for the most part shallow and manipulative.

Insights from evolutionary biology, cognitive psychology and other disciplines now allow us to understand why people so often seem to act irrationally when it comes to politics. These insights may allow us to develop better systems of government — systems which are less polarized and more democratic.

Human suffering persists today on a colossal scale. Government is certainly not the only means we have for fighting suffering, but it is one of our most important. Government failure and inefficiency can have a huge toll in terms of human suffering (witness the aftermath of Hurricane Katrina in New Orleans). This book is dedicated to the hope that we can reduce human suffering by fighting political irrationality.

I wanted in this book to pay homage to the great collaborative effort of biology, psychology and the social sciences to the understanding of human nature. Although the academics who have influenced my thinking are too numerous to note here (see References), I would like to draw special attention to the work of Daniel Kahneman, Amos Tversky, John Hibbing, Elizabeth Theiss-Morse, John Alford, Carolyn Funk, Michael Fowler, Frans de Waal, Ellen Langer, Drew Westen, Bryan Caplan, Paul H. Rubin, George Lakoff, Michael Huemer, Cass Sunstein, Philip Tetlock, Morris Fiorina, Samuel Abrams, Robert Trivers, Susan Blackmore, E. O. Wilson, Louann Brizendine, David Buss, Robert Cialdini,

Geert Hofstede, Robert Levine, Robert Sapolsky, David Sloan Wilson, Jonathan Haidt, Nolan McCarty, James Fishkin, Ned Crosby, Robert Gastil, George E. Marcus, Martha Stout, John Matsusaka and Kevin O'Leary. Gratitude to Bert Hölldobler for teaching such a wonderful introductory class on evolutionary biology at Harvard, and to my great legal teachers, Stefan Riesenfeld and Richard Buxbaum of Cal-Berkeley, Roy Goode of Oxford, Jan Ramberg of the University of Göteborg, and Fabio Bortolotti of the University of Torino.

Aside from my academic influences, I would also like to thank the friends and family who have shaped not only my political thinking, but my way of being. Special thanks to my high school English teacher, Christian Smith, who first encouraged me in the craft of making sentences, and who was still encouraging me decades later on this project. Thanks for their endurance and patience to my family, my wife Consuelo and sons Nico and Pablo. Thanks for their support to my parents, Cesar and Virginia, my brothers and sisters, Edward, Pilar, Rosa, Lilia, Licha, Beatriz and Cesarito. Thanks to all the friends and mentors with whom I've argued politics and philosophy over the past thirty years, Frank Konstantynowicz, Michael and Mary Barbara Alexander, Paul Bloom, Brett Obermann, Gary Monzon, Mark Worrell, Dave Jaffe, Ron Ortiz, Glen Hayes, Ian Marshall, Clarke Parker, Ramsay Al-Salam, Carlos Guerra, Glenn Terrones, Ed Gonzalez, Steve Young, David Lewis, Kenny Walton, Terence Kenny, Alberto Rosa, Michael Pollack, Bowman Hastie, Carlos Moreno, Albert, Chris and Bruno Karoly, Thomas and Felix Legrand, Dominique Foray, Azouz Begag, Wendy and Joyce Klemperer, Oliver Keserue and Francois-Gabriel Ceyrac.

For comments on the manuscript thanks especially to Gene Stone and Mark Goldblatt. Finally, thanks to my indefatigable and erudite publisher and editor, Jim Fleming.

Brooklyn, New York
April 2009

CHAPTER 1

The New Science of Political Irrationality

> Nowhere are prejudices more mistaken
> for truth, passion for reason, and invec-
> tive for documentation than in politics.
> — John Mason Brown, *Through These Men*

DARK TRUTH #1
*Most of us like to think that we come to our political
opinions as the result of calm, reasoned reflection, and not as the
result of instinctive, irrational, or emotional bias.
Most of the time, we're wrong.*

The Importance of Watching TV

I used to spend too much time watching the Sunday-morning political talk shows on TV. In particular, for one long campaign season, I joined the ranks of the political junkies. After living in France for a dozen years I had returned to the U.S. in the fall of 1998, just as the 2000 presidential campaign was getting under way. The boiling partisanship that had emerged during President Clinton's impeachment trial puzzled me, as it did much of the nation. I looked on this strange American political landscape with the renewed and heightened interest of an outsider.

During that time I would get up early on Sunday mornings (early for me being a little after 10 a.m.) to watch the Democratic "talking heads" debate their Republican counterparts. The talking heads talked and talked, until about noon, but I soon came to see that nothing was ever clarified or resolved, no matter how much yammering got done. A typical example was the popular "McLaughlin Report." Here, the supposedly neutral announcer orchestrated nothing more than competing rants. No one seemed to be listening to anyone else. These political debates might as well have been conducted in different languages, so great was the lack of mutual comprehension or dialogue. As opposed to the stylish debates I had seen in France, which placed great value on verbal fencing and required the participants to think on their feet, these American free-for-alls often seemed more like teen-age mud-splashing contests.

And yet there I was, every weekend, watching them. Which led me to ask myself, why? Why do I derive enjoyment from watching this political version of professional wrestling? And what does this reveal about the state of politics in America?

These were important and difficult questions...so I watched more TV. One day, I felt I achieved a sort of breakthrough epiphany. I was watching Senator Orrin Hatch on a particular talk show. I was marveling at the Senator's hair, which had clearly been cut by a very conservative, Christian barber. Hatch's grizzled locks had been beaten into submission and then molded into a chipper little helmet of gray *gravitas*.

His white collar was so stiff it seemed made of starch. I forget what the Senator was talking about, but I will never forget his stern demeanor. He had the narrow-eyed expression of the small-town pharmacist who suspects the kid in the leather jacket is shoplifting comic books. Hatch was debating something with another politico, a wooly-headed Democrat from out West. I could sort of understand what the Democrat was saying, but I could not comprehend Hatch at all. He seemed to be spouting nothing but absurdities, although he did so with a convincing arrogance.

It suddenly occurred to me, as I marveled at Hatch's words, and to a lesser extent, hair: these people, these Republicans, they must be from a different species. Just look at their hair. They may even be from a different planet. All I know is — they are not like us. I remembered the title of John Gray's popular marital psychology book, *Men are from Mars, Women are from Venus*. That's right, I thought. In a very real way, Republicans are from Mars, Democrats are from Venus.

As I watched the Utah Senator, I realized that there was something about his very essence that repelled me to the marrow of my bones. It wasn't just what the man said, it wasn't just his hair, it was everything about him. I was annoyed by his dress, his accent, his collar, his facial expression. On the deepest levels I rejected him. My DNA recoiled at his DNA.

Any reader with a knowledge of American politics will have been able to deduce from the above that I am probably a liberal, ideologically speaking. In fact, I grew up in a family which tilted toward the far-left Democratic side of the political spectrum, while the Utah Senator is well-known to tilt toward the other extreme.

I stopped observing Hatch and started observing myself (I'm not sure why — perhaps there was a commercial break). In all fairness to the conservative Senator, I had to admit that my reaction was too excessive to be based purely on his politics. I really did not know that much about Hatch, so my reaction had to be emotional rather than logical. If my reaction to the Republican Senator were that visceral, I felt I had to allow that the reactions of Republicans to Democrats should be equally so. "It's only fair," I mused, "They get to hate us as much as we hate them."

I wondered whether I had a Republican *döppelganger* — like a long-lost twin, a person like me in every way except conservative — somewhere out there across the heartland, watching the same television show, but expressing sentiments exactly the opposite of mine:

"Who the heck is that crazy Democrat? That boy can't even comb his own damn hair — how does he expect to run the country?"

I sensed that if I were ever to meet Hatch face-to-face there would be little that we could agree upon. There was something about watching Hatch that reminded me of unpleasant, futile political arguments I had had in my life. I wondered whether such political disagreements did not issue from underlying, perhaps even innate, characteristics. Certainly, experience teaches us that when we encounter another person whom we instinctively dislike, constructive political dialogue is not likely to follow. Humans can intuitively sense through a variety of subtle clues (i.e., dress, accent, gestures), when another person possesses a mix of cultural and psychological characteristics that is so substantially different to our own that political discord is also likely. Put otherwise, a liberal can usually smell a conservative, and vice versa. Moreover, the smell is not a pleasant one.

When it came to the issues being discussed on the television show (tellingly, I have forgotten what they were), I was still certain that I was correct and that Hatch was wrong. Nonetheless, upon further reflection I had to admit that Hatch would be equally certain that he was right and that I was wrong. One could predict a fundamental insolubility to any political disagreements I might have with the Senator. We could argue for a lifetime and not move each other's position an inch.

Neither the strength of my feeling against Hatch, nor my certitude as to my own correctness, provided any proof that I was actually right.

Here, I felt I had stumbled upon a truly engaging puzzle. Where did my political certitude come from? How could I be so sure that I was right? And why were my political certitudes aroused so emotionally and instinctively by the mere sight of a conservative politician?

These were important and difficult questions, but this time I did not find the answers on TV.

In Pursuit of Political Irrationality

Eventually, my curiosity led me to spend several years researching the academic literature on the interplay of emotion and reason in political judgment. This book is the product of that research. In particular, I discovered important recent studies in neuroscience and behavioral genetics which helped explain many of the more puzzling aspects of political behavior.

I now believe that my negative emotional reaction to Senator Hatch was but a personal example of a universal, biologically-grounded syndrome, which I refer to as *political irrationality.*

Political irrationality is the tendency to arrive at biased political judgments emotionally and instinctively, while nonetheless attributing such judgments to logic and evidence. Political opinions come from the heart, so to speak, but the head claims the credit.

The first grand (or grandiose) claim I will make in this book is that coping with political irrationality is one of the world's most important challenges. All attempts to manage humanity's other problems (war, disease, environmental degradation, poverty, etc.) will be hampered by ineffective government. Government failure, in turn, is an inevitable by-product of political irrationality. An irrational electorate is like sand in the gears of democracy, and irrational politicians just make things worse. If we want to tackle the world's problems effectively, we will have to learn to overcome, or at least minimize, political irrationality.[1]

First, though, we need to understand it. Political irrationality is exhibited primarily as follows:

Partisan bias: In any political debate or dispute, we assume that our political side is the "correct" one;

Political gullibility: People tend to adopt the political beliefs of their peer group, regardless of the existence or strength of the supporting evidence;

Over-confidence: In politics, we are very sure we are right (again, regardless of the evidence);

Hostility: We don't like our political adversaries and disdain them as morally or intellectually inferior;

Self-deception: We fool ourselves by denying and ignoring the existence of the above tendencies within ourselves (though we are able to detect them in others).

Social mythology: The above tendencies combine with patriotism to generate a number of national political myths (e.g., patriotic citizens tend to believe that their nation's system of government is superior to all others).

Let us now briefly introduce each of the key elements and manifestations of political irrationality:

Biology. One of the central arguments of this book is that political irrationality is at least partially innate or biologically-grounded. Thus, for example, we will review scientific studies that suggest that humans are born with an underlying political orientation. Even as infants, long before our family and community get a chance to indoctrinate us politically, we are already predisposed towards conservatism or liberalism. The biological reality underlying our red-state/blue-state polarization is that some babies are born blue, some red (and quite a few are in between, varying shades of purple).[2]

Research in behavioral genetics confirms that some people have an instinctive preference for "tough" social relations, involving rigid obedience to hierarchies and rules (red babies). Others just as instinctively prefer "soft" social relations, which allow exceptions to rules and emphasizing equality over hierarchy (blue babies). This genetic heritage, though crucial, is not the end of the story, but merely the beginning.

Later, family and culture get a chance to work on us. Our social environment is extremely important in our political development, and I will not deny its crucial role here. Sometimes political nurture overcomes political nature; a person's upbringing or education may outweigh their innate predispositions. A blue baby may yet grow into a red adult, or vice versa. However, that is the minority case. It is much more likely that our social and cultural programming will *reinforce* our underlying biological leanings. After all, our most important social influence is the family, and we usually share a common genetic heritage with family members. Families themselves tend to self-segregate, seeking out communities with like values. Red families prefer red neighborhoods, which blue families shun. Ethnic neighborhoods, common in most cities throughout the world, are a manifestation of this phenomenon.

Now let's return to the purple babies (the ones who are born with a mix of red and blue). What happens when they grow up? Statistically, they should be the most numerous cohort. However, there is no "purple party" waiting to receive them. Our dualistic system forces a choice between red and blue, which most children have absorbed by age ten. Over time, the purple population shrinks, its members recruited and brainwashed by the encroaching red and blue armies. In the end, the remaining purples retreat to feed the ranks of the so-called "independents" and "moderates," people who find themselves strangely alienated from our red-and-blue political battlefield.

Why insist so much on biology, if culture has a powerful impact which can in some cases totally over-ride our biological programming? I argue that we need biology because it helps us understand why political disagreement is so *intractable*: in most cases our political prejudices are rooted both in biology *and* culture.

Emotional, instinctive reactions. The existence of a biological substratum to our political outlook helps explain why people can be so automatic and rigid in their politics (though we all deny it). When exposed to a political stimulus we react by feeling rather than by thinking. These emotions work like sharp commands from our bio-cultural programming. Most of the time, they are reflexively obeyed.

If you doubt the power and reach of irrational emotion in politics, and are willing to try an easy thought experiment that may reveal the depth of your own red vs. blue divide, attempt the following. If you tend to consider yourself a conservative or otherwise lean towards the Republicans, imagine yourself going through a whole day admiring and supporting everything Hillary Clinton says or does (or choose another liberal standard-bearer). If, on the other hand, you place yourself on the liberal side and usually vote Democratic, try to do the same, but with Rush Limbaugh (or another conservative archetype) — imagine yourself enthusiastically approving hi-severy utterance. If you are like most Americans, you will find the above to be an excessively demanding task. We all pay lip service to the concepts of tolerance and bi-partisanship, but asking us to love and admire the buffoons who lead the opposition political party — that is asking too much.

"I'd rather kiss a toad," might sum up the sentiment of many Americans asked to perform such an experiment. Why do we find opposition political leaders so *disgusting*? They are, after all, Americans, too. Yet, despite their extremely impressive resumes, we cannot shake the feeling that they work for the "Dark Side."

If our political attitudes were based solely on logic, we would not feel so strongly; but politics is also very much about emotion. A popular book on Buddhism tells a story dating from the 1960's, of a young American Buddhist nun reporting on her efforts to extend loving-kindness and forgiveness to all sentient beings in the universe. "We have to forgive everyone," she said, "Even Nixon." That last bit must have been quite a challenge for her! Political neutrality is difficult to attain even for those on the arduous path to Nirvana.

Partisan bias. Modern psychology has revealed that our brain is hard-wired to take sides. The best explanation for this is evolutionary. As humans evolved, the capacity to perceive the world in a distortedly self-interested and partisan fashion was actually helpful. The biases of individual self-interest, such as optimism, kept our ancestors going through hard times. The biases of group self-interest, fore-runners of today's political partisanship, helped ensure the survival of small groups and tribes. For our ancient predecessors, bias worked.[3]

The result is that humans have been programmed by evolution to habitually break the world down into a black-and-white diagram: the good guys (us) against the bad guys (them). We have inherited an overwhelming instinct for solidarity. Today, the political party system allows isolated city-dwellers to satisfy that primal need for belonging. Supporting the Republicans or Democrats is like joining a tribe that refuses entrance to no one, although there is an implied oath of allegiance at the door. Every party supporter gets to enjoy the full benefits of tribal membership (rooting and cheering for victory, mocking the opposition tribe, gloating when your tribe wins an election). And it's all for free, America's greatest bargain in group affiliation.

In an age in which many other forms of traditional affiliation, such as religious or neighborhood groups, have waned, partisanship has become increasingly prominent as a secular alternative. Today, in our multicultural society, we tend to think of religion only as a spiritual practice, and have forgotten the socially unifying role it once played. The word "religion" is derived from the Latin *religio*, "to bind together." If religion is *that which binds us together*, then politics is the modern religion. Elections have replaced church ceremonies as our most widely accepted national rites, with this notable innovation: we now can choose (and indeed, *must* choose) between a red church and a blue one.

Gullibility. If you take some time to observe your friends and colleagues (and even yourself, if you can stand the scrutiny), you will see that most people do not really "think" about political issues. Few of us stop to analyze political issues before coming to a political opinion. Instead, we swoop past the possibility of dispassionate analysis on our way to soothing conformity. When a new political issue achieves prominence (for example, the regulation of financial markets), the average voter briefly goes "opinion shopping," considering the viewpoints of trusted parties like politicians, broadcasters and columnists. As soon as we figure out what our political peer group is saying, we tend to adopt that viewpoint without further reflection.

In short, we like to take the easiest and most pleasant path out of the thicket of political uncertainty. In a sense, it is always a path *home*, because it involves finding the orthodoxy of those people we identify with. In contrast, it would be very hard to confront and challenge the political orthodoxy of our peer-group. Not only would it require a huge amount of effort to analyze political issues in depth, doing so could put us out of tune with family and friends. So it should not be surprising that humans are generally willing to adopt political views virtually without reflection. This docility stems from our need for social belonging, the most basic of human drives. If we fail to integrate ourselves politically, we risk ostracism, which throughout evolutionary history was the worst of all human fates.

Our political opinions have a strong social component, which we routinely underemphasize. Political opinions are not like answers to algebra problems, the value of which depends solely on the correctness of the answers. Rather, our politics are an essential part of our social *persona*, like an intellectual version of clothing.4 Without our politics we would feel naked. Going to the office in the morning without bringing our political views would be like going without a shirt or shoes. It helps us pass the time with co-workers if we can refer to something we read in the *New York Times* or *Wall Street Journal,* or watched on "The Daily Show" or the "O'Reilly Factor." Most of our political beliefs are like trendy attire we wear because our social peers are wearing the same thing (though we may all look ridiculous). In politics, birds of a feather flock together. Like birds, we don't even have to think about it.

Unfortunately, if it is true that people possess a partisan belief-drive, it is also likely that people, on occasion, will be quite easily convinced of political beliefs which are erroneous, preposterous, or even evil. If, as the price of belonging to a social group, we are prepared to *believe* just about anything, the group can also convince us to *do* just about anything.

> It ain't what you don't know that gets you into trouble. It's what you know for sure that just ain't so. — Mark Twain

> **Positive**, adj. Mistaken at the top of one's voice. — Ambrose Bierce, *The Devil's Dictionary*

Overconfidence: Our certitude and vehemence in political argument are way out of proportion to our knowledge. Political scientists have established that most people acquire political opinions rapidly and without much reflection, though afterwards they may emotionally defend those opinions.

Listen to the *tone* of any political argument, editorial, or campaign speech. What do you hear that is common to all of them? Each is marked by that supreme and swaggering *confidence* that characterizes political discourse. People involved in political arguments do not advance their opinions timidly and with qualifications. They speak boldly and aggressively, practically declaiming their positions. In politics, everybody is always very sure that they are right.

But they simply can't be. When the Democrats and Republicans take opposed positions on an important issue, they can't both be right. One side must be wrong, though you would never know it from observing their uniformly cocky demeanor. Thus, on any critical policy debate, it follows that about half the electorate and half the politicians are completely *wrong*, yet are blithely and majestically assured that they are *right*.

This self-confidence is all the more remarkable in that it remains unfazed by exposure to contrary facts. This is particularly true in the case of politicians who are responsible for any major public act or decision — they never admit they were wrong. Consider the sad case of the U.S. invasion of Iraq, which is still staunchly defended by Dick Cheney, Donald Rumsfeld and Paul Bremer, though the consensus of world opinion is that the U.S. occupation has proven a fiasco. It took thirty years for Robert McNamara, the architect of America's Vietnam debacle, to admit his obvious and monumental errors, which makes him, relatively speaking, a model of political repentance.

Hostility. Unfortunately, our modern political religion seems to require that society be cleaved into antagonistic armies, liberals versus conservatives. Academics tell us that political parties are *helpful* because they simplify a complex political spectrum, which makes it easier for citizens to express their preferences at the ballot box.[5] However, since this alleged benefit has been achieved only at the cost of perennial social conflict, we should now ask ourselves whether it is worth it, or whether there is not some better way.

The conflict between left and right in modern republics is a sort of perpetual-motion mechanism and negative spiral at the same time. When we support political parties, it is regrettably more than just a matter of adopting certain political beliefs. We are also expected to agree that our party's beliefs are *better* than those that are held by the other party. Feelings of hostility and superiority are an inevitable byproduct of partisan competition. The media encourages representatives of both sides to vent their emotions, because this sells papers and boosts ratings. When we hear that others disagree viscerally with us, we tend to return the feeling of emotional dislike. Political hostility leads to further social polarization and to habits of legislative gridlock.

Self-deception. We make our political decisions instinctively and emotionally, but attribute those decisions to reason and logic.

The capacity for *self-deception* is thus an essential component of political irrationality, and one reason that the syndrome is so troublesome: we can't observe it in ourselves. However, we can easily spot it in our neighbors and rivals.

If it were impossible to overcome our own political self-deception, there would be no point in writing this book. But I think that we can learn to break (or at least weaken) our habits of political irrationality. The first step is to confront the fact that we are probably a lot like other people, and susceptible to the same flaws. The scientific studies presented later in this book will show that most people have "cognitive blind spots." We can learn to be attentive to our own blind spots, which should make us a bit more cautious in political judgment-making. We can learn to cultivate an openness to new ways of looking at things, a state of non-judgmental awareness that one psychologist refers to as "mindfulness" — the opposite of our habitual, automatic behavior, mindlessness.[6]

Social mythology. Political partisans are willing to believe whatever their group culture requires. Some of the time, inevitably, they get things wrong. Patriotic citizens, likewise, buy into a whole set of beliefs, some of which must also prove mistaken. Many of the things that patriots believe are true; but history tells us that some patriotic beliefs are probably mistaken. Every country maintains some popular beliefs that are not grounded in history or reality, and these mistaken beliefs I deem the nation's "social mythology."

Social myths are political irrationality writ large. They involve self-deception at the national level. Social myths prevent progress, because they prevent citizens from perceiving reality, which is often unpleasant and depressing. However, it must be our duty to identify and eradicate social myths. Problems can't be fixed if they aren't admitted.

In order to expose social myths, we should proceed like homicide detectives working with uncooperative, deceptive witnesses. Our first inquiry should be as to *motive*. What realities would our nation, or its leaders, prefer to ignore or conceal? What would it make sense for us to try to hide?

I will argue that the main American social myths are related to our vaunted democracy: the power and effectiveness of voting, the wisdom of the

Founding Fathers, the virtue of politicians, our national commitment to equality, and the value of modern elections and electoral campaigns.

More than we would like to admit, these beliefs are mythical and erroneous. America's Founding Fathers made serious mistakes, our modern politicians are often just self-serving hucksters, our nation's power structure is profoundly oligarchic and anti-democratic, and our elections commonly devolve into farcical marketing contests between elite interests. These are not pleasant realities to acknowledge, but we cannot hope to improve matters without an unsparing diagnosis.

Costs and dangers of political irrationality. Our political irrationality is dangerous in two ways. First, it fosters polarization. Second, it distracts our attention from a more serious underlying problem — the fundamentally undemocratic reality of our nation.

Ultimately, the biggest cost of our innate group-bias is that it sustains America's two-party duopoly. The Democrats exploit hostility toward Republicans in order to monopolize liberals. The Republicans exploit hatred of liberals in order to monopolize conservatives. Americans become like the citizens of two parallel, Soviet states, with most voters turning out at every election to vote for the same party that they did in the previous election. Consequently, our Congressional incumbents are re-elected at the Soviet-style rate of 98%.

Despite this, the electoral conflict is irresistibly compelling. Citizens become hypnotized by the scorpion-like combat, enjoying the drama — unfortunately, at great social cost. Like victims of a card hustler, the citizens are so mesmerized by political theatrics that they don't realize their pocket is being picked.

Studies show that Congressional productivity declines in times of intense partisan polarization.[7] A political system marked by high levels of partisanship is not only inefficient, it is just plain dangerous, because partisan antagonism has been known to flare unpredictably out of control. Many social commentators trace the current American partisan conflict, the so-called Culture War, back to the 1970s or 1980s. This is very short-sighted. In truth we should look much further back — to the *1770s* at least.

This country was born in an upheaval of violent partisanship. The Revolutionary War was actually the first Civil War, pitting neighbor against neighbor in the bloody schism between Patriot and Loyalist. On several occasions, for example, when Patriots re-took towns previously held by Loy-

alists, British collaborators were ruthlessly executed by their fellow towns-
men. Again and again, repeatedly throughout our history, from the Civil
War to the Civil Rights era, we have witnessed eruptions of violent civil conflict based on partisan politics. Extreme partisanship is thus, in my view, one
of the most dangerous manifestations of political irrationality. Any highly-po-
larized society is a ticking time-bomb, as we have seen in the recent examples of Iraq, Rwanda and the former Yugoslavia.

Political irrationality is thus costly and dangerous. Fortunately, there
is something very powerful we can do about it. We can begin to confront
our own political irrationality. We can "snap out" of the trance of mass political conformity. We can make long-term, structural improvements to our
system of government that will bring us closer to our democratic goals.

By understanding and accepting our hard-wired irrationalities, we
can craft innovative electoral processes that minimize the opportunities for
irrational behavior. Our current election-based democracy makes it difficult
to escape the human penchant for partisan bias, but in the future we can
hope for progress with the implementation of alternative mechanisms such
as *citizen juries* and *deliberative polls*, democratic innovations described in the
concluding chapter.

Explaining the Futility of Political Debate
(& 14 Other Political Mysteries)

People are usually willing to believe that members of the *other* political party are irrational, but it is hard to get the average voter to look in
the mirror.

"Irrational, *moi?*"

As an incentive to make the effort, I now wish to provide a hint of
the great explanatory power of the concept of political irrationality. In
the last section I suggested that political irrationality was extremely important — let me insist here that it is also a lot of fun. When you understand political irrationality, you finally understand politics. It is like
having a pair of magic X-ray glasses. Political irrationality allows us to
decipher many of the puzzles of modern politics.

The first of and foremost of these is our near-universal discontent with
modern systems of government. Particularly acute in the United States, this

is a worldwide phenomenon. Surveys show that ordinary citizens are unhappy with their elected officials. Pundits and political scientists have expressed an even broader frustration — with our politicians, our electorate, and even with the basic workings of our government.

Consider the (typical) titles of these popular political books:

Why Americans Hate Politics

Politics Lost: How American Democracy Was Trivialized By People Who Think You're Stupid

Hostile Takeover: How Big Money and Corruption Conquered Our Government

You Call This an Election? America's Peculiar Democracy

The Broken Branch: How Congress Is Failing America

Presidential Power: Unchecked and Unbalanced

The Best Democracy Money Can Buy

Democracy in Peril

Democracy at Risk

Is Democracy Possible Here?

Why is there so much frustration? Should we accept political sour grapes as an enduring characteristic of a free press? Perhaps the jeremiad is a necessary staple of political publishing?

The frustration expressed in these book titles represents a discontent which is both rational and healthy. History tells us that governments are only forced to improve when dissatisfaction becomes general. The above book titles collectively point to a growing public awareness that our modern system of government is neither democratic nor efficient.

Our political malaise stems from the rational mind's incomprehension of a political system thoroughly permeated by traditional irrationalities. As the poets have often reminded us, humans are capable of both rationality *and* irrationality.

This book will use the concept of political irrationality to shed light on a great number of previously-perplexing political phenomena:

Mysteries of Political Behavior

The Mystery of Futile Debate: Why do we engage endlessly in futile political debates? We can argue politics forever, with nary a hint of progress. The likelihood of anyone changing his or her mind as the result of a political argument is negligible; but we debate anyway. Whether on the street corner or *Meet the Press*, political discussions go on and on, and are only rarely resolved by polite compromise. As comedians have pointed out, it would be astonishing if a presidential candidate were to decide, mid-debate, that the other candidate was right:

> CANDIDATE: "You know, Senator, I never looked at it that way before, but you're actually *completely right*. Since it's such an important point, I guess I'll just concede the whole election to you right now — you are definitely the better candidate. Congratulations!"

If a candidate actually did say something like that, he or she would soon face overpowering citizen anger* – at having violated the unspoken rule that debates are *supposed* to be futile.

By convention, political discussion is regarded as a logical process. However, the studies cited in this book suggest that in the political arena we do not respond to each other's logic so much as we express and defend our sense of personal and group identification. Our political opinions emanate from deep cultural and biological sources.

It is therefore about as easy to change our overall political orientation as it is to change the shape of our bodies or our taste in clothes (not impossible, but extremely difficult, especially as we get older). This explains why we get so emotional about politics and why political compromise is generally impossible. When someone criticizes our politics, they attack our very being. Political debate is futile because it is based on the naïve premise that we can be convinced by the logical arguments of our enemies to change our inner selves. Following the analogy of John Gray's marriage counseling, it is as if women expected men to behave like

---

* Not to mention, a free one-way ticket to a psychiatric institution.

women, or vice versa. That kind of dialogue is sure to end in failure. Why then, do we engage in it?

The Mystery of Passionate Ignorance: In politics, ignorance is no bar to passion — frequently, it is even an indispensable ingredient. When pressed on a topical political issue (e.g., the war in Iraq, abortion, immigration reform, global warming, etc.) most people will defend their opinions with assertions based on reason, logic and evidence (or more accurately, feeble attempts to locate any shred of reason or evidence). Most people would be highly offended if you were to suggest that their political opinions were based purely on intuition, emotion or partisan bias. However, surveys show that the average person is stupendously ignorant of political issues (one-fourth of Americans can't even name the vice-president). Although most citizens claim that politics is important, they have evidently neglected to learn very much — if anything — about political issues. If our knowledge of politics is so shallow, how can the depth of our passions run so deep?

Why are we so politically ignorant, and how does that square with our self-professed fascination with politics? How can we explain that?

Can a democracy be run by people who don't know the facts?

The Mystery of Bad Policies: of Wars and Panics: Why do governmental leaders adopt foolish policies and make stupid decisions? Perhaps even more puzzling — why do the citizens so often go along? Examples:

In the case of the Iraq War, the U.S. was warned by virtually all of its major allies that an invasion was imprudent and unnecessary. The president's own father, through his surrogates, attempted to warn his son of the danger. After failing to discover the weapons of mass destruction which were the ostensible cause of the war, the U.S. armed forces nonetheless remained in Iraq despite the overwhelming hostility of Iraqis. The U.S. suffered the loss of over 4,000 soldiers, with an estimated cost to the economy of as much as three trillion dollars, not to mention the cost in Iraqi lives and the huge burden on the global economy. Yet, when the public was allowed to vote on this fiasco in 2004, it confirmed the error by re-electing George W. Bush. Why?

The global financial panic of 2008 was novel in terms of its scope, but financial panics are not a new phenomenon. Their colorful history, from Holland's famous tulip mania to the Mississippi stock schemes that bankrupted

France in 1718, had already been recounted by 1855 in Charles Mackay's history, *Extraordinary Popular Delusions and the Madness of Crowds*. The world economy has experienced, and overcome, a great number of financial panics in the last century. There have been so many opportunities to learn from mistakes. We are left wondering, how can the so-called "experts" continue to get it wrong, over and over again?

Schizophrenic, or Just Bi-Polar? The Mystery of Zig-Zag Government: In 2008, the U.S. electorate brought a Democratic president, senate and congress to power. It was widely anticipated that this would lead to a new era of "progressive" (meaning liberal) policies on issues as diverse as foreign relations, the environment and civil liberties. However, to achieve its liberal objectives the new administration would first have to unweave a conservative fabric carefully and methodically woven throughout the eight years of the George W. Bush administration from 2000 to 2008. Bush, similarly, had spent much of his administration trying to undo what Bill Clinton had achieved in 1992–2000, while Clinton had labored to wipe out the achievements of Ronald Reagan and George H.W. Bush in 1980–1992, and so on.

Every eight years or so, the American polity lurches from left to right, or back again. Each reversal is hailed by half the nation as the long-awaited re-awakening of civic reason, while the other half demands a recount. Our foreign allies are alternately placated and mystified by our good-cop, bad-cop routine, but they can't complain about it without being hypocrites, because most of them are playing the same game.

Mysteries of Polarization

The Mystery of Political Hatred: Why does it seem that Democrats and Republicans *hate* each other? If Americans really are patriotic, why is one half of America mocking and heaping abuse on the other half? George W. Bush aroused undeniable emotions of hatred amongst many liberals, while Bill and Hillary Clinton did the same for conservatives. Why have so many presidents been hated by half the country?

The Mystery of Illusory Differences: Numerous studies show that Democrats and Republicans actually *do not* differ politically as much as they think they do. On most key political issues, there is a general consensus of opinion across the parties. Why, then, do we speak so much about partisan polarization? If we don't really disagree on political issues, what is the basis of the "culture war"? Is our political divide merely a contrast of underlying *cultures* — e.g., that Republicans like country music while Democrats prefer brie?

The Mystery of the Gaps: the Gender Gap, Race Gap and Generation Gap — Why do we see the landscape so differently depending on our sex, race or age?

On average, women are more liberal than men. A clear gender gap in female political support for the Democrats has been repeatedly confirmed since 1964, reaching a contemporary high of fourteen percentage points in 1996.[8]

Latinos are more liberal than whites, but more conservative than African-Americans or Jews.

Young liberals overwhelmingly and passionately supported the presidential candidacy of Barack Obama in 2008, while their liberal parents and grand-parents tended to support Hillary Clinton. Young conservatives flocked to Ron Paul while their elders gravitated to John McCain.

Presuming that all of these different segments of the population are equally rational, why are they attracted to different candidates?

Mysteries of Parties and Politicians

The Mystery of Political Duopoly: Why do Americans accept to be represented exclusively by only two parties? Many citizens agree with the Democrats on some issues, but support the Republicans on other issues. How can such citizens vote for president without contradicting themselves? Why can't a citizen order vanilla *and* chocolate? If America needs to have 128 different kinds of granola, why is it satisfied with only two political parties? Why do we need political parties to aggregate our preferences at such a crude, mass level? Why don't we have proportional voting systems the way they do in Europe?

The Mystery of "Public Service": Politicians claim they enter politics to "serve the public," but surveys show that many citizens think politicians are out to exploit the public. Who is right, the politicians or the citizens? Who is getting serviced, and by whom? And if the citizens are right, why do they keep electing the politicians?

The Mystery of Neurotic Oligarchy: Since the political campaign process is so onerous, expensive and humiliating that normal people won't put up with it, and since a political career provides so many incentives for megalomania and duplicity, it is reasonable to expect that over time the pool of politicians will become polluted with neurotic, immoral and perhaps even emotionally-dysfunctional people. Why do citizens accept to be governed by these kinds of persons? Is this not government by nut-cases, a kind of nutocracy?

The Mystery of Political Elitism: Why are so many politicians tall, wealthy, thin, white and male? Why does a diverse America accept that it can be "represented" by such a blandly homogenous group from a tiny, privileged minority? Why is it that so many wealthy liberal politicians — like FDR, JFK, John Kerry, Al Gore, John Edwards — have been categorized as "champions of the poor"? Is it believable that very wealthy people can somehow *represent* the poor? Are the poor that gullible?

The Mystery of "Representative" Democracy: Americans are proud of their Founding Fathers, and also proud of having a "democracy." However, the historical record shows that the Founding Fathers thought "democracy" was an extremely bad idea. The Founders clearly distinguished a republic from a democracy, and did not hide their contempt for the latter. How is it that George W. Bush could talk of exporting democracy when George Washington would have frowned at its importation? We have turned the terminology of the Founders on its head, by adopting a modern euphemism for republic: "representative democracy." In reality, though, we just kept the system of government the Founders called a republic, but went along when politicians began to call it a democracy. Why is it so acceptable to dispense with a verbal distinction that the Founders considered fundamental? True — the populace seems happy with the name change, but they also report a sneaking suspicion that somehow the wool is being pulled over their eyes. Does our elective oligarchy merit the term "democracy"? Or is it really just a form of placebo democracy, a simulacrum?

Mysteries of Voting

The Mystery of Voting: Why do people vote at all? You might think the answer is obvious, but generations of economists and political scientists have formally tried to figure out the reasons and haven't been able to come up with an answer. Academics refer to this as the "Voter's Paradox": statistically, the probability that your vote will affect the next presidential election is virtually zero, but you will probably vote anyway.[9] Why? There are good reasons, but they are not the ones that you would expect.

The Mystery of Political Proselytizing: Why do we try to convince apathetic people to vote, when there is strong evidence that they don't know anything about politics and won't learn anything from the experience? What makes us think the country will be better off if we harass the politically ignorant into voting? If we borrow the concept of "marginal voter" from economics, it follows that the marginal voter will always be the most ignorant. Is it not therefore irrational to encourage the undecided to vote? Would we not be better off with lower turnouts?

The Mystery of Sensationalized Elections: Why do we think elections are the only way to choose political representatives, when there is so much evidence that elections can be won by manipulative and deceptive advertising techniques (or by outright theft)? Why are important elections decided by such seeming irrelevancies as whether one candidate sighed too much during a debate, or whether his rival sweated under the television lights? Why is there no alternative to the elaborately staged ritual of phony campaign events meant to indicate that the candidates are locked in an ongoing "horse race"? Why do we need to think that the candidates are racing — do we really believe the candidates are somehow changing from day to day?

It is my promise to the reader that each of the above mysteries (and even a few more) will be illuminated by the theory of innate political irrationality, An understanding of political irrationality allows us not only to unravel the above mysteries, but also to propose solutions. Irrationality, like the grain in the oyster, may help us produce the pearl of true democracy.

For the impatient reader, I offer an advance hint. All of the above mysteries can be understood through the application of the following simple principles:

1. People tend to believe what their peers believe.

2. People tend to believe whatever makes them feel good about themselves.

3. People are born with a slight bias toward liberal or conservative thinking.

4. People naturally take sides, supporting their group and expressing hostility toward other groups.

5. Politicians exploit all of the above tendencies to maintain power in a system built on conflict.

The Politics of Irrationality — Starting at Neutral

In 2005, President George W. Bush's approval rating reached a high of 92% amongst Republicans while it languished at 18% for Democrats — the largest recorded gap in the history of the Gallup Poll.[10] What was going on in the brains of the American electorate at that point in time? By April 2009, these positions had reversed, with 88% of Democrats approving of President Barack Obama's performance, while only 27% of Republicans agreed. How is it possible that Americans can look at the same person and come to such radically different viewpoints? Most observers place the blame on our unprecedented culture war, the yawning chasm between red and blue states. This book accepts the importance of culture, but argues that culture is rooted in biology.

Recent research from a number of different disciplines — psychology, neuroscience, economics, political science, anthropology — provides a powerful, multi-disciplinary perspective which I refer to as the "New Science of Political Irrationality." Although many scholarly and popular works address specific aspects of human political irrationality, there is no single work that provides an overview of the entire field. My first objective here is to provide an introduction to that new science.

However, I first have to situate this new approach within the context of an old debate. The emerging science of political irrationality has already become a political football, with each political wing accusing the other of irrationality. This has been going on for some time.

Indeed, the new science confirms an age-old schism. Plato's parable of the cave was an elitist metaphor for the irrationality of the citizenry, a theme to which conservative thinkers have perennially returned. James Madison and the other architects of the U.S. Constitution were influenced by the Platonic tradition in their design of the American government. Some historians have argued that the American government's vaunted "checks and balances" were really intended as bulwarks against the citizenry's presumed irrationality.

This book starts with the neutral premise that all humans are to some extent susceptible to political irrationality. It may indeed be true that at a certain point in time, and on a specific range of issues, one party tends to be more reasonable than the other. However, the difficulties of proving even such a simple assertion are formidable. Whom are we to ask? Even the U.S. Supreme Court, in its president-making decision of 2000, showed it was subject to political bias. When society's most eminent judges fail so spectacularly at neutrality, where are we to find a trustworthy, dispassionate arbiter?

The irrationality of Democrats and Republicans is probably not symmetrical, but my primary objective in this book is not a partisan one. There is a more important point to be made. Political irrationality is at some level a fundamental human characteristic and, therefore, omni-partisan. Democrats, Republicans, Independents and Apathetics, all are to some extent susceptible (though perhaps not to the same degree; more about that later).

Where to Begin

Cease being the slave of a party and you become its deserter — Jules Simon, 1864 (*Viking Book of Aphorisms*)

An understanding of the concepts in this book can change your life for the better, but not without a certain risk. In the interests of full disclosure, let me sound a note of caution. If you are dearly attached to your own political hatreds, proceed with caution. Sometimes a little knowledge can be a dangerous thing, especially if it puts you out of tune with your fellow citizens. This book will help you understand politics from a more rational perspective, which sounds nice, but most of the people around you will continue to discourse in the same emotional, irrational manner.

To give you an idea of possible outcomes, I will confess how things ended up with my old friend Senator Hatch. First of all, I don't see him on TV quite so often, because I spend less time watching the mass media and their shallow and distorted treatment of political issues. Understanding political irrationality is like knowing the secret behind a magic trick. Afterwards, the trick is less amusing. I do not enjoy the old political mud-wrestling shows the way I used to, and I must admit to some sense of loss.

Conservatives no longer bother me the way they used to. After years of research on the topic, I have come to accept that conservatives could not help being born and brought up the way they were, just as I had no impact on my own genetics or upbringing. Of course, that means that much of the pleasure I used to feel in condemning conservatives has dissipated, but perhaps that is a small price to pay for seeing clearly. I no longer hang around the office with my colleagues ridiculing Republicans endlessly, the way I used to. I still ridicule them for a few minutes, out of perfunctory camaraderie, but then I move on. When Republicans decide to ridicule Democrats, I listen briefly before I change the channel. They are not always wrong.

If you wish to seriously examine the rationality of your own politics, you will eventually have to face the issue of party loyalty. Any attempt on your part to look at political issues from a disinterested or neutral perspective will look, to your partisan friends, like a worrisome hint of treachery. You may be accused of being a deserter, or worse, a closet conservative (or liberal). My wife told me recently that a friend of hers had asked if I was conservative or liberal. My wife had answered, "He used to be a liberal, but lately, I don't know, I'm not sure any more…"

I tried to re-assure her that I am still a liberal (though I'm not sure I succeeded). I don't think rationality requires you to abandon your ideology. However, I now try consciously to examine my own political beliefs, and I think I have managed to loosen the automatic hold that those beliefs used to have on me. Overall, this makes me slightly more cautious in coming to political judgments. Finally, I try take my own political opinions — and those of my friends — a bit less seriously, which leads to fewer arguments.

I doubt that we will ever rid humanity of political irrationality, and in fact it would not be a good idea to try. To use a "Star Trek" analogy, we are more like Bones, the irascibly irrational medical officer, than we are like Spock, the coolly rational Vulcan. Humans will never become political robots, nor should the important role of the heart in politics be disparaged or neglected. However, as we will see, we pay a heavy and unnecessary cost for our excessive political irrationality.

CHAPTER 2

The Psychology of Political Irrationality

> The typical citizen drops down to a lower
> level of mental performance as soon as
> he enters the political field…. He becomes
> a primitive again. His thinking becomes
> associative and affective. — Joseph
> Schumpeter, *Capitalism, Socialism and
> Democracy* (1942)

DARK TRUTH #2
*In politics, the heart makes decisions but the head takes the credit.
That's why "talking heads" so rarely agree.*

Political Irrationality 101: Emotion and Irrationality

What does it mean to say that someone comes to a political decision "rationally," "irrationally," or "emotionally"? Let us consider a few possible cases:

MARK adores Hillary Clinton with a veneration bordering on worship. Not surprisingly, he was a big supporter of Hillary Clinton's 2008 presidential campaign. As the primary season progressed, Mark developed an antipathy for Barack Obama. When Obama received the Democratic nomination, Mark was disgusted. Although he agreed that Obama's policy platform was much closer to Hillary's than to John McCain's, Mark decided to cross party lines and vote for McCain. *Rational or irrational?*

SALLY is trying to decide whether to vote in the U.S. presidential election. Her 7-year old daughter is home sick with the flu and the doctor told Sally to check her daughter's temperature at least once an hour. Sally always votes Republican, though a Republican presidential candidate has not carried her state in fifty years. The last polls showed the Democrat ahead by thirty points. Despite this, Sally has never failed to vote in a presidential election in her adult lifetime, and after taking her daughter's temperature one more time (it was 100.1), she rushed off to the polls. When she got to the polling booths however, she could see from the length of the line that it would be at least *two* hours before she could cast her ballot. Despite her concerns about her daughter's flu, Sally decides to stay in line to vote. Voting is *that* important to her. *Rational or irrational?*

ANDREA, who is 21, is not interested in politics, but she has been harassed by all her friends so much that she decides to vote. As she waits in line to cast her ballot, Andrea doesn't know what to do, because she has no preferences amongst the candidates or parties. When she finally gets in the voting booth, she reads the names of the candidates and tries to figure out which one "feels better." She remembers that one of the candidates had a more sincere, reassuring smile than the other. She votes for the candidate with the better smile. *Rational or irrational?*

A LARGE WEALTHY COUNTRY prides itself on being a "democracy." For the past fifty years, polls show that a clear majority of the citizens have been in favor of universal health coverage. Despite that, the country's legislature has not passed any of the numerous proposed laws that would have created universal health coverage. The citizens continue to pride themselves on being members of a "democracy." *Rational or irrational?*

When we say someone makes a "rational" decision, we mean that in our opinion they have made the right decision, and that they first thought about the problem (by implication this takes time), using logic and evidence.

When we say someone has acted "irrationally," we mean that they have made a bad decision through a kind of self-contradiction (acting contrary to their knowledge or professed objectives).

We say of those who have acted irrationally that they have "weren't thinking," "were thoughtless," "didn't think it through," or "didn't think straight" (or sometimes we just ask ourselves, astonished, "What were they thinking?"). Underlying our conception of irrationality is the conviction that people *could* have made the right decision. If you make a bad decision purely out of ignorance, strictly speaking that is not irrational — you just didn't know better. Academics say that such decisions have been made under conditions of "bounded rationality" (meaning limited rationality, due to a limited access to perfect information). Scholars who focus on bounded rationality argue that we are generally as rational as we can be, given our limited knowledge, so we shouldn't use the term "irrationality" at all.

Irrationality is thus an inherently paradoxical concept, because it suggests that sometimes we choose the wrong answer when the right answer is within our grasp. The philosopher Donald Davidson has demonstrated that we can lose ourselves in semantic riddles when we try to define irrationality because, theoretically, it shouldn't exist. Why would we ever do the wrong thing if it was really our intention to do the right thing? It is very hard to come up with an example of pure irrationality.

Consider the example of Sam, an alcoholic man who continues to drink even though it is apparent that drink is destroying his life. Is Sam's alcoholism "irrational"? If we learn that Sam has made numerous, unsuccessful efforts to stop drinking, then it becomes clear that it would be unfair to accuse Sam of irrationality (perhaps he is weak-willed, but certainly not irrational). It is not irrational to succumb to an irresistible compulsion, no more than it would be irrational to contract a serious disease.

Irrationality is always in the eye of the beholder. We call someone irrational when we can see that their actions contain some element of self-contradiction, but the person who is accused of irrationality must either be *unaware* of that irrationality (otherwise, they would stop) or they must be acting under some sort of compulsion.

When we use the term "irrationality" in politics what we really mean is "different rationality." People are motivated by different reasoning systems and different objectives. Most people follow a social rationality (partisan loyalty) in politics but when questioned will pretend to be following an abstract, theoretical rationality. I will distinguish these two types of rationality by referring to the first as *social rationality* and the second as *abstract rationality*.

Political irrationality is usually a matter of social rationality masquerading as abstract rationality. Most of the time we blindly follow the party line (social rationality) but pretend that we are servants of logical truth (abstract rationality).

In the final analysis, is such behavior rational or irrational? Strangely, one cannot say. In fact, it is rational from one perspective but irrational from another. I use the term "political irrationality" to describe such behavior because I deem it irrational to act out of instinct and pretend that you are acting out of reflection.

However, I must concede that those I accuse of political irrationality are, from another perspective, completely rational. Such individuals prefer social rationality, which is easy and fun, to abstract rationality, which is difficult and dangerous.

> In all disputes, so much as there is of passion, so much there is of nothing to the purpose; for then reason, like a bad hound, spends upon a false scent, and forsakes the question first started.
> — Sir Thomas Browne, *Religio Medici*

Emotion. What about emotion? The pundits are now prone to observe, for example, that a given campaign advertisement was carefully crafted to evoke emotions (for example, Hillary Clinton's famous "middle-of-the-night-phone-call" advertisement was interpreted as an appeal to fear).

Emotion is thus popularly connected with irrationality, but this is a mistake. When we say that someone has made an "emotional" decision, what we really mean is that they have made a *bad* decision under the influence of a momentary surge of emotion. One might conclude from this everyday understanding that a good, "rational" decision is one which is devoid of emotion.

However, contemporary neuroscience has revealed that all human decisions have some emotional content. As we go through the day our experiences transpire over a background hum of emotion, what psychologists call "affect," sometimes referred to as the "faint whisper of emotion." The general tenor of this hum, either positive or negative, reflects our disposition to take positive or negative decisions. We tend to do things that make us feel good and refrain from doing things that make us feel bad.

Because of this, it is sometimes said that our emotions not only precede but determine our decisions. In other words, it is suggested that our emotions make decisions for us but that our rational, conscious mind takes the credit.

This is probably somewhat of an over-simplification, given recent research which indicates that our brain makes decisions as much as ten seconds before our consciousness becomes aware of the decision. It may that emotions don't drive decisions, but rather signal them.[11] Emotions may be harbingers of decisions that have already been sub-consciously made and are about to be brought to conscious awareness. Rather than driving our decisions, emotions may serve a role in activating our conscious awareness to deal with decisions that require immediate action

In either case, it is clear that the human brain mechanisms for emotion and decision-making are closely-linked. When those parts of the brain that regulate emotion are damaged by injury or tumor, the patient may lose the ability to make any decisions at all. Neuroscientist Joseph LeDoux discovered the dual role of the brain area known as the amygdala in generating emotions and making decisions.[12] He observed that patients who had suffered injury to the amygdala lost all sense of the significance of events. One man, whose amygdala had been surgically removed, lost interest in human contact, forgot the faces of his friends and even his mother, failed to react to her anguish, and withdrew into a passive, hermetic existence. We need our emotions in order to act at all.

Strictly speaking, therefore, it is just as possible to come to a good emotional decision as a bad one. The reason for our popular misunderstanding is that we are all familiar with what author Daniel Goleman refers to as an "emotional hijacking," an extreme emotional event. Certain emotions, particularly anger and hatred, predictably lead to negative social consequences. Emotional outbursts have given emotion an undeservedly bad name.

Although our everyday confusion of emotion with irrationality is understandable, we must be more precise here. Any "rational" political decision, like an "irrational" one, is associated with some level of underlying emotion, so it makes no sense to simply disparage "emotional" political thinking.

However, on a common-sense level, we are probably right to suspect that *strong* political emotions correlate with political irrationality. Not all emotions are created equal.

It is as healthy to enjoy sentiment as to enjoy jam.
— G.K. Chesterton, "On Sentiment"

Wise Emotions / Foolish Emotions. Clearly, emotions have a major impact on our decision-making, including our political decision-making. On the whole, is this a good thing or a bad thing? Should we fight, resist or suspect our own emotions, or should we "go with the flow," trusting their intuitive wisdom?

Modern science has revealed that our emotions *can* be wiser than our conscious mind. Swiss psychologist Gerd Gigerenzer, who has studied the accuracy of intuitive reactions, provides an explanation. By using rules of thumb, combined with the evolved capacities of the human brain to handle social interactions, we are able to make much quicker choices than if we rationally calculated every action. Emotions enable us to make decisions speedily, without having to tabulate all relevant data.[13]

Our conscious mind represents an extremely-focused filtering of all the millions of possible sensations, memories and thoughts which are perpetually buzzing in our brain. We would never get anything done if we weren't able to exclude the vast majority of brain activity from our ordinary consciousness. However, much of that subconscious information can still be relevant to a given decision that we face. Emotions are one of the ways that our subconscious mind uses to communicate with our consciousness. It therefore makes a lot of sense to pay attention to your feelings.

When we suddenly say, "I've got a bad feeling about this," we are admitting, in effect, that our conscious, rational mind has gotten us into a predicament that our subconscious, emotional mind recognizes as dangerous. Gigerenzer believes that in such cases you should definitely heed your emotional warnings (*get the heck out of there*), because your subconscious mind is probably working faster and more efficiently than your rational mind.

Does that mean, therefore, that it is all right for citizens to react emotionally to politicians? If we simply *like* one politician more than another, perhaps that is enough. Perhaps we should accept that our emotional attraction reflects a deep, intuitive wisdom, even in cases where we are unable to draw any rational distinction between the candidates?

Consider, for example, that psychologists have discovered that the human face generates thousands of different "micro-expressions," fleeting gestures that are usually not perceived by others at the conscious level (unless they receive special training), but which are excellent indicators of whether someone is lying or not.[14] This explains why we sometimes are able to sense that someone is not being honest with us, though we cannot say what aroused our suspicions. When citizens react emotionally to a political figure, perhaps they are actually performing a highly-accurate but subconscious analysis of the candidate's facial micro-expressions? Perhaps the feelings of emotional trust generated by some politicians are an accurate reflection of their political integrity?

I will argue that on the whole emotional reactions to political figures are *not* wise, because they are so heavily conditioned by pre-existing partisan bias. It is hard to imagine now what else, other than bias, could have prompted Democratic voters to cheer enthusiastically for Dukakis or Mondale, or Republicans to root fervently for Ford or Dole. Emotions can be genuine, but they can also be manufactured, manipulated, feigned and counterfeited. Emotions can be wise, but they can also be astoundingly stupid.

If voters are such wonderful intuitive analysts of candidates' facial gestures and other non-verbal communication, how is it that Americans elected Richard Nixon to an overwhelming landslide victory in 1972? Nixon's face was such a twitchy, quivering, sweating, conflicted mask of repressed dishonesty that the sobriquet "Tricky Dick" was nothing if not inevitable. America would never have bought a used car from Dick Nixon, but they voted for him by the tens of millions.

In many important areas of life, you should definitely trust your emotions. Politics is not one of those areas.*

---

* I do not wish to deny the insights of thinkers such as political scientist George Marcus (2000, 2003), who has written persuasively as regards the potential for emotional wisdom in politics. However, I am not convinced that such potential is commonly realized. Emotional wisdom in politics is the exception rather than the rule. We are most likely to find it in those contexts that most resemble those of our evolutionary history, i.e., small group dynamics.

> The heart errs like the head; its errors are not any the less fatal, and we have more trouble getting free of them because of their sweetness. — Anatole France, *Little Pierre*

Fear and Loathing. There are two sets of emotional responses that merit our special concern — those associated with fear and loathing. Human beings have evolved an extraordinary touchiness when it comes to the sensation of fear. We are guilty of "over-fearing" and "mis-fearing." We fear the wrong things (insignificant risks) too much, and the right things (serious dangers) not enough.

Take the example of my old friend, Irrational Sam. Sam, who was an alcoholic in my last example, is not what you would call "a big health fiend." On weekends, Sam likes to go out to Brighton Beach, where he sits on a towel all day smoking cigarettes and eating donuts. Sam never goes swimming because he has been terrified of shark attacks ever since he saw the movie "Jaws" in 1976. Ever since 9/11 Sam has refused to travel to any foreign beaches because he fears terrorist incidents. Actuarial statistics can conclusively prove that Sam faces a much greater risk of mortality from cigarettes and donuts than from a shark attack in Brooklyn or a terrorist bombing in Cancun, but Sam won't listen. Sam is guilty of over-fearing (he's too afraid of sharks and terrorists) and mis-fearing (he's not sufficiently afraid of cigarettes and donuts). Most Americans, like Sam, have more to fear from a donut than from a terrorist, but our emotional perceptions are different. The terrorist and the shark are made to look scary, while the donuts look so soft and inviting (especially Krispy Kremes, dear reader; but resist their siren call — they're dangerous).

Politicians and political parties learned long ago to exploit our extreme susceptibility to fear. They learned that this technique works best if the object of terror is presented to us in a vivid, frightening way (as in "Jaws," or the endless documentaries on 9/11). Instilling fear is one of the basic tools of the propagandist, as in Nazi Hermann Goering's famous formulation:

> Voice or no voice, the people can always be brought to the bidding of the leaders. That is easy. All you have to do is tell them they are being attacked, and denounce the peacemakers for lack of patriotism and exposing the country to danger. It works the same in any country.

It has been persuasively argued by one psychologist that American politicians and the media routinely act as "fear brokers" who try to flip our "paranoia switch."[15] Republicans foment fear of terrorism to support legislation which restricts civil liberties, while Democrats rightly denounce this fear-mongering — and strive mightily to replace it with terror of climate change. One of the worst things about the paranoia switch is that (once flipped) it tends to stay on. Irrational fears can persist for a very long time, as any adult knows who has ever had to descend alone into a dark basement (I still won't do it).

Recently-published research indicates that conservatives may be more physiologically-sensitive to fearful imagery than liberals. A group of research volunteers was tested to see how easily they startled when exposed to stimuli such as loud noises or frightening images. The people who were most easily-frightened also tended to endorse the most conservative political positions. While this result might cheer my liberal colleagues (or at least make them feel relatively brave), partisans should in general be cautious about celebrating scientific "victories." A we will see, there is enough irrationality to go around, and no one escapes unscathed. Let us not be too quick to conclude that "your irrationality is bigger than my irrationality."

While conservatism may correlate with fearfulness and hence with greater susceptibility to propaganda, it does not follow that liberals are immune from political fear-mongering. Moreover, there are other psychological studies which suggest that conservatives' fearfulness may not be such a bad thing — it also correlates with a significantly higher degree of reported life happiness. For the past 30 years, American conservatives have enjoyed a "happiness gap" over liberals, with the discrepancy widest between extreme conservatives (48 percent of whom reported themselves to be very happy) and moderate liberals (only 22 percent of whom reported themselves to be very happy).[16]

It may be that the fearfulness (and the need for structure and traditionalism) that seems to mark the conservative predisposition compels conservatives to structure safer, more well-ordered lives than their free-wheeling liberal counterparts. Alternatively, the happiness edge may result from the fact that American conservatives are more likely to be white and wealthy, and therefore to benefit from racial and class privilege than liberals, who are more likely to come from ethnic minorities or the lower economic strata.

Are conservatives happy, rich cowards, while liberals are brave, poor grouches? Leaving that complex debate to more partisan scribblers, I will conclude here only that both liberals and conservatives are too susceptible to fear-based political brainwashing.

Loathing, or political hatred, is even more dangerous than fear because it so often has been the precursor to crimes against humanity. As witnessed most recently in Rwanda and Darfur, genocide begins with a dehumanizing contempt for the enemy. Even on the smallest, subtlest scale, such emotions are rightly to be feared.

The hatred that opposing partisans felt for the presidencies of Bill Clinton and George W. Bush, for example, can hardly be interpreted as an expression of the "wisdom of gut feelings." Even when it comes sincerely from the gut, hatred is rarely wise.

Two Ways of Thinking: Fast/Emotional and Slow/Rational

> What is the hardest task in the world?
> To think.
> — Ralph Waldo Emerson, *Journals*, 1836

The human brain continually uses two different modes of thinking, a fast mode (intuitive and emotional) and a slow mode (reasoning). By convention, psychologists refer to these as System 1 (fast, easy, intuitive, emotional) and System 2 (slow, difficult, rational).[17]

System 1 — The fast way of thinking was inherited from our ancient ancestors (hence, it is sometimes referred to as our "reptilian brain"), and is popularly associated with our limbic system. System 1 is always turned-on and ready for action. Its lightning speed allows us to interact with our complex environment in real time. All large animals share some kind of System 1 capacity because it is so useful. If one of your prehistoric ancestors came across a tiger, System 1 got your progenitor safely up into a tree long before System 2 had a clue as to what was going on. System 1 is extremely fast, but that virtue is also its vice — because System 1 has a nasty habit of coming to hasty, erroneous decisions. System 1 is also sometimes quite thick-headed. Thus System 1 quickly acquires new habits, bad as well as good, but then refuses to budge from them.

Our core political problem is that most of our political thinking is governed by System 1, the realm of intuition and emotion, while we all pretend that it is subject to System 2, the realm of logic.

System 2 — The slower type of thinking, reason, is uniquely human. Our evolutionary siblings, chimpanzees, might have a little capacity for it, but no other species on the planet has anything like the System 2 capacity that humans possess. System 2 processes occupy the neo-cortex, the surface layer of brain tissue which was the last part of the brain to develop in evolutionary time.

System 2 is conscious, deliberate, methodical, and requires a huge amount of effort (which is why we are so lazy about using it). Using System 2 is just plain hard work. System 2 is good at doing things like solving algebra problems, making sense of Ikea assembly instructions, or organizing a wedding — things we would rather not do. Since System 2 is so onerous a form of cognition, we only call it into play when absolutely necessary. There has to be some message from the environment telling us that it's time to rev up the Brainiac. Usually this message comes from System 1, when it finds itself in dire straits. A sense of anxiety, urgency or panic coming from System 1 is like the Commissioner's call to Batman — "We need you now, masked avenger!"

System 2 likes to think that it controls System 1, but this is wildly unrealistic, as anyone knows who has ever tried to quit smoking, stick to a diet, or fulfill some other such "New Year's resolution." Most of us conceive of our rational brain as a kind of CEO in charge of our life. We believe that orders issued by the CEO (e.g., "put down that beer," "close the fridge") will be followed. However, a better analogy is proposed by psychologist Jonathan Haidt, who likens the rational brain to an ineffectual jockey riding on the back of an unruly elephant. The jockey likes to think it is in control, but in reality the emotional elephant tramples anywhere it pleases.

Despite the rational brain's hubris, our lives are largely ruled by the unconscious urges and impulses of the intuitive brain and it would be naïve to think it could be otherwise. System 1 was there first and is never going to go away. We are all basically animals and a healthy System 1 allows us to express our natural animal vitality. That's a good thing, because all enjoyment of life depends on System 1. As we saw with the patient who suffered damage to his amygdala, life without System 1 isn't worth living. Thus the great skeptical philosopher David Hume keenly observed, "We speak not strictly and philosophically when we talk of the combat of passion and reason. Reason is, and ought only to be, the slave of the passions, and can never pretend to any other office than to serve and obey them."

We arrive at our political opinions through System 1 processes but, like the self-deluding jockey on the back of the unruly elephant, we pretend that it was System 2 that came up with our political philosophy. In truth, when we bring System 2 into play it is usually to help *defend* the initial positions taken by the System 1 elephant.

Kahneman-Tversky:
Towards A Psychology of Political Stupidity

> Thought is not a gift to man, but a
> laborious, precarious and volatile
> acquisition. — Jose Ortega y Gasset,
> "In Search of Goethe from Within"

Princeton psychologist Daniel Kahneman won a 2002 Nobel Prize for his systematic exploration of the "susceptibility to erroneous intuitions of intelligent, sophisticated, and perceptive individuals." Kahneman's research is unique in the extent of its dual impact on both psychology and economics. Working with long-term partner Amos Tversky of Stanford, Kahneman's "heuristics and biases" model of thinking transformed our modern view of human mental fallibility. Although initially derided by one American philosopher as offering nothing more than a "psychology of stupidity," the Kahneman-Tversky research has been extremely influential, earning thousands of academic citations and helping create a thriving new academic field known as behavioral economics.

People (even smart ones) are predictably stupid under certain conditions. Kahneman and Tversky sought to precisely chart those situations in which System 2, the reasoning system, failed to correct gross errors made by System 1. Their approach is often referred to as the "heuristics and biases" school of psychology. "Heuristics" are quick-and-speedy rules of thumb that System 1 relies on automatically. By definition, heuristics usually work, and if they don't, we are supposed to have System 2 standing by to let us know. System 1 is always guessing but it gets a pretty good number of its guesses correct, so we humans have a developed the lazy habit of believing in our guesses even when a moment's reflection would tell us that they are way off. We know that System 2 is smart enough to help us out, but it is puzzlingly inert in many situations.[18] Kahneman was the senior member of the team (and poignantly, the only one to receive the Nobel, Tversky having passed away of cancer in 1996). Let's set the scene for their revolutionary accomplishments.

When Kahneman graduated from Tel Aviv University in 1951 with a B.A. in psychology and began his military service, he was surprised to find that his college degree made him the top-trained psychologist in the Israeli army. At 21, he was assigned to a unit conducting psychological testing for officer recruitment.

Kahneman was disturbed by the feedback concerning the reliability of the officer recommendations made by his personnel team. The statistics showed no correlation between his team's predictions and actual officer performance in the field. The officer-screening mechanism was useless. In retrospect, this should not be surprising, since the Israelis evaluated officer capacity in a bizarre fashion inherited from the British Army. Each group of officer candidates was told to find a way to transport a telephone pole over an eight-foot high barrier without touching the barrier. The candidates' response to this challenge was carefully observed, recorded and analyzed, and officer recommendations were formulated accordingly. It was assumed that candidates who were brilliant in organizing telephone-pole transport would prove equally effective in combat. No one ever thought to challenge this basic assumption, which was sadly mistaken. The Israeli army was not frequently called upon to attack the enemy with telephone poles.

Kahneman was forced to accept the disconcerting fact that the army would be better off without his personnel team's "expertise." He was further struck by the fact that the proof received from the field did not lead to any elimination or revision of the process. The personnel team ignored the feedback and the army continued choosing officers on the basis of telephone-pole acumen. Kahneman realized this was highly illogical and later considered it the first "cognitive illusion" he had discovered.

When the army finally assigned Kahneman the task of coming up with a better way of screening candidates, Kahneman's reading brought him to Paul Meehl's classic 1954 monograph, "Clinical versus statistical prediction."

Meehl's meta-study established that simple statistical tabulations were generally superior to the intuitions of clinical experts such as doctors or psychologists. Meehl's findings have now been accepted by the medical community, although your family doctor may still diagnose you on the basis of his or her personal wisdom (the worse for your health). Were our doctors to reveal the truth it would spoil the shamanic aura surrounding their diagnoses, which may have a powerful placebo effect. However, if your doctor is following current medical orthodoxy, he or she should be running through a standard mental checklist — called a decision tree — for any suspected diagnosis. Like pilots trained to rely on instruments rather than on intuitions of what the sky looks like, good doctors should pay greater heed to the outcome of the clinical tabulations than to their own intuition.

Meehl's findings were published at a time when "expert opinion" was revered and unquestioned, particularly in medicine. The top of the medical pyramid was occupied by eminent physicians who had spent their lifetimes relying on their intuitions and had come to believe that their unchallenged "expert opinions" were the most reliable predictors of medical outcomes. Meehl established that expert opinion was not only surprisingly stupid, the experts had no idea how bad they were. In areas as diverse as brain trauma diagnosis, psychiatric triage, criminal parole predictions, and even college admissions, the so-called "experts" routinely over-estimated their predictive accuracy, which was consistently inferior to that achieved by simple statistical methods. This was pretty shocking. No one wanted to believe that a "shopping list" could be smarter than a brain surgeon, but that is what the data suggested.

Taking Meehl's conclusions to heart, Kahneman tried to implement a screening mechanism based on a simple questionnaire. This enraged his personnel team, the members of which felt reduced to the role of automatons. Kahneman negotiated a compromise — the personnel team could add their own subjective analyses — after considering the statistical tabulation of responses to the questionnaire. Reassuringly, Kahneman found that this last method produced the highest predictive correlation. In other words, it was only by forcing his personnel team to make use of both intuition and reason that he was able to arrive at the best results.

Later, as a young psychology professor, Kahneman began to experiment with a research methodology he called a "psychology of single questions." He learned the technique from Walter Mischel, whose research was based on asking children such simple questions as, "You can have this lollipop (a small one) today or that lollipop (a large one) tomorrow — which do you choose?" Kahneman was greatly impressed that the childrens' answers to such simple questions had a very high correlation with psychological traits and life outcomes (chidren who are willing to wait for the larger lollipop show greater ability to delay gratification, and they do better in school and in life).

Kahneman had now discovered a theme worthy of a life's work (human cognitive illusions) and a methodology (single questions asked to groups). All that this combustible mixture needed was a spark, and that was provided by Amos Tversky, Kahneman's junior colleague. Kahneman and Tversky were a great example of that wonderfully irrational human phenomenon, the team that is stronger than the sum of its parts. Although both researchers had successful independent careers, publishing numerous papers separately, none of their independent work came close to matching the success of the dozen papers they published together (their 1979 article on prospect theory in *Econometrica* is the most-cited article in economics history, impressive for a couple of psychologists).*

Part of the great popular appeal of the Kahneman–Tversky research program is that it was based on the "psychology of simple questions" — so the average reader can easily follow the argument (not so easy with Einstein's theory of special relativity). Let us try a few of the classic questions ourselves, as an introduction to the world of cognitive bias.

* Were it not for his untimely death, Tversky would doubtless have shared the Nobel podium with his old friend Danny. Fittingly, Kahneman devoted a portion of his Nobel lecture to a eulogy for Tvsersky, in which he recollected their collaboration movingly:

"Amos was often described by people who knew him as the smartest person they knew. He was also very funny, with an endless supply of jokes appropriate to every nuance of a situation. In his presence, I became funny as well, and the result was that we could spend hours of solid work in continuous mirth."

The dynamic duo's working method validates the Nietzschean motto that the greatest work is produced in the highest spirits.

TEST YOUR I.Q. (IRRATIONALITY QUOTIENT)

1) A bat and a ball cost $1.10 in total.
The bat costs $1 more than the ball. How much does the ball cost?

Most people answer "10 cents," which is clearly *wrong* if you think about it for more than ten seconds. The correct answer is: the ball costs a nickel. If you answered incorrectly, don't feel bad — more than half of a group of Princeton students got the answer wrong as well. Why are we so dumb when it comes to such a simple question? In Kahneman's words: "The respondents offered their responses without checking. People are not accustomed to thinking hard and are often content to trust a plausible judgment that comes quickly to mind." Since $1.10 divides neatly into $1.00 and ten cents, respondents leaped to this "obvious answer," though it was incorrect. Kahneman theorized that such errors derive from the "availability" heuristic — we rely on a mental shortcut to choose answers from the most obvious (available) options.

Kahneman has amusingly illustrated a variant of the availability bias called the "anchoring bias." When asked to estimate anything numerically, we have a tendency to over-rely (to "anchor") on any number that has recently been suggested to us, regardless of its relevance. Kahneman asks an audience to think of the last four digits of their social security number, and then asks them to estimate the number of physicians living in New York City. To a remarkable and entirely illogical extent, people's subsequent estimates of the number of New York physicians correlated with the last four digits of their own social security number (this even held true when the audience was composed of math teachers). Numbers hold a mystical sway over the human brain and it appears we are frighteningly suggestible when it comes to arguments based on data, even when the data is irrelevant. The implications for political propaganda are obvious. Next time you hear a political candidate quoting statistics, beware the anchoring bias.

2) Tom is an individual chosen randomly from the American population. He has been described as follows: "interested in politics, likes to participate in debates, and is eager to appear in the media." From the following options, what is the most likely profession for Tom?

a. Congressman
b. Salesman

Since there are hundreds of thousands of salesmen in America, while there are only 435 Congresspersons (and only 370 Congress*men*), it should be obvious that there is a much greater likelihood that Tom is a salesman than a congressman. However, a large majority of respondents choose A. (Congressman) as the correct answer. Why?

Kahneman refers to the cause as the representativeness heuristic — most people chose the group which seemed most representative of Tom's personality (he sounds like a Congressmen) instead of choosing the group to which he had a greater probability of belonging. People gave the right answer, but to the wrong question. They asked themselves how similar the portrait of Tom was to their mental picture of an average Congressman (a simple question, easily handled by System 1), instead of asking themselves what were the relative proportions of Congressmen and salesmen in the general population (which is a tiny bit harder, and requires us to fire up System 2).

3) How would you rate your personal attractiveness — above or below average?

If you answered "above average," it could be that you look like Brad Pitt or Angelina Jolie, but the research suggests you would answer the same way even if you looked like Prince Charles or Camilla. In general, people are wildly over-optimistic and over-confident when it comes to their own personal qualities. Obviously, by definition 50% of all people must be below average in looks, intelligence, sense of humor, kindness, education, and athleticism, but few people care to admit membership in the lower category.

If you answered questions 1 and 2 above correctly,* you may be a highly-rational exception to the general public (or you were smart enough to figure out that the context of the questions demanded a counter-intuitive answer). Whatever your personal case, most of your fellow citizens are highly-susceptible to these kinds of errors. What are we to make of this?

---

* I can't tell if you answered question 3 correctly unless you send me a recent picture.

Politics: The Land of Bias

> Where misunderstanding serves others
> as an advantage, one is helpless to make
> oneself understood. — Lionel Trilling

1. The "Ego" Biases: Sources of Political Irrationality

The essential driver of political bias is our need to boost and protect our fragile human ego. One writer refers to the constellation of ego-related biases as our "vain brain":[19]

"Lake Wobegon Effect" (also referred to as "over-confidence bias" and "self-serving bias") — This is the tendency to overestimate our own achievements and capabilities in relation to others, immortalized in fictional Lake Wobegon's pride that it is a town where "all the children are above average." This classic bit of humor from radio-land anticipated psychological research. People generally rank themselves as far above average, regardless of the criterion. Thus, 80% of respondents rated themselves in the top 30% of all drivers. When high school students were asked to rate their own ability to "get along with others," less than one percent rated themselves as below average, while one-fourth rated themselves in the top one percent (either proving something about the ubiquity of unjustified self-esteem, or demonstrating that our young people are even worse at math than we feared).

When a group of adult men were asked to rank themselves as either above or below average in athletic ability, not a single respondent ranked himself below average. The Lake Wobegon effect helps explain why American politicians always refer to America as the "greatest country in the world" — any less than that would seem distinctly below average.

The over-optimistic bias is characteristic of all healthy humans and does us more good than harm. Clinical depressives are less subject to the over-confidence bias than the rest of us, but their rationality has been purchased at too high a price — a happy life. In politicians and partisans, on the other hand, we see a case of the optimistic bias on steroids, a ridiculous hypertrophy of confidence and certainty in the face of contrary evidence. A candidate twenty points down in the polls on the eve of the election always assures his supporters that victory is still certain. Under these circumstances, rationality would seem cowardly.

Vast over-confidence has become a mandatory characteristic for political candidates. Is this rational? We select from the general population those people who are most afflicted with excessive personal optimism and self-love, then we entrust these brazen souls with the key to the treasury and command of the armed forces. The rest, as the saying goes, is history.

Political partisans, like rabid sports fans, are especially prone to wishful thinking. Republican voters expect and anticipate Republican victories, regardless of what the polls say, while Democrats are sure of the contrary. Over-optimism becomes progressively more pronounced amongst the more zealous.

As Paul Meehl first demonstrated, the so called "experts" are even more disturbingly prone to overconfidence bias than the rest of us. While Meehl's research focused on doctors, psychologists and social workers, political scientist Philip Tetlock extended the findings to a group of "political experts," who were asked to give opinions on the expected outcomes of various political scenarios.

Tetlock compared the predictive accuracy of the political experts with a theoretical "monkey" who would randomly pick answers from a short list of possibilities. In Tetlock's analysis, the combat between man and simian yielded a tie, suggesting that political experts had little to feel smug about (although the theoretical monkey was probably quite pleased). Despite their comeuppance, the political experts maintained a towering confidence in their own abilities. Remember this the next time an "expert" gives you his or her "professional" opinion. Many Americans fear that direct democracy would take government away from the experts, the "policy wonks" who run Washington. Tetlock's research suggests that the citizenry should also be wary of the wonks.[20]

Self-serving bias is a variant of over-confidence bias: it refers to the tendency to interpret events in a way which is most soothing for our egos. While overconfidence bias is rooted in an excessive optimism toward the future, self-serving bias allows us to view the past and present through egotistically rose-tinted glasses. Our memory is a willing conspirator of the self-serving bias. Psychologists have established that we constantly re-write and over-write our memories in order to make ourselves look and feel better. In the political sphere, self-serving bias leads partisans to write completely different histories of the same events. For liberals, the Reagan era was marked by disastrous budget deficits and the corruption of the Savings & Loan crisis and the Iran-Contra affair. For conservatives, Reagan made America feel good again and he defeated communism in his spare time, between naps. American politics has two, parallel histories — red and blue — and no one can finally say which is right.

Partisan Bias: The Un-Wisdom of Teams — Partisan bias is the extension of self-serving bias and overconfidence bias into the world of groups and teams. Partisan bias is the most important source of irrational political behavior. As soon as we feel we belong to a group, we begin to view that group as superior to other groups. It is so easy to elicit partisan bias that psychologists have proposed the existence of "implicit partisanship" — a hard-wired human predisposition to take sides and then prefer that side.

If people are shown a list of names and asked to study it for as briefly as a few minutes, they develop a preference for the names on the list and consider them superior to other names.[21] If a group of students is told that they are being randomly assigned to one of two teams to watch a taped basketball game, the students immediately develop a clear preference for their assigned team and later will argue that the referee was unfairly calling fouls against their team.[22]

If a group of people are told that they will be assigned to Group A or Group B according to a coin toss, they begin to prefer their group even *before* they are sure they are assigned to it. Those to whom it has been merely hinted that they may have been assigned to Group B begin nonetheless to express a clear preference for the members of B and a belief that B is generally superior to Group A.

While the existence of the partisan bias has been confirmed by recent research, it has long been apparent to perceptive observers of political argument. Thus Socrates noted (in Plato's *Phaedo*): "The partisan, when he is engaged in a dispute, cares nothing about the rights of the question, but is anxious only to convince his hearers of his own assertions."

Bandwagon effect — Also popularly known as the "herd instinct," this term is based on the observation that people tend to follow the crowd, even when the crowd is doing something irrational (drinking poisoned Kool-Aid, for example, or buying a thong bathing suit). The bandwagon effect is the broad social manifestation of the human desire to conform. Human beings desire so desperately to conform that they will engage in clearly irrational activity. In one of the most famous experiments in the history of psychology, Stanley Milgram found it disturbingly easy to induce ordinary citizens to torture a human research subject with electric shocks (the citizens wanted to conform to the experimental context).[23]

In politics, the bandwagon effect is absolutely crucial and all campaign managers rack their brains trying to figure out how to induce it amongst the electorate at just the right time. We can observe the bandwagon effect lurch predictably into operation every four years, just after the first presidential primaries — in the sudden snowballing of support for the early winners.

2. Confirmation bias: the motor of political irrationality

Like an Iago of the political soul, the confirmation bias should be cast as the evil culprit of this book. The "confirmation bias" is the human tendency to discredit or ignore information which contradicts our beliefs, while we uncritically adopt information that supports our beliefs. Studies have demonstrated that people are only open to hearing new information if it confirms their previously-held beliefs.

Confirmation bias explains why information-exchange tends always to strengthen and reinforce our latent biases. The more we learn about political issues, the more biased we become. The confirmation bias is thus the motor of political irrationality. Once we get a tiny bit biased one way or another, the confirmation bias pushes us further and further in that direction. Increased political awareness and education just ends up making us all more deeply biased.

In one classic study, a group of pro-death penalty students and a group of anti-death penalty students evaluated two "opposing" studies on capital punishment. In fact, the studies were identical, except that they carried different titles and came to different conclusions. The students concluded that the study which supported their pre-existing views was clearly superior in its facts and methodology to the other study, and they were able to present a number of highly specific examples to support their evaluations. Since both studies were based on exactly the same information, the students' preference for one study over the other could only be derived from bias.[24]

When we receive mixed information, part of it supporting our views and part of it contradicting our views, we are attentive to that the part that supports our views, which we accept as accurate and true, while the part that contradicts our views barely registers in our consciousness, and if it does, is quickly explained away. If we are forced to confront a strong argument, our emotions compel us to find an even stronger rationalization for our prejudice against it. Each argument we face only reinforces our biases. The stronger the adversary argument, the more stubbornly we rationalize our point of view. This is why highly-educated people can be so obnoxiously opinionated and closed-minded when it comes to politics.

Consider the recent controversy over whether the press is subject to a liberal or conservative bias. The confirmation bias teaches us that even if partisan voters were provided with perfectly unbiased reporting, indeed even if they were provided with exactly the same information, their opinions would still grow further and further apart, driven by the inexorable force of the confirmation bias. In politics, we pick and choose what we want to hear and believe; and we want to go on believing what we already believe.

Once you understand the power of the confirmation bias to make people irrationally stubborn in their beliefs, you will begin to see evidence of it everywhere — even (sigh) in the mirror. Most of us fall prey to the confirmation bias every day. The clever reader will have realized by now that if confirmation bias is really so widespread, it might even have spread to... us.

Once I had developed the thesis that human beings are systematically irrational when it comes to politics, I scoured the academic literature for confirmation and corroboration. I found so much confirmation that I was greatly comforted — until I had had a chance to fully absorb the implications of the confirmation bias. I was not following my own advice — to check carefully for disconfirmation. If anybody should avoid falling into the trap of the confirmation bias — it is someone writing a book chapter about the confirmation bias! All scholars are supposed to know that one disconfirming study is more valuable than a hundred confirming studies, because a single disconfirming study can disprove a model, while a hundred confirming studies may not be sufficient to remove all doubt. Sadly, in my view, many of the authors in this field have failed to face up to their own confirmation bias (e.g., Lakoff, Westen, Gore, etc., all of whom go in search of scientific support for their ideological positions and then — surprise — find it).

I have tried to face up to the "confirmation bias challenge" by critiquing my own biases (admittedly, there are serious philosophical limits to this approach). I reviewed authors critical of the Kahneman-Tversky model and did the same for other studies cited in this book. Acting as my own devil's advocate, I repeatedly asked myself if I was ignoring contrary evidence or reasoning. This is the lesson of the confirmation bias, and it is especially relevant to all political reflection — we have to continually re-examine our beliefs, making a special effort to be honest with ourselves. If we want to overcome our own political irrationality, this is our first assignment. The essence of political rationality is a determination to confront one's own confirmation bias.

My own confirmation-bias challenge yielded a greater appreciation of counter-arguments to my initial thesis (that people are systematically irrational when it comes to politics). Below, I try to summarize the most compelling arguments *against* my thesis. We should sincerely explore the best counter-arguments to our own political beliefs.

THE COUNTER-ARGUMENT

The strongest critique of political irrationality is found in the daily functioning of a large society.

The "gut rationality" underlying our instinctive, emotional, herd-like behavior is sufficient to sustain our civilization and even allow it to slowly progress. This instinctive rationality is the flip side of the coin of political irrationality; we could call it the "political heuristic." Political irrationality is what you call it when the political heuristic doesn't work — but most of the time, it does work.

In politics, System 1 is "crazy like a fox." It doesn't waste time and brainpower on political issues that don't really matter in our everyday lives.

Taking the "confirmation-bias challenge" has allowed me to come to a more nuanced view of political irrationality. Although I still argue that most of our political thinking is System 1 thinking (and therefore susceptible to logical error), I must admit our political system functions anyway.

My point here is that it can function much better.

Conclusion: Living With Political Irrationality

> Yes, man is a highly-reasonable, brain-using animal. But he also has distinct biological tendencies to act in the most ridiculous, prejudiced, amazingly asinine ways. He is, quite normally and naturally, inclined to be childish, suggestible, superstitious, bigoted and downright idiotic about much of his personal behavior, particularly about his relations with other people. — Albert Ellis, with Robert Harper, *A Guide to Rational Living in an Irrational World* (1961)

Kahneman and Tversky's research shows us that we frequently misperceive the world around us. The main causes of our erroneous views are:

1) Habitual Mental Laziness — We resist the effort involved in turning on System 2, the analytical part of the brain; and
2) Bias — Our view of the world is warped by self-interest, and that self-interest is in turn aroused by political partisanship, ideology and patriotism.

Humans move through life instinctively and emotionally, living (and dying) by the snap judgment. Most of the time, our intuitive judgments are correct. System 1 is like a crude but effective auto-pilot, a cruise-control system for life that allows us to economize on effort and attention. This allows brainy System 2 to relax and drowse most of the time. The easiest way to satisfy our laziness and group bias at the same time is to drift along with the herd, which is what most people do when it comes to politics.

Since most political issues are complex, our mental laziness provides a strong predisposition toward political bias. Political issues are inherently difficult. Bias makes them simple. To achieve true understanding of a single political issue can be the work of a lifetime. Alan Greenspan spent fifty years engaged in the intense study of the regulation of financial markets, only to discover at the end that there were still a few things left to learn. Thinking about politics is so hard, while following the herd is so easy.

If we are loyal partisans, System 1 takes care of politics for us, and System 2 can nap all day. The second irresistible virtue of partisan loyalty is that it promotes social harmony. Our friends are always much happier with us when we are loyal to the team. Despite these benefits, allegiance to the herd does have a countervailing drawback. Under certain circumstances, herds are known to stampede over cliff-sides. The suicidal plunge of the lemmings is thus the archetypal symbol of political irrationality.* If you are unfortunate enough to be part of a stupid, stampeding herd (global financial investors prior to 2008, for example), group loyalty may prove to be your downfall.

Abstract rationality becomes noticeable when there is a trouble-maker in the herd. When a Democrat annoys her friends by pointing out the benefits of free trade agreements, or when a Republican irritates his co-workers by arguing that racial bias is pervasive enough to require affirmative action — we may suspect that someone has been thinking.

Political rationality is thus doubly taxing. Not only does it require great effort (thinking is hard), it annoys and worries our friends. People who engage in too much political rationality may find that friends are becoming scarce. Socrates, for example, was history's greatest master of impromptu rationality — which is precisely why the Athenians forced him to drink poison. Socrates' pesky rationality was so annoying to Athenian society that he literally talked himself to death.

Perhaps we should be careful to respect the herd? After all, when the herd goes in the right direction we have a case of successful political heuristics, what we might call "gut politics." Surely it is rational to follow the herd when they are headed in the right direction? There must be times when gut politics makes the most sense, while at other times abstract rationality is better.

Some people feel most at home in the heart of the herd (conservatives), while others are natural loners and outsiders (liberals). Red herds and blue herds follow different rules. Red herds like to run in tight formation, even when they're plunging over the edge of the cliff. Blue herds are more chaotic, with lots of stragglers, but they, too, plunge regularly over cliff-sides.

In either case, passionate intensity of feeling is the key warning sign that your political herd is about to lead you astray. Political judgment is most questionable when it is most passionate. When the herd seems particularly

---

*The lemming should be the mascot of all political parties everywhere.

emotional — whether greedy, frenzied, angry or fearful — take your distance. Sometimes the passionate herd is correct, but it is not a safe bet.

Let us return to the examples that opened the chapter:

MARK was the frustrated Hillary fan who crossed party lines to vote for McCain because he was still fuming that Obama had defeated Hillary. From the perspective of abstract rationality, Mark's vote was irrational, because Hillary's policies were much closer to Obama's than to McCain's. However, from the perspective of social rationality, Mark's vote could make sense if Mark usually hangs out with a crowd of equally insanely-rabid Hillary supporters (maybe he's hot for pant-suits and policy vixens). The intensity of Mark's passionate support for Hillary was a warning sign that his final vote might lack abstract rationality. When Hillary accepted Obama's nomination to be Secretary of State, Mark felt foolish.

SALLY was the super-patriotic citizen who decided to stay in line to vote even when she had a sick daughter at home. From the perspective of abstract rationality, Sally was nuts. Sally had no chance of changing the election (the Democrat was up thirty points in the polls), but she did have a small chance of killing her daughter. Even from the perspective of social rationality, Sally's vote was irrational. Perhaps she thought her action would earn praise from her flag-waving peers, but instead they scolded her for being a careless mom. Sally's passionate patriotism clouded her maternal judgment (since I wrote this example, I can report to worried readers that Sally's daughter survived anyway).

ANDREA was the clueless young voter who cast her ballot purely on the basis of a candidate's smile. From the perspective of abstract rationality, we can criticize Andrea's decision to vote at all. What did Andrea think she was contributing to the public sphere, given her admittedly total ignorance of politics? However, from the perspective of social rationality, Andrea's vote made perfect sense. Now, when her friends ask her if she voted, Andrea can say, "Yes!" Her friends will congratulate her and they will all happily go out for drinks in a bar which is too noisy to permit conversation. The media will wax eloquent about the influx of young voters. Most importantly, Andrea no longer has to worry about the scorn her friends would have poured on her if she hadn't voted. Andrea's friends are very passionate about voting. Perhaps someday they will become equally passionate about acquiring political knowledge and judgment.

THAT LARGE RICH COUNTRY (the one that went fifty years without enacting universal health coverage, though the majority of its citizens favored such coverage): This country really should think twice before it calls itself a "democracy." From the perspective of abstract rationality, we cannot accept a country's claim to democracy when it consistently fails to heed the desires of the citizenry. On the other hand, from the perspective of social rationality, this self-flattery is perfectly understandable. If "democracy" is a good thing (we are invariably told that it is), then it makes sense for citizens to refer to their country as a democracy (whether it is or not), especially if doing so makes them feel superior to citizens from other countries. That is why so many countries call themselves democracies when the obvious reality is that their governance is anything but democratic.

Fortunately for humanity, our penchant for political irrationality is often attenuated and counter-balanced by the wisdom of gut politics. Otherwise, the world would be in even worse shape than it is today. Some people might argue in consequence that political irrationality should simply be tolerated and accepted as part of human nature. However, as we will see in the next chapter, political irrationality is far from harmless.

CHAPTER 3

War, Ruin, Panic: Cases of Irrationality

Dark Truth #3:
Sometimes, our political irrationality is harmless.
Unfortunately, the other times include times of war, depression and panic.

The Varieties of Irrational Experience

In reading the history of nations, we find that, like individuals, they have...their seasons of excitement and recklessness....Millions of people become simultaneously impressed with one delusion, and run after it, till their attention is caught by some new folly... We see one nation suddenly seized, from its highest to its lowest members, with a fierce desire for military glory.... Money, again, has often been a cause of the delusion of multitudes. Sober nations have all at one become desperate gamblers, and risked almost their existence upon the turn of a piece of paper.... Men, it has been well said, think in herds; it will be seen that they go mad in herds, while they recover their senses slowly, and one by one. — Charles Mackay, *Memoirs of Extraordinary Popular Delusions* (1852)

Political irrationality is manifested by all of the players in the political arena:

Citizen irrationality — Most people's political thinking is clouded by chronic mental laziness and bias. Partisanship magnifies that irrationality. We should never expect extreme partisans to be fully rational about the current president, for example. During the George W. Bush administration, Republican die-hards worshiped the president as an icon of American decency and toughness, while Democrats despised him as a mean-spirited moron. When Barack Obama achieved electoral victory in 2008 he was promptly acclaimed as a Messiah of social change by choirs of Democrats; right-wing Republicans grumbled that he was an effete socialist with America-hating tendencies.

Elite irrationality — Social elites — politicians, "experts," and business leaders — are also susceptible to different forms of irrationality.

Politicians, like everyone else, tend to believe whatever their self-interest compels them to believe. Inevitably, politicians must choose between their personal self-interest and the public interest (e.g., should I accept large campaign contributions from a dirty corporation?). The self-serving structure of human nature suggests that the politicians will tend to follow their own self-interest but rationalize their choices as actually being in the citizenry's interests. Consequently, it would be naïve to expect any other political landscape than the one we have —e.g., politicians touting the public interest while catering, behind closed doors, to the wealthy and powerful.

"Experts" are particularly subject to overconfidence bias. Economists, scientists, business leaders and government officials are all very smart people who become progressively unused to criticism and self-criticism as their careers advance. Most of the time, the experts are right; but that's no help when they are colossally wrong, as they were in the financial crisis of 2008.

Partisan irrationality — Political parties, like people, strive to project an appearance of consistency, even when they are really internally-conflicted. Since political parties represent diverse interests, they are always forced to contradict themselves, sooner or later. Republicans, for example, have always marketed themselves as the party of small government and fiscal responsibility. However, Republican presidents like Ronald Reagan and George W. Bush proved to be military spendthrifts who presided over unprecedented federal deficits. The Democrats present themselves as the defenders of the poor and the middle-class, but this leads inevitably to conflict. The poor pay little in taxes while the middle-class pays quite a bit. When pressed, as in the case of welfare reform in the mid-1990s, the Democrats abandon the poor in order to hold on to the middle class — then, of course, adamantly deny having done so.

National irrationality — There are times in a nation's history when the entire populace, or at least the great majority of the populace, becomes unified in its commitment and dedication to a particular goal or ideal. Unfortunately, this national unity has frequently corresponded with the most extreme irrationality. Several of the horrific genocides of the 20th century were sustained by patriotic or ethnic unity. One might have hoped that by now the world would have learned to be wary of patriotism, but it is still extolled everywhere as the very essence of civic virtue (good news for arms merchants, at least).

Bias in Action: The War Bias

> How good bad music and bad reasons
> sound when one marches against
> an enemy! — Nietzsche, *The Dawn* (1881)

A "war bias" has been confirmed *ad nauseam* throughout history, most recently in Iraq. Although I will refer to it as a single bias, it would be more accurate to speak of a large group of biases working together.

The war bias predisposes our national leaders to overestimate the likelihood of military victory and to underestimate the possibility of compromise. In an article entitled "Why Hawks Win," Kahneman observed that every single one of the cognitive biases discovered in the past forty years favored "hawks" over "doves."[25]

One key bias is the "fundamental attribution error," the tendency to attribute bad motives to adversaries even when there is evidence that they are acting under constraint. Under the sway of the fundamental attribution error, we rationalize away our own bad actions by attributing them to bad luck or compulsion, but if other people do bad things to us, we attribute their actions to bad motives. Kahneman explains how the fundamental attribution error can operate in the pre-war context:

> A policymaker or diplomat involved in a tense exchange with a foreign government is likely to observe a great deal of hostile be-

havior by that country's representatives. Some of that behavior may indeed be the result of deep hostility. But some of it is simply a response to the current situation as it is perceived by the other side. What is ironic is that individuals who attribute others' behavior to deep hostility are quite likely to explain away their own behavior as a result of being "pushed into a corner" by an adversary. The tendency of both sides of a dispute to view themselves as reacting to the other's provocative behavior is a familiar feature of marital quarrels, and it is found as well in international conflicts.[26]

In the case of the Iraq invasion, the Bush administration interpreted Saddam Hussein's refusal to cooperate with U.N. weapons inspectors as evidence that he had weapons of mass destruction (W.M.D.s). Actually, Saddam Hussein had dismantled his W.M.D. capacities, but left the impression even amongst his own senior command that he had hidden weaponry. Hussein probably felt that the illusion that he still possessed some weapons would both intimidate enemies and cower his own people. If so, Hussein could have thought that a complete show of cooperation with inspectors would have revealed his deception. Reasonably or not, Hussein may have felt himself constrained by circumstances to maintain some level of doubt as to whether he still had W.M.D.s. Falling prey to fundamental attribution error, the Bush administration took Hussein's intransigence as a sign of his determination to keep and eventually use W.M.D. (*viz.* Condoleezza Rice's ominous references to the danger of a mushroom cloud).

The Bush team compounded this error with a large dose of overconfidence bias. In retrospect, Vice President Cheney's assurances that the conflict would be quick and easy and that American soldiers would be greeted as liberators seems absurdly overconfident. Sadly, though, it is typical. Military history is strewn with examples of spectacularly unrealistic optimism. In his book *Overconfidence and War: The Havoc and Glory of Positive Illusions*, Dominic Johnson cites a number of examples.[27]

At the beginning of the Civil War, residents of Washington, D.C. brought picnics to the first major battle, expecting to celebrate a decisive Union rout which would promptly end the conflict. In a darkly comic example of optimism, Union General John Sedgwick inscribed his name in military history when, watching enemy artillery, he calmly predicted: "They couldn't hit an elephant at this distance..." (sentence permanently interrupted when an enemy bullet penetrated the General's highly optimistic brain). At the outset of World War I, the leaders of every nation involved predicted a quick and complete victory, in what turned out to be history's bloodiest war.

The war bias not only helps start wars, it keeps them going and prevents the negotiation of peace. There is evidence that we tend to reject compromises made by an adversary even though we would have found the same compromise acceptable if it had come from our side. Our tendency to believe that "my compromise is better than your compromise" is known by psychologist as the bias of "reactive devaluation" (sometimes known as the "not-invented-here" syndrome).

As Kahneman puts it: "The very fact that a concession is offered by somebody perceived as hostile undermines the content of the proposal. What was said matters less than who said it." In one experiment a group of Israeli Jews was presented with an actual Israeli-authored peace plan. Some respondents were told it was authored by the Palestinians, while the rest were told the truth. Respondents viewed the plan much more negatively when told it came from the Palestinians than when told it came from the Israeli government.

A final war bias element is the irrational bias against cutting losses. Kahneman and Tversky demonstrated this bias by asking individuals to choose between the following options:

A. — A sure loss of $890
B. — A 90% chance to lose $1000 and a 10% chance to lose nothing

Statistically, your odds are better with Option A, but the majority of respondents take the gamble in Option B. Irrationally, people prefer a large potential loss to a smaller certain loss.

Humans hate to admit defeat and so we will snatch at any straw that promises a possible victory, even when there is a good chance it will only lead us to a worse defeat. When a conflict is going badly and it looks like we're going to lose, our instinct is to hold out and hope for a miracle rather than to accept the bad news. This bias may partially explain why the American army is still in Iraq as I write this.

Economic Biases

One theory of political irrationality holds that in practice irrationalities cancel out, and are therefore harmless. For every irrational voter with an extreme view of the world, there is some other equally irrational voter with the opposite view. The extremes cancel each other out, leaving political outcomes to be decided by the rational minority, no matter how small. Even if 99% of voters were politically irrational, the government could still function rationally so long as the voters' irrationality was randomly distributed. The remaining 1% of rational voters would make the correct choice.

The economist Bryan Caplan presents strong evidence that at least in the economic sphere, political irrationalities do not cancel each other out but instead cumulate. Caplan posed the same questions to two different populations — "ordinary" citizens and economists. By comparing the average popular opinions on economic issues to the consensus view of economists, Caplan generated a list of popular economic misconceptions.[28]

Critics have pointed out that Caplan does not really prove that the citizens are wrong — he merely establishes their disagreement with economists. Indeed, economists are rarely unanimous on economic issues. Despite this, Caplan's evidence for the existence of persistent economic biases is robust. The gap between the popular view and the view of professional economists is too large to be easily discounted.

For example, Caplan finds:

Anti-foreign bias — Most people don't like and don't trust foreigners, though we are loath to admit it. A number of popular economic misconceptions stem from a general anti-foreign bias, which is but a patriotic variant of partisan bias. Caplan's survey showed that the biggest disagreement between professional economists and the general public was over the proposition, "Foreign aid spending is too high." Citizens overwhelmingly agreed, economists disagreed. Citizen ignorance appears to explain the divergent opinions. Citizens estimate that 10% of the U.S. government budget goes to foreign aid, while the true figure is closer to 0.7%. Aware of the true figures, economists are not at all concerned about foreign-aid spending, while the average citizen is convinced that America is too generous.

Similarly, the proposition "There are too many immigrants," was widely supported by the public and just as widely rejected by economists. Caplan attributes the disagreement to the public's anti-foreign bias combined with a failure to appreciate the positive economic impact of immigration. For economists, immigration is a form of international trade in labor, which theoretically should increase the wealth of the country receiving the immigration.

Make-work bias — The general public is greatly concerned about the overseas "outsourcing" of jobs by American corporations. The economists, however, are not as upset. Economists believe that the public focuses only on the jobs being lost to the economy without paying comparable attention to the jobs being created.

Caplan says the public's concerns arise out of the "make-work" bias: the mistaken premise that it is better to make people work at unproductive jobs rather than allow the unproductive positions to be terminated and replaced by jobs in more productive sectors. Thus, the general public believes that "companies sending jobs overseas" is negative for the economy, while economists believe that manufacturing jobs go overseas when American capital has found a more profitable use for American labor, which is a good thing.

In fact, statistics show that job losses are seven times more often attributable to technological innovation than to outsourcing, but no one complains about nifty new products. If someone calls you on an iPhone to complain about job losses due to outsourcing, they are contradicting themselves.

Anti-market bias — A number of disagreements between economists and the general public are based on the public's general suspicion of markets and corporations. Thus, the public believes that business profits are too high and that corporate executives are overpaid. In his 2008 campaign for the Democratic nomination to the Presidency, Senator John Edwards made his pledge to fight against "corporate greed" the central plank in his political platform. His argument resonated strongly with a large sector of the American public which is deeply anti-corporate. The issue of corporate greed returned to the forefront when it was reported that huge bonuses had been paid by financial firms that been bailed out by the government.

Economists are less bothered by the issue of corporate greed because economic theory holds that high profits will inevitably attract competitors and new products, with the long-term outcome being higher-quality products and services at lower prices for consumers, with lower average profits for producers.

Caplan has been criticized for coming to un-democratic conclusions. Indeed, Caplan argues that governments follow bad economic policy primarily because politicians are constrained to carry out the irrational directions of an economically-illiterate populace. Consequently, he believes that voter examinations are a good idea because they would create an electorate with a higher educational level (Caplan's research shows that education decreases economic bias). If he could, one infers, Caplan would turn the running of our economic affairs entirely over to economists. He is certainly no fan of greater democracy in economic policy-making.

I agree that the citizenry holds a number of economic misconceptions, but it is a mistake to focus only on economic irrationality while failing to address the underlying political irrationality. Citizens have been indoctrinated to believe that an elitist system that presents them with no real choices is "democratic." In such an environment, they have little incentive to acquire the economic sophistication which Caplan expects of them.

Political Irrationality and the Financial Panic of 2008

> When things began to go wrong, there was a truly bovine stampede for the exits. The result was a massive, synchronized downturn in virtually all asset markets. — Niall Ferguson, *Wall Street Lays Another Egg* (2008)

The Mysteries of Panic

Irrationality was the leitmotiv of the global financial panic which began in September 2008. During the heat of the 2008 crisis, politicians, bureaucrats and economists vied with the citizenry in displays, and counter-accusations, of irrationality. When the dust settles, whom should we blame?

In the last section we encountered the argument that bad economic policies are the inevitable result of too much democracy — the politicians make mistakes because they are forced to heed an irrational public. We would all be better off, in this view, if the politicians could just ignore the citizens and only listen to economists.

The economists were therefore hard-pressed to explain the financial meltdown of 2008, which occurred under the watchful eye of some of the world's most brilliant economists. In particular, the previous Fed Chairman, the legendary Alan Greenspan (known to Congress by the modest nickname of "the Oracle"), had striven mightily for over a decade to prevent the financial regulation of derivatives.

Today, it is widely conceded that Greenspan blew it (he admitted so himself to Congress), but in the early 1990s Greenspan was so revered as a demi-god of economics that he easily out-maneuvered Congressman Edward Markey and the General Accounting Office when they called for strict oversight of derivatives. In the late 1990s Greenspan once again went to war, this time with Brooksley Born (another bureaucrat). Once again, Greenspan's clout as the nation's economic wizard-in-chief enabled him to block the derivatives regulation that might have avoided the eventual catastrophe.

How can an economist like Caplan explain that in the most important economic debacle of the last eighty years, the non-economists were right, while the great Oracle was wrong? If anyone was well-prepared to steer the nation clear of economic catastrophe, it was Dr. Ben Bernanke, Greenspan's successor as Chairman of the U.S. Federal Reserve. Bernanke was a recognized academic expert on the Great Depression, the author of scholarly articles on the topic. Though Bernanke may yet shepherd the country through its financial tempest, he certainly did not do a good job of avoiding dangerous waters.

His failure cannot be excused by the supposed unpredictability of the sub-prime meltdown. Financial panics are not a new phenomenon. The global financial panic of 2008 was in many respects similar to a credit crunch described by the Roman historian Tacitus, which occurred in 33 C.E.

In that episode, Roman property values crashed as the result of a regulatory error, loans were called in which could not be paid, and panic ensued as fortunes were destroyed until the Emperor finally stepped in with state funds to guarantee interest-free credit to restore order — which came quite slowly. Sound familiar?

The U.S. experienced serious financial panics in 1785, 1792, 1819, 1837, 1873, 1893, 1907 and 1929. The world has dealt with a number of financial panics in recent decades, notably the Mexican peso crisis of 1994, the East Asian crisis of 1997, the Russian meltdown of 1998, and the U.S. bailout of Long Term Capital Management in 1998. There have been abundant opportunities to learn from mistakes.

Dr. Ben Bernanke, the Chairman of the U.S. Federal Reserve, knew this history very well from his academic studies of the Great Depression. Quite confident that he knew what he was talking about, Bernanke made the following toast (and boast) at Milton Friedman's 90th birthday party in 2002: "Let me end my talk by abusing slightly my status as an official representative of the Federal Reserve System. I would like to say to Milton...: Regarding the Great Depression. You're right, we did it. We're very sorry. But thanks to you, we won't do it again."

Bernanke over-estimated his own ability to foresee and prevent economic calamity. Like stampedes, panics can have consequences that are both tragic and unnecessary. Human lives are trampled underfoot, when everyone might have survived if people had kept their calm. In such circumstances, to paraphrase FDR, the main thing that we have to fear is irrationality itself. Why then, did the fabulously-knowledgeable Bernanke rush to present an indecipherable bailout plan to the U.S. Congress (and public) in the most terrifying and ominous of tones? Isn't this like a fireman yelling "fire" in a crowded theater? While waving a can of kerosene and flicking a Zippo? How could Bernanke have failed in a task for which he was so exquisitely well-prepared?

While Caplan blamed the citizenry for irrationality, this book blames human nature, as the capacity for irrationality afflicts economists, politicians and bureaucrats as thoroughly as it does the ordinary citizen. As the 2008 financial crisis developed, each of these players became infected with one or more strains of the irrationality virus:

Bandwagon Effect & Herd Instinct

Financial bubbles and panics are classic examples of the herd instinct in action. We should always be particularly vigilant as to their potential negative effects. Aside from physical safety, nothing motivates humans more powerfully than greed or the fear of financial ruin. As David Hume noted in 1741, "Avarice, or the desire of gain, is a universal passion which operates at all times, in all places and upon all persons." When the bandwagon effect takes over in financial markets, we can witness the most violent stampedes, reminiscent of the charge of the bulls in an old Merrill Lynch commercial. Consequently, de-regulation of financial markets is always risky. How is it possible that we have not yet fully absorbed that lesson, after dozens and dozens of panics? Why do we continue to listen to the "experts"?

Over-confidence Bias / The "Expert Problem"

As Paul Meehl and Philip Tetlock established, it can be dangerous to rely on "experts." Most of the time they give good advice, but they are bad at noticing when they are off track, and they have no idea how far off they can be (they can be very far off). Economists argue that we should routinely defer to the advice of economic experts, but Meehl's research (confirmed by the 2008 panic) suggests that this would be a recipe for disaster.

Of course we should consult experts, but we should never abandon our common sense when we do so. Sometimes the experts are offended when we dare to question them (Greenspan bristled when challenged by Markey and Born). The arrogant self-assurance of experts often intimidates the ordinary citizen. Despite this, we non-experts must learn to hang tough. Every time a surgeon accidentally cuts off the wrong leg, or an airline pilot steers his plane into a mountainside despite the timidly-expressed reservations of his co-pilot, we have more concrete evidence of the danger of the Expert Problem. It is one of the main reasons we need more democracy, not less.

Deciding What Happened: Red History, Blue History

When something calamitous occurs in a human life, a rational person seeks to understand the nature of the occurrence, so as to be able to avoid it in the future. This elementary form of rationality is almost impossibly challenging for modern republics because our bi-polar political structure forces us to take a schizophrenic view of history. Whenever something momentous happens, we construct alternative red vs. blue histories.

After the financial crisis broke in September 2008, each political party claimed it was the other party's fault: "We saw this coming. We called out warnings to no avail."

Democrats pointed out the Bush administration's failure to regulate derivative markets. Republicans harped on the Clinton administration's decision to promote sub-prime mortgages. Who was right? If you want a clear view, don't ask a partisan historian (and good luck finding any other kind).

Confirmation bias

Ideologues are even more subject to the confirmation bias than the rest of us, and many economists are ideologues. Alan Greenspan, in his blanket refusal to consider any regulation of the derivatives markets, was too dogmatic in his loyalty to the libertarian ideals of Ayn Rand and Milton Friedman. Chairman Greenspan was exposed to plenty of disconfirming evidence (smart people warned him under Congressional oath that unregulated derivative markets were dangerous). Even Warren Buffett, the ultimate financial pragmatist, had publicly stated that unregulated derivatives were "financial weapons of mass destruction." Securely coddled in layers of confirmation bias, Greenspan ignored all the alarm-bells.

Self-serving bias

Wall Street bankers had learned by 1998 that trading in sub-prime mortgages was immensely profitable. Therefore, we should not have been surprised when those same investment bankers argued that further regulation of derivatives markets was unnecessary. The mistake was to listen to them.

Unfortunately, the investment bankers were impossible to ignore. Treasury Secretary Henry Paulson, like his predecessor Robert Rubin, was a former CEO of Goldman Sachs. Both men had earned hundreds of millions of dollars on Wall Street, gambling in the very derivatives markets that the well-meaning bureaucrats and politicians now threatened to regulate. Investment banks (like Goldman Sachs) generously funded the political campaigns of key politicians from both parties. Blinded by self-serving bias, the bankers fought against the regulations that would have preserved the stability of the global economy (and upon which they, too, depended).

Acting out of self-interest, the politicians helped them. It is extremely unlikely that there would ever be a recession so severe that it would result in a decrease in Congressional salaries. From a self-interested perspective, a member of Congress has more to fear from campaign funds drying up than from an economic depression.

Partisan bias

When Paulson and Fed Chair Ben Bernanke presented their first bailout plan to Congress, they were strongly supported by President Bush, by both presidential candidates and by the party leadership of both parties. The government's top leaders were then shocked to find their rescue plan voted down by a Republican revolt. Why did the Republican politicians, so loyal to their president when he led them into war, now refuse to go along when he tried to save the economy?

Partisan bias provides the answer. Large government takeovers and bailouts are in principle anathema to strict conservatives. Partisan bias can force a person into an irrational consistency. Asking the Republicans to vote for the bailout was like asking a country-music band to play hip-hop.

Conclusion: Political irrationality matters...

Humans are certainly capable of political rationality, but the opposite is all too often the case. Economists and politicians are just as susceptible to political irrationality as the rest of us. Political irrationality can be costly. It can start wars and financial panics and, what is worse, aggravate those catastrophes once they're underway.

Despite thousands of years of experience with wars and financial panics, society has not yet learned how to avoid or manage them. In order to do so, we will have to confront the deeply intractable nature of political irrationality. This will require us to track irrationality to its biological sources.

CHAPTER 4

The Biology of Political Irrationality

> Residents of Red States are ignorant racist fascist knuckle-dragging NASCAR-obsessed cousin-marrying road-kill-eating tobacco-juice-dribbling gun-fondling religious fanatic rednecks, while Blue State residents are godless unpatriotic pierced-nose Volvo-driving France-loving Communist-loving latté-sucking tofu-chomping holistic-wacko neurotic vegan weenie perverts. — Dave Barry

DARK TRUTH #4
Democrats and Republicans are just different kinds of people; their disagreements are not based on logic, reason or facts.

Inherited Partisanship: The Biology of Bias

> Every boy and gal
> That's born into the world alive
> Is either a little liberal
> Or else a little conservative
> — W.S. Gilbert, *Iolanthe*

John Hibbing, a University of Nebraska political scientist, had long been professionally intrigued by voter behavior that seemed irrational. Although research shows that Americans do not know or care much about political issues, people often express virulent disliking for politicians of the opposing party. Hibbing asked: Why? If you didn't show much interest in politics, why did the opposition leader bother you so much? Hibbing was also puzzled that voters would identify themselves as Democratic or Republican, then express views contrary to the official platforms of those parties.

Working with Rice University political scientist John Alford, Hibbing began to test the hypothesis that there is a genetic basis for political preferences. Genetics could explain why political disagreements can seem so intractable — people might just be hard-wired for different ideologies. Together with Virginia Commonwealth colleague Carolyn Funk, Alford and Hibbing published a ground-breaking 2005 paper entitled "Are Political Orientations Genetically Transmitted?"[29]

Their research was based on analysis of pre-existing surveys of identical and fraternal twins (the researchers relied principally on a survey of 30,000 twins conducted under the auspices of Virginia Commonwealth University). Using standard correlation analysis to compare the rate of agreement on political issues between identical and fraternal twins, the research team was able to estimate the influence of genetics on ideology. When identical twins agree on political questions to a greater degree than fraternal twins, they provide us with a metric for estimating the impact of genetics on political ideology.

The researchers concluded that genetics accounted for about 53% of differences in ideology, an extremely strong influence. In particular, attitudes on such issues as school prayer, property taxes and the draft were strongly influenced by inheritance.

The data further suggested that genes affect not only individual political opinions but rather "clusters" of political attitudes on a number of issues. As a result, the report concluded that people probably fall into "broad but distinct political phenotypes." A "phenotype" is a term for the physical expression of a genetic trait, while the genetic code itself is called the "genotype." Thus, if you have blond hair, the section of your DNA that codes for that blond hair is the genotype; the blond hair itself is the phenotype. Alford and co. are suggesting that liberalism and conservatism are the outward behavioral expressions — phenotypes — of two different genotypes.

The research paper's description of the two genetic groups reads like a summary of our own red vs. blue cultural divide:

One [phenotype] is characterized by a relatively strong suspicion of out-groups (e.g., immigrants), a yearning for in-group unity and strong leadership, especially if there is an out-group threat ("Do not question the president while we are at war with terrorists"), a desire for clear, unbending moral and behavioral codes (strict constructionists), a fondness for swift and severe punishment for violations of this code (the death penalty), a fondness for systematization (procedural due process), a willingness to tolerate inequality (opposition to redistributive policies), and an inherently pessimistic view of human nature (life is "nasty, brutish and short").

The other phenotype is characterized by relatively tolerant attitudes toward out-groups, a desire to make a more context-dependent rather than rule-based approach to proper behavior (substantive due process), an inherently optimistic view of human nature (people should be given the benefit of the doubt), a distaste for preset punishments (mitigating circumstances), a preference for group togetherness but not necessarily unity ("We can all get along though we are quite different"), suspicion of hierarchy, certainty, and strong leadership (flip-flopping is not a character flaw), an aversion to inequality (e.g., support for a graduated income tax), and greater general empathic tendencies (rehabilitate, don't punish).[30]

Alford, Funk and Hibbing's research leads to the conclusion that many of us are simply born liberals or conservatives.

The researchers' dualistic categorization of humans into left-wing and right-wing "phenotypes" echoes findings in other disciplines. In cross-cultural anthropology, for example, societies around the world are grouped into "tough" or "soft" types. Tough societies are more masculine, have greater gender inequality and authoritarianism, and accord more social status to wealth. Soft societies are considered more feminine, with greater gender and social equality; wealth is relatively less important and relationships relatively more important.

Psychologists, similarly, have long known that aspects of personality are highly heritable and that some of these personality characteristics correlate with positions on the left-to-right ideological spectrum. Thus, for example, cross-cultural research on psychological needs and values has established that right-wing political orientation is often associated with a need for traditionalism and rule-following: "People embrace right-wing ideology in part because it serves to reduce fear, anxiety and uncertainty; to avoid change, disruption and ambiguity; and to explain, order and justify inequality among groups and individuals."[31]

Working with a large team of researchers, Hibbing published a 2008 paper entitled "Political Attitudes Vary with Physiological Traits," which provides further corroboration that ideology has a hard-wired component. Hibbing recruited a group of 46 highly-partisan research subjects. Each subject underwent a battery of political surveys which allowed the researchers to determine the subject's political orientation. Later, the subjects were exposed to stimuli intended to startle them – loud noises, gruesome photographs – and their physiological responses were measured. Hibbing used measurements based on involuntary reflexes (speed of eye-blinking and level of increased skin-conductance).

The research found that people who were less sensitive to sudden noises and threatening images were more likely to support foreign aid, liberal immigration policies, pacifism and gun control. Conversely, those who had a more instinctively fearful reaction were more likely to support defense spending, capital punishment, patriotism and the Iraq War. Hibbing concluded that in general people who are more physiologically sensitive to fear-inducing stimuli are more likely to advocate policies that protect the status quo from external and internal threats.

That two completely opposed poles of behavior can subsist in the same species has also been corroborated by biologist John Maynard Smith's classic "hawk-dove" analysis of a hypothetical bird species.[32] "Hawks," in this thought-experiment, are birds that always fight to the death over resources, while "doves" are birds that always concede resources to a competitor. If there is only one hawk in a given bird population, that trait will soon be so successful that in a short while much of the population will be hawks. However, at some point diminishing returns will set in, because hawks will have to fight continuously with other hawks. At this point, one begins to see the sense of the dove strategy. Doves always concede to hawks, avoiding the risk of a fight. They lose a little nutrition, but they stay alive. When there are lots of hawks around, it makes good sense to be a dove. The hawks tend to kill each other off until there is a stable balance between hawks and doves. Over time, the species may evolve into what Maynard Smith called an "evolutionarily stable" state with two distinct phenotypes.

This phenomenon has been observed in nature. Among Harris sparrows, darker birds tend to be dominant while the lighter birds are submissive. Maynard Smith found evidence that both strategies (light and dark) were conducive to evolutionary fitness. The twin research suggests that human beings may be like big, featherless versions of Harris sparrows.

Are we a species divided into two breeds, conservative (hawks) and liberal (doves)? Ironically, the answer may have been provided by that most charming and concrete of all human dichotomies: twins.

The Power of Twins

All current research into the genetic sources of human behavior owes a large debt to the ground-breaking "Minnesota twins" project begun by Thomas Bouchard at the University of Minnesota in 1979. Bouchard, a Minnesota psychologist, had long fantasized about the scientific possibilities of studying identical twins who had been raised apart. Bouchard realized that such twins would provide a unique tool for determining how much of human behavior is inherited and how much is derived from the environment. The scientific orthodoxy among Bouchard's fellow psychologists was that human behavioral patterns were principally determined by the childhood environment and that genetics played a minimal role. Bouchard was not convinced.[33]

He understood that previous twin studies had been discredited because it was felt that they were tainted by environmental influences. Bouchard knew that a study of twins reared apart, however, would not be subject to that criticism — there could be no social influence to act like an absent twin. If a study of twins reared apart were to confirm the findings of twins reared together, this would validate and in a sense resuscitate the earlier studies (a much larger body of data). Thus it was that in 1979 Bouchard was on the lookout for twins separated at birth and reared in different homes.

One evening Bouchard received a phone call informing him of a newspaper article about male twins in Ohio who had been separated at birth and re-united at age 39. The article spoke of many remarkable similarities between the men. Bouchard immediately contacted the two men, who agreed to come to Minnesota for testing.

Bouchard was amazed by the twins, as was everyone who worked with them. The two men were shortly to attain near-legendary status due to the remarkable similarities in their lives. They soon appeared on the "Tonight Show," where their case helped draw popular attention to the world of twin studies. Although Bouchard went on to study more than seventy sets of twins reared apart, and although the research has been duplicated elsewhere, the first set of "Minnesota twins" remains an unparalleled example of the potential link between genes and behavior.

"The Case of the Twin Jims"

Jim Lewis and Jim Springer were identical twins born in Ohio, given up for adoption at birth and raised in separate families eighty miles apart. They had no contact with each other. If human behavior is based more on culture and upbringing than on genetic inheritance, we would expect the two Jims to have led fairly different lives. There would be no reason for them to share any behaviors unusual for men of their age and social background. Nevertheless, the list of behaviors shared by the long-separated twins was striking.

Both had a nervous habit of chewing on the fingernail of the same finger. Both had worked as sheriff's deputies. Both chain-smoked Camels. Both liked all sports except baseball. Both married women named Linda, divorced them, and then both re-married women named Betty. Each had a habit of leaving love notes to his wife around the house. Both had the same hobby, wood-working, and they had nearly identical work areas. Both had decided to build a circular white bench around a tree in their front yards. Both had undergone vasectomies. Each had become overweight at the same point in their lives and both had leveled off in weight at the same time. Both had sons named James Alan. Both had owned dogs they had named Toy.

Although the case of the twin Jims suggests that human lives follow a sort of pre-set script or computer program, neither Bouchard nor Hibbing would argue that humans are mere robots to their genes. However, if human behavioral patterns as disparate as choice of hobbies, pet names, or preference for a given sport are to some extent derived from DNA, as the Minnesota studies suggest, then it is but a small step to hypothesize that political beliefs are also to some extent innate.

Obviously, if one of the twin Jims had been raised in rural Pakistan rather than Ohio, it is rather unlikely that he would have married women named Linda or Betty, or named his son James Alan, or his dog Toy. Clearly, culture and environment must play a role at some level. I am not aware of any serious scientist who maintains a contrary point of view.

While most proponents of biological influence accept that humans exhibit a mix of biologically- and culturally-determined behavior, many social scientists continue to stubbornly insist that biology has no influence whatsoever on political behavior. This point of view is now outdated. Alford, Funk and Hibbing's scientific evidence is too persuasive. In politics, culture is not everything. The testimony of biology must be heard.

Red Genes, Blue Genes

Molecular biology techniques suggest intriguing possibilities for the future of political science, as science fiction becomes reality. We should eventually be able to track ideology to a specific origin in sequences of DNA. Consider that the twin research found a very high heritability-correlation for attitudes relating to the death penalty. Does this imply the existence of a "death penalty gene"? Could such a gene be turned on or off?

As opposed to physical traits, behavioral traits are harder to trace to specific genes. When Mendel worked out the basic laws of genetic transmission, he focused on traits which were linked to single genes. This led to the common popular conception of genes being directly linked to outward markers. In this view, the pathway from genotype to phenotype is simple and direct: one gene = one trait. This is known in genetics as the single major locus (SML) or single-gene model. Although developed to explain observed physical traits, the SML model has also been proven correct in a small number of cases related to behavioral traits. Notably, in 1993 the Dutch geneticist Hans Bruner traced the origin of inherited aggressive behavior in a single Dutch family to a defect in the gene that produced monoamine oxydase-a, an enzyme that helps brain cells regulate levels of neurotransmitters.

Despite the success of the single-gene or SML model, a more complete understanding of human behavior is promised by what is known as the multi-factorial-polygenic (MFP) model. In this model, a given behavioral trait may be produced by a combination of several genes, but the expression of the trait may depend further on certain environmental triggers. Thus, instead of a single gene coding for conservatism or liberalism, it may be that we have dozens or hundreds of genes which, when present in certain configurations and triggered by certain external stimuli, will produce varying degrees of the observed trait of conservatism or liberalism. In this model, the pathway from genotype to phenotype is complex and supposes a number of feedback loops and interactions with the environment.

The complexity of the MFP model suggests that it will be many years before the full behavioral implications of the genome can be deciphered. However, one day they will be. What a strange, new world that will be. Imagine this commercial:

ANNOUNCER: "Do you want to determine whether your fiancé is really a committed liberal or just pretending? Just take a strip of our special Pol-i-Test™ paper, brush it against his skin when he's not looking, and wait five seconds. If the paper turns blue — he is for you, a true liberal. But if the paper turns pink or red, don't wed — he is a closet conservative."

What if some day it becomes possible to activate, or block, the genetic-molecular pathways to liberalism or ideology? Would a conservative husband of the future consider purchasing an unobtrusive spray that would temporarily disactivate his wife's preachy liberalism? Would the liberal wife be willing to take a pill that would make her a Republican for a day, so that she could tolerate Sunday dinners with her right-wing in-laws?

The potential for Orwellian mind-control is disconcerting. If a certain number of random stimuli, say certain smells and colors, were someday determined to be conducive to conservatism, wouldn't one expect the ruling party to ensure that such smells and colors permeated the polling booths on Election Day? How would we outlaw such conduct — with a Fairness in Campaign Smells Law?* Outlandish though the above examples may seem, future generations will have to deal with real questions that lie at the uneasy intersection between biology, science fiction and politics.

Political scientists James Fowler and Christopher Dawes have identified two genes that appear to play a role in political participation. In a 2008

---

* There is already a substantial body of research which indicates that people's moods and decision-making can be affected by exposure to particular smells.

paper entitled, "Two Genes Predict Voter Turnout," Fowler and Dawes reported findings that people with one variant of the MAOA gene were significantly more likely to vote in the 2000 presidential election. The researchers also found that possession of a variant of the 5HTT was linked to levels of voter turnout.[34]

Fowler and Dawes looked specifically at MAOA and 5HTT because these genes were known to be involved in the production of serotonin, a neurotransmitter which regulates fear, trust and social interaction. The 5HTT gene in particular was further cross-linked to the behavior of church attendance, which is also known to influence voting behavior. This was the first study to implicate specific genes as influencing political behavior, but it will certainly not be the last. This research does not amount to the discovery of a "religion gene" or a "voting gene," but it renders those concepts less far-fetched than they previously seemed.

The Alex Keaton Theory of Partisan Development

> CHILD: Mamma, are Tories born wicked, or do they grow wicked afterwards?
> MOTHER: They are born wicked, and grow worse.
> — G.W.E. Russell, *Collections and Recollections*

Party affiliation is less influenced by genetic inheritance than is ideology. While genetics accounts for roughly half of our political ideology, it only explained 18% of party affiliation. We may instinctively lean toward the progressive or conservative side, but we still tend to choose the same political party chosen by our parents, friends or co-workers.

In politics, it seems, social pressure to conform outweighs our inner political voice, but does not suppress it entirely. This would explain the appeal of terms such as "compassionate conservative" or "Reagan Democrat." They are revelatory of self-conflicted partisans. Political "conversions" are more often due to an elimination of this internal self-contradiction than to the exercise of logic. Over time, if your genetic inheritance puts you far over toward the liberal side of the spectrum, someday you may even come out of the closet, declaring to startled in-laws at Thanksgiving that you'll be voting for the Democrats in the next election.

This suggests a two-part or two-layer model for the choice of political party. The first part is composed of an initial biological layer, but then an even thicker layer is put on top of that, a cultural layer. Sometime the two layers will be congruent (a "dyed-in-the-wool Conservative" or "bleeding-heart Liberal"), but sometimes the two layers will conflict. If all of your peers are Republican, then you probably have affiliated yourself with the Republicans, though deep inside you might be a "closet Democrat." The twin-based research suggests that a small but significant proportion of Americans are probably in the "wrong" party, in the sense that their internal ideological leaning runs contrary to that of the party they publicly support.

We are each born with a genetic predisposition that places us at a certain starting point on the left-right political spectrum. Let's call this the Liberalism-Conservatism Spectrum and set the maximum liberal score at 0 and the maximum conservative at 100. On this scale, Democrats represent people who fall between 1 and 50, and the Republicans represent the population between 50 and 100.

The odds are that your initial partisan predisposition will be close to that of your parents, because if you have any genes, that's who you got them from. If we were able to measure the strength of your innate ideology, we might find that you were born at about a 65 level of conservatism, for example, in which case we would not be surprised to discover that your father was a 72 and your mother a 61. Thus, in the normal case, our biological predisposition to a certain ideology will be reinforced by our upbringing, which is usually carried out by people who share our biological leanings.

However, because political behavior is complex and the number of genes involved may be large, it is possible that you will develop a political phenotype that is different from that of your parents. It does happen that a redhead is born to a husband and wife who are both blonds (even in cases where the mailman was not a redhead). When a number of genes together are required to produce a trait, and when those genes are present in both dominant and recessive alleles, it becomes possible to generate a very wide range of phenotypes. The pressure of DNA does not always dictate that we look like our parents (though people usually do). The same is true of inherited political disposition — there is a general tendency, but there are lots of exceptions.

Generation X'ers will remember Alex Keaton, the character played by Michael J. Fox in the TV show *Family Ties*, an ultra-conservative Republican teen-ager at odds with his left-wing hippie parents. Many of us know of similar cases — conservatives that grew up in liberal households, and vice versa. How can our genetic theories accommodate this observed reality? Recall the multifactorial-polygenic theory of genetic transmission. The complex mixing of genes and environment that occurs at each generation can easily lead to a phenotype that is somewhat distant from the parent's phenotype. Unless our own genetic predisposition is, like Alex Keaton's, unusually remote from that of our parents, we will probably succumb to their indoctrination and adopt political views close to theirs. However, when we leave home, begin to fend for ourselves and encounter new social environments in the workplace, we are granted a second opportunity to express our inner partisan predispositions (or conform to external social pressures).

If the twin-research data is accurate, you hold about half of your political beliefs just because you were born a certain way. Logic and reason had surprisingly little to do with the formation of those political opinions, though the political scientists do not go on to explain why none of us will ever admit it.

Confirmation from Neuroscience: Brain Scans Reveal Hard-wired Bias

Neuroscience has now provided us with the equivalent of photographs of political irrationality in *flagrante delicto*. Dr. Drew Westen, Director of Clinical Psychology at Emory University, conducted a ground-breaking 2004 study in which the brains of partisan voters were subjected to fMRI-scans while the voters were asked a series of political questions. Functional magnetic resonance imaging (fMRI) scans allow us to literally "watch people think." We can see which parts of the brain are activated when people are asked about certain topics, and we can determine whether or not the subjects are reasoning or merely reacting emotionally (because we know which part of the brain is associated with emotional reaction, and which part is associated with logical reasoning).

In Dr. Westen's experiment, the subject's brains were monitored while they reflected upon political issues and were asked to evaluate information from the 2004 U.S. presidential campaign.

Westen reported:

We did not see any increased activation of the parts of the brain normally engaged during reasoning. What we saw instead was a network of emotion circuits lighting up, including circuits hypothesized to be involved in regulating emotion. None of the circuits involved in conscious reasoning were particularly engaged. Essentially, it appears as if partisans twirl the cognitive kaleidoscope until they get the conclusions they want, and then they get massively reinforced for it, with the elimination of negative emotional states and activation of positive ones.[35]

Apparently, when humans participate in political discussion they are first careful to disconnect the thinking parts of their brains. This is like the elderly husband who, when informed that his irate wife "wants to talk," calmly unplugs his hearing aid and says, "OK, honey, go ahead."

In Westen's study, the partisan subjects were exposed to statements from candidates George W. Bush and John Kerry and from neutral controls such as actor Tom Hanks. Each statement was then followed by a statement which apparently contradicted the first statement, suggesting that somewhere the candidate was either lying or pandering to the audience. The subjects were then asked to rate the extent to which the statements were self-contradictory. Westen and his colleagues watched the MRI scans while subjects "reflected."

The answers were clearly determined by partisan bias.* Each subject denied that his own preferred candidate had contradicted himself, but was able to detect the contradiction in the statements made by the opposing candidate. When asked about the contradictions expressed by their own candidate, the subjects showed activity in the orbital frontal cortex, which is in charge of the management of unpleasant feelings. One part of the brain remained eerily quiet throughout the questioning — the prefrontal cortex, associated with reasoning as well as with conscious efforts to suppress emotion. Westen interprets these results to indicate that emotional bias operates outside of awareness. In Westen's view, when we feel threatened by an opposing political belief, emotionally-biased reasoning quickly and unconsciously

---

* Neuroscientists have complained on occasion that the press is too quick to attribute scientific validity to brain-scan research that is still embryonic. Some researchers may indeed have been guilty of over-reaching, claming abilities little short of mind-reading. The huge amount of brain-scan research currently underway will soon corroborate or discredit these early claims.

"stamps in" a defensive belief, generating positive feelings and elimination of distress. All this happens without our noticing.

The result is that, in Westen's words, "partisan beliefs are calcified and the person can learn very little from new data." Thus neuroscience corroborates the existence of the confirmation bias. Even when we are exposed to evidence that contradicts our beliefs, we somehow use that very evidence to quickly spin to a comforting rationalization, followed by a deep internal "ahhhh" of relief. Each exposure to an opposing argument merely reinforces our pre-existing, internal bias. The more we argue, the more partisan we become. Instead of clearing things up, providing more information is like pouring oil on the fire instead of water.

Constitutional scholar Cass Sunstein has suggested that the proliferation of biased news media, including web-based zines and blogs in addition to talk radio and cable TV, makes it increasingly possible for Americans to obtain their political information exclusively from biased sources. Thus a conservative can listen to Rush Limbaugh on the way to work, read the *Wall Street Journal* once there, visit Ann Coulter's blog once home, and lull himself to sleep watching Fox News. Sunstein believes that the availability of partisan media products is a dangerous catalyst for further polarization. Westen's research suggests that the problem is actually worse than that. Even if the information were perfectly impartial, the two sides would still be driven further and further apart over time by the inexorable forces of human nature.

Detecting Hidden Bias: The IAT

A number of other psychological research methods have been developed to pick up the unconscious motivations and biases that explain our political leanings.

One such tool is the Implicit Associations Test (IAT) developed by psychologists at Harvard, the University of Virginia, and the University of Washington.[36] I always encourage my students to take a few of the tests available on the IAT website, as this provides a fascinating way to reveal your own subconscious biases. IAT tests are taken over the Internet on your own computer monitor. Essentially, you are asked to rapidly pair a word with a picture. For example, you might be asked to pair the word 'good' with a picture of a smiling baby. Evidence shows that if you have a negative attitude toward the pairing, your reaction time will be slightly slower or you may make a mistake, and this will be recorded by the computer. Thus, when the computer asks us to pair the word 'good' with the face of an old man, we may hesitate or choose the wrong answer, revealing that we have a slight bias against old people. As it turns out, most young Americans do have an anti-elderly bias (the little jerks).

In one study, the data of 130,000 whites who had volunteered to take the IAT online was analyzed. The data indicated that substantial majorities of Americans, whether liberal or conservative, possessed some level of anti-black bias. It would seem that African-Americans are not wrong to fear that Democrats are only slightly less racist than Republicans. However, when the IAT data was correlated with voting behavior in 435 congressional districts in the 2004 presidential election, it was found that districts that registered higher levels of racial bias tended to support Bush.

Yale psychology professor Mahzarin Banaji, one of the researchers, said that the data showed that George W. Bush was appealing as a leader to those Americans who harbored greater anti-black prejudice.

This conclusion was supported by Stanford professor Jon Krosnick, a specialist on the psychology of political affiliation:

> If anyone in Washington is skeptical about these findings, they are in denial. We have 50 years of evidence that racial prejudice predicts voting. Republicans are supported by whites with prejudice against blacks. If people say, 'This takes me aback,' they are ignoring a huge volume of research.[37]

It is slightly unsettling to think that, deep inside, each of us harbors an inner racist; it is even more discomforting to think that it is the inner racist who casts our ballots.

CHAPTER 5

The Evolution of Political Irrationality

> When our ancestors first became human, they
> already had in place a set of rules and social
> institutions. — Paul H. Rubin, *Darwinian Politics*

DARK TRUTH #5
We have a good excuse for our political irrationality: we inherited it.

Monkey Machiavellis: The Birth of Politics

There is a popular misinterpretation of Darwin according to which humans "descended" from chimpanzees. The correct view is that both chimpanzees and humans have descended from a common ancestor. Genetically and evolutionarily, chimps are our siblings, not our parents. About 4.5 million years ago humans and chimpanzees diverged, like brothers moving to different states. One of the families evolved into modern humans, while the other became chimpanzees. The other siblings in our primate family tree — bonobos, gorillas and orangutans — are all classified as apes (humans are sometimes said to be the "fifth ape"). At a much earlier point in evolution, the *ape* family had already separated from the *monkey* family — the folks with tails. This occurred about twenty million years ago.

When looking for clues as to the evolutionary history of humans, apes provide hints as to possible behaviors we may have inherited from our common ancestor.

Studies of chimpanzee societies provide us with an intriguing perspective on the possible origins of political behavior. Primatologist Frans De Waal has eloquently depicted the rich social life of a captive troop of chimpanzees.[38] In one particularly dramatic episode, the power struggles of three male chimps assume a sort of Shakespearean majesty. In order to appreciate De Waal's "Chimp MacBeth," we need to know the following cast of primate characters (this is a true story):

Yeroen: A wily old leader, this alpha male chimp had enjoyed for many years all the perquisites of power (mainly, sexual) at the chimp colony of the Arnhem zoo.

Luit: This powerful upstart grew big enough to knock Yeroen off the top position, replacing him as alpha male and leaving Yeroen to nurse the brooding grudge of the dispossessed tyrant. As the new alpha male, Luit was described by De Waal as the "most magnificent" chimp he had ever observed, a natural leader. In contrast, the defeated Yeroen was described as utterly forlorn and deflated, rather like Nixon after impeachment.

Nikkie: This younger competitor was described by De Waal as "dopey but brawny." On his own, he was no match for the magnificent Luit, but the cunning Yeroen detected some raw potential in the youngster and forged a strong partnership with him. Backed up by Yeroen, Nikkie was able to dethrone Luit for top position. Working together, the wily Yeroen and the mediocre Nikkie were able to exclude Luit from power for a period of four years.

The final drama involving these players exploded one tense summer, triggered by an act of treachery. Normally, the alpha male's main perquisite is to have first sexual rights to attractive females in heat. As the new leader, the dopey Nikkie could have claimed his *droit de seigneur*. However, realizing that he owed his victory to a partnership with Yeroen, he prudently agreed to share mating privileges with Yeroen. And so things passed for a very long time, until one day Nikkie became ungrateful and stopped sharing females with Yeroen. Outraged, Yeroen abandoned Nikkie, leaving him vulnerable to a renewed attack from Luit, which promptly occurred. Luit quickly toppled the solitary Nikkie.

Luit once again reigned supreme, but his reign was a nervous one because he clearly remembered the collaboration that had reversed him before. He became extremely agitated whenever he saw Yeroen and Nikkie approaching each other. Luit's dominant position depended on Yeroen holding his grudge against Nikkie. As if to teach his former partner Nikkie a lesson, Yeroen kept him at a distance for some time, allowing Nikkie to learn what it felt like to be toppled from power. Apparently, it feels terrible. When the time was ripe, he approached Nikkie again, showing he was ready to resume their old partnership.

This *rapprochement* threw Luit into a panic, as well as the human zookeepers who were watching the drama unfold. The potential danger was clear to everyone, especially Luit, who tried to stay between the two conspirators. One evening the three males were practically clinging to each other as they were put into the same cage at night.

The next morning Luit was found fatally wounded, his body a mass of wounds. Toes had been bitten off, bones broken, testicles mashed and squeezed out of his scrotum. The attack had been coordinated and vicious, with Yeroen holding Luit down while Nikkie pounded and bit from the other side. Murder most foul, with political ends. Two mediocre leaders got together for selfish purposes to defeat a brilliant rival. Instructively, they were successful. As Jonathan Swift tartly observed, "When a true genius appears in this world you will know him by this sign: that all the dunces are in confederacy against him." The morning following the attack Nikkie was harassed by outraged females who had witnessed the incident, but he was able to wait out the storm. Nikkie and Yeroen resumed shared leadership, and Luit's battered remains were disposed of.

De Waal draws several lessons from this drama. First, De Waal believes that human males are subject to the same power lust that drove these chimpanzees (he cites amusing personal examples from the world of academia, but this is probably not the only place that men act like chimps). The power drive is not only visible in large-scale politics but also in everyday confrontations between males. "Pecking order" is a relevant concept in biology derived from the behavior of chickens. Two chickens never waste time pecking at the same grain of food because each chicken has learned its relative hierarchical status and subordinate chickens automatically yield to a higher-status rival. De Waal observes that human and chimp males act similarly. When males meet, they first bluster at each other as if to determine their pecking order in a dominance hierarchy. Chimps do this by hooting, stamping and charging at each other. Human males do it by arguing, often about politics. Once the hierarchy is established, things can relax.

A friend provided me with an example from a trip to France. He had been invited to dinner by a French family. The family was hosting a visiting Italian professor. At dinner, discussion turned to a governmental proposal to revoke a French tax on the ultra-wealthy. The French husband supported the tax, but the visiting male colleague politely pointed out a potential economic critique — the law had forced many French millionaires to set up tax residence in Monaco, leading to an overall loss of tax-revenue to France.

Although the husband was reportedly an equable fellow, he suddenly became very angry at the visitor and lost control of himself, creating an embarrassing scene. My friend found the incident strange, but I told him it was not unusual, from a biological perspective. When unfamiliar men encounter each other they often feel pressed to test each other, as if in a dominance contest. As with chimps, this sometimes involves a certain amount of hooting and bluster, which only rarely generates into fisticuffs. What made the French incident worse, I suggested, was that it had happened on the host's home turf. It is as if the host were challenged for alpha status in front of his own mate. When one man tries to out-argue another in front of the latter's wife or girlfriend, there is an evolutionary sub-plot being played out that makes me want to leave the room (before anybody's toes get bitten off, or their testicles mashed).

Another key lesson that De Waal derives from the saga of Luit, Yeroen and Nikkie is that the acquisition of power in chimp societies requires true political skills. Although Yeroen comes across as a balding, murderous Iago, one must acknowledge the remarkable intelligence and social cunning that his plot demanded. First, Yeroen had to find the emotional maturity to get over his initial disappointment at being knocked off by Luit. Then, he had to realize that Nikkie was strong enough, if assisted, to defeat Luit. Although it may sound far-fetched, I believe Yeroen's strategy even required an intuitive understanding of Nikkie's personality ("brawny but dopey"). If Nikkie had been too assertive, he would not have been the type to share access to females, and the plot would not have worked. As it was, when Nikkie tried to renege on their partnership agreement, Yeroen knew exactly how to use his leverage to get the deal re-instated.

Early human or proto-human tribes probably witnessed countless political dramas similar to that of the Yeroen-Luit-Nikki triangle. In fact, the intellectual demands of such competition may have been partially responsible for the remarkable growth of the human brain in the time period from about 1.6 million years ago until about 10,000 years ago. It was during this period, referred to as the Environment of Evolutionary Adaptedness (EEA), that humans evolved from creatures who looked a lot like chimpanzees to modern humans.

During the EEA, humans probably were constantly entering into and leaving coalitions of various sizes with a view to exploiting collective power for mutual gain. Any candidate for alpha male status always faced numerous competitors, equally cunning and determined. Consequently, power in human groups has probably always been based on what is called "reverse dominance" hierarchies. In such a hierarchy, power can only be obtained with the consent of some crucial segment of the governed. In order to forge the necessary coalitions, it helped to be intelligent. Political chess battles were waged for hundreds of thousands of years on the African savannah, with victory, if Yeroen is any indication, going more often to brains than to brawn. For the sake of comparison, consider that gorilla males are as much as four times heavier than gorilla females, while human and chimpanzee males are only about 15% larger than females. This suggests that for human males evolving in the EEA, size and muscle alone were no guarantee of ascendancy — political skills were equally important.

Our astonishingly capacious human brain is in part the evolutionary by-product of a million Machiavellian power struggles fought by our scheming ancestors. We are wired for politics, and well-wired.

The Evolution of Political Irrationality

Humans evolved from creatures like chimpanzees into creatures like us over a 1.6 million year period we call the EEA.[39] The first 1.5 million years of that period occurred in Africa. The social behavior of chimpanzees provides us with something like a chalk-mark close to our evolutionary starting point, while the behavior of hunter-gatherer tribes marks the finish line (we have not evolved much in the past 10,000 years).

In between, there is a vast uncharted area with only slender archaeological evidence to help guide us. Regrettably, we can only hypothesize the trajectory of human evolution.

Evolutionary psychologists begin with informed guesses as to how humans may have lived in the EEA, then seek to test these hypotheses on modern humans. The conjectural nature of evolutionary psychology will always leave it open to critics. Despite this, the accumulation of corroborating evidence amassed by evolutionary psychologists suggests we can now make a few well-informed guesses about the likely evolution of political structure in the EEA. Our confidence in these conjectures arises from the strength of analogies to the common behavior observed in chimpanzee and hunter-gatherer societies, as well as from corroborating evidence provided by modern techniques such as DNA analysis and brain scans. However, evolutionary psychologists must always admit the frustrating fact (until a time machine is invented) that it is impossible to directly observe the behavior of one's ancient ancestors.

Evolutionary psychology is a political hot potato because it suggests some disturbing facts about human nature (disturbing for some people). For example, evolutionary psychologists believe that human lives and human societies follow a finite range of pre-determined tracks. The key fear aroused by this view is that biological determinism can be used to justify and perpetuate human inequality. Critics argue that evolutionary psychology justifies human inequality and exploitation. This view is misguided and counter-productive.

If humans have innate tendencies which facilitate social discrimination, an understanding of the underlying mechanisms may allow us to propose effective remedies. By understanding the structure of human nature, we can identify those impulses and structures which are easy to manage and distinguish them from those which are more intractable. We will have a better chance of overcoming social inequities if we understand their evolutionary origins.

Why We Care About Politics: The Evolution of Political Participation

Humans evolved in small groups ranging in size from about 15 to about 150. We have observed from existing hunter-gatherer tribes that when populations reach a certain upper limit, they split, or "fission."

It has been suggested that the figure of 150 represents a sort of natural maximum capacity of the human brain to manage social relationships. For example, in corporations and in bureaucracies, when departments grow much larger than 150, they tend to split up into sub-units. When people get into the habit of sending out holiday greetings cards they rarely send out more than 150.

Let us go back in time a million years or so. In a group of perhaps fifteen or twenty adults, it made sense for every adult to participate in "political" decisions. The political decisions of pre-history were tribal decisions. What does our little tribe do? Even the smallest tribes repeatedly had to face a number of complex social decisions:

1. Shall we stay here or shall we move?
2. Shall we fight that tribe, or run away?
3. Shall we stay together, or split up into separate tribes?

How did the group come to a collective decision on such matters? Decisions were probably mediated by a small power group of males and another of females. However, it made sense for everybody to be interested and informed. Small groups of men or women gossiping about what the group was going to do next — such were the first political conclaves. At times, there must have been quite dramatic debates as tribal leaders and their challengers tried to persuade the group of alternative courses of action. During such debates, it made sense for all adults to participate, because the individual participation of any single adult might conceivably have been sufficient to change the outcome. Consequently, it seems natural for humans to believe that we should have a political voice, and that that voice will be heard.

It made great sense in the EEA for every tribe member to be well informed on upcoming group decisions and social events ("We will be moving to a new tree tomorrow; Grok is now mating with Yarp"). It seems likely that we have evolved a "celebrity gossip module" in our brains, an innate sensitivity to the actions of high-status individuals. In the life of a small tribe, the actions of a particular political celebrity could have a very real impact on our lives. For hundreds of thousands of years, it was prudent to gossip about politics. Now it just seems natural to us, and rather irresistible. Even when we get disgusted with our tawdry political apparatus and disappointing candidates, we still cannot help being fascinated by their struggles and foibles.

Political scientists James Fowler and Christopher Dawes have established that possession of a variant of two genes correlated significantly with voter turnout. They also found in a separate, twin-based study that the predisposition to vote is highly heritable. Matching public voter-turnout records in Los Angeles to a twin registry, they demonstrated that up to 70% of the variance in turnout figures can be attributed to inheritance.[40]

Fowler and Dawes suggest that a specific brain mechanism accounts for at least part of the variance in people's desire to participate in politics. Serotonin is a brain chemical that is released by neurons when they fire, as in response to stress or fear. Normally, the neurons have a mechanism for re-absorbing the serotonin. However, in some people, this mechanism doesn't function well, either for genetic reasons or due to trauma. The inability to regulate serotonin levels has been linked to anti-social and aggressive behavior. Animals that have a defect in their serotonin-processing mechanism have a tendency to react impulsively and fearfully to social stressors. Fowler and Dawes established that people who have genes which are linked to less efficient re-uptake of serotonin are also less likely to vote. By implication, if you were born with serious anti-social tendencies, you probably don't give a damn about elections.[41]

Serotonin mechanisms may provide the molecular keys to understanding left-to-right political variation. If one compares humans to other social animals, like bees, ants or wolves, one is struck by how disobedient humans are. Humans accept the chains of society, but only up to a point. The degree to which we tolerate, or need, social cohesion is probably genetically-based.

As bands of humans spread across the planet, two divergent social strategies emerged. Sometimes it made sense to be very tight and close-knit with the members of your band, showing absolute loyalty and deference to power figures. Conversely, at other times this must clearly have been a bad strategy, such as when your group was threatened by larger rivals, or when your leader was evidently exploitative or incompetent.

The human brain has probably evolved cerebral mechanisms — very likely involving the maintenance of a serotonin balance — which allow us to instinctively calculate the trade-offs between obedience to group norms and individualistic defection to pursue selfish goals. People with a sensitive serotonin mechanism, from this perspective, will feel relatively more disturbed by actions that threaten social harmony. These people are more likely to become conservatives. Other people's brain chemistry leaves them less sensitive to social harmony, and they are more likely to subvert rules, traditions and hierarchies, to leave the group to pursue individual goals, and to permit others to do likewise. These people are more likely to become liberals.

Evolution has left even our neurons tinted red or blue.

The Evolution of Partisanship

Ironically, partisan bias can best be explained by concepts developed in the study of its apparent opposite: altruism (behavior involving self-sacrifice or generosity).

Altruism was long considered a mystery and a great challenge to Darwinism. Why would any animal, or human, help another? If the basic principle of Darwinism was that only traits conducive to reproduction were likely to be inherited, how could one explain altruism? Humans have been known throughout history to go to extraordinary lengths to help other humans. News reports of house fires commonly are accompanied by tales of heroic bystanders who rush in to save children or animals at great risk to themselves.

Altruism remained perplexing until the great English biologist W. D. Hamilton unlocked its secrets by applying the concept of "kin selection." Kin selection refers to evolution based on cooperation between related organisms. J.S.B. Haldane famously summarized the principle as follows: "I would gladly give my life for two brothers or eight cousins." Haldane was humorously but accurately referring to the proportion of genes shared in a family: identical twins share 100% of genes, brothers and sisters share 50%, nephews 25% and first cousins 12.5%.

W.D. Hamilton argued that what appeared to be selfless altruism by many animals was in fact a form of prudent calculation at the level of the gene. If we consider that evolution occurs at the level of the gene and not just the organism, then we can appreciate that it is all the same to the gene whether it is this organism or that one that provides the conduit to the next generation. The gene's-eye perspective is the basic premise underlying the most popular book ever written on evolutionary biology, Richard Dawkins's *The Selfish Gene*, which expounded upon Hamilton's findings.[42]

Hamilton suggested that the incidence of altruism could be predicted from a basic formula involving just three variables: the degree of relatedness of the parties, the benefit to the receiver, and the cost to the giver. In simple terms, if two individuals are closely related and one of them can at small cost do something that has great benefit to the other, then altruistic behavior should be expected. Anyone knows that much who has sought to borrow a small sum of money from a rich relative. Altruism thus requires an organism to calculate the genetic relatedness of the two parties (called "kin recognition") and analyze the cost/benefit ratio of the altruistic behavior. It as if the genes in one body say, "Hey, those genes in trouble over there look a lot like our genes! Let's go help them out, as long as it doesn't cost too much." Altruism is teamwork between identical genes that happen to be in different bodies.

Observation of human and animal behavior confirms that altruistic and cooperative behavior does in fact occur in direct proportion to the genetic relatedness of the parties involved. Blood *is* thicker than water. One of the most common examples of supposed altruism amongst animals is warning behavior. When animals make loud noises to warn of the approach of a predator, they make themselves more visible to that predator. Why do animals take that chance? Why does warning behavior exist?

Hamilton's hypothesis prompted field biologists to carefully observe and measure the warning behavior of squirrels, birds and monkeys. They found that the frequency of risky warning behavior exhibited was in direct proportion to the proximity of genetically-related individuals. It makes sense, genetically speaking, to stick your neck out for a brother, nephew or cousin.

All parents are expected to show altruistic concern for their children. Hamilton's theory, however, suggested that step-parents could be expected to show a lower level of altruistic concern than biological parents. Sadly, the statistics bear this out. Step-children and adopted children have a higher incidence of childhood accidents and suffer a greater amount of domestic violence than do biological children.

Thus we arrive at the dark side of the genetic equation. If it made sense for our ancestors to be altruistic to those who were genetically similar, it also made sense, on occasion, for them to harm or exploit those who were genetically distant. Genetically-distant individuals from our own species are the worst sort of competition. Their genes are well-suited to our ecological niche, but they're not our genes. Any assistance we render such individuals will just tend to displace lots of our own genes from future generations. Our genes don't like that.

Instead of trying to help outsiders with altruistic behavior, evolving humans may have obeyed a darker evolutionary imperative — aggression, even homicide. From an evolutionary perspective, altruism and homicide are the two extreme poles of social behavior available to humans. From the gene's-eye view, altruism made sense when the cost was little and the receiver was a close relative. Regrettably, by the same token, murder made evolutionary sense when the victim was genetically distant and a tough ecological competitor. Hamilton referred to the latter sort of behavior — reverse altruism, if you will — as "spiteful."

In the primate world, evidence of the spiteful, murderous instinct was first observed in 1974 in groups of wild chimpanzees at Gombe stream in Kenya, the research camp established by famed primatologist Jane Goodall. At Gombe, one large party of chimpanzees fissioned into two sub-groups, which then moved apart. One day, members from the larger group formed into what appeared to be a hunting party, which set out silently in search — as it turned out — of a solitary member of the smaller band of chimpanzees. When the unlucky member of the smaller band was found, he was savagely murdered. Methodically, the larger group exterminated the smaller group, a small-scale primate example of ethnic cleansing. Field biologists elsewhere have confirmed that chimps tend to form murderous raiding parties, like gangs of thugs, who set out in search of isolated males from other troops. In humans, of course, history is also replete with examples of gang violence and the massacre of minority out-groups.[43]

While Hamilton focused on altruism between individuals that are directly related, an important extension of Hamilton's theory applies to altruism and cooperation between members of different groups. This approach, known as Genetic Similarity Theory, is an extension of the gene's-eye view to larger groups of related individuals. It is based on the notion that individuals do not have to be directly related to have a high degree of genetic overlap. In any human population subjected to long in-breeding (as in the island populations of Iceland or Japan), there will eventually accumulate a great deal of genetic overlap even between people not known to be directly related. Estimates of the degree of genetic-relatedness in such homogenous populations suggest that ethnic nationals are as closely related to each other as cousins. Put otherwise, it is almost as if all Icelanders or Japanese were first cousins within their respective communities. Evolutionary theory predicts a high degree of cooperation in such societies.

The choice of which course of behavior to engage in depends on what biologists call "kin recognition." Social animals — those most likely to benefit from cooperation and altruistic behavior — should develop outward markers of their genetic traits, so that genetically-related individuals can recognize each other and help each other out. People should be very attentive to markers by which they can recognize their kin. Indeed, it is a commonplace that brothers and sisters look alike.

From an evolutionary point of view, we could say that siblings resemble each other so that they will remember to cooperate. The need to differentiate genetic cousins from genetic outsiders may be why people have developed such highly-visible markers as bright hair and eye coloring or prominent noses and ears. Humans are capable of incredibly fine discrimination between individuals (which is why twins are such fun: they confound our natural capacity to tell people apart). We have all had the experience of being able to pick out a friend in a crowd from very far away, just by the way the person stands or walks, or from the shape of the back of their head, or their ears.

In the EEA there arose situations when a potentially altruistic person had to make a difficult decision as to whether a given person "deserved" altruistic behavior. At a distance, you can see that a child is under threat of attack from a panther. Do you run over, at risk to your life, to save the child? If the child has those funny ears that run in your family, you run over.

Sometimes, however, two people look similar even when they have different genetic makeup. There is the possibility of being fooled in one's altruism by a deceptively similar outsider.

Consequently, it would make sense if humans could also discriminate between individuals on the basis of behavioral cues that would be shared only by those who had actually lived together. Just as teen-agers everywhere are quick to invent slang and their own private languages, early groups of humans may have used language-cues to distinguish insiders from outsiders. This may explain why making fun of foreign accents is universally considered to be hilarious, and a staple of comedians everywhere. In many countries, even a trace of a foreign accent can be considered shameful. Culture itself, in its myriad forms of behavior and display, may have originated in the need to carefully mark a shared genetic legacy.

A classic example of culture as a tool for discriminating genetic outsiders is found in the historical use of the "shibboleth." 'Shibboleth' is a

Hebrew word found in the *Bible's* "Book of Judges," in an account of a conflict between the Ephraimites (who used the word "shibboleth") and the Gileadites (who were unable to pronounce the sh- sound). After their defeat, many Gileadites tried to sneak across the Jordan river, where they found themselves seized by Ephraimite soldiers and given the following, terrifying order: "Say 'shibboleth'!" Those who were unable to pronounce the word correctly were immediately killed. As your mother told you, it pays to study languages.

Shibboleths of various sorts have been used throughout history for similar military purposes (American soldiers in the Pacific asked unidentified parties to say "lollapalooza," an American slang term difficult for native Japanese speakers). The concept of shibboleth can be taken very broadly, to indicate any kind of sign or behavior by which group members can distinguish outsiders. Thus we see that cultural artifacts such as accent, slang, clothing, and gesture, etc., may have arisen as means of distinguishing genetic insiders from outsiders. Culture itself can be seen as a massive accumulation of shibboleths.

The broader implication of genetic similarity theory for political life is that evolution has wired us for tribal partisanship. We are programmed to figure out which people are genetically close to us and which are not, and to treat the former better than the latter. We can often afford to be altruistic and generous — because we are usually pretty good at figuring out when it makes sense to be altruistic. On the other hand, we just as instinctively tend to detect and punish outsiders.

In a large, multi-cultural society like the U.S., the two-party system allows citizens to express their ethnocentric, spiteful impulses in a socially-sanctioned manner. Our culture war is a form of internalized xenophobia. Instead of hating the neighboring cultures (Canadians, say, or Mexicans), we just divide our own country in two, and hate ourselves. Members of the other political party are regularly derided as fools and suckers. We hoot and holler at each other like two colonies of estranged chimps, and no one gets hurt.

At least, not since 600,000 were killed in the Civil War.

The Evolution of Political Gullibility and Self-Deception

> We lie loudest when we lie to ourselves.
> — Eric Hoffer, *The Passionate State*

The greatest deception men suffer
is from their own opinions.
— Leonardo Da Vinci, *Notebooks*

An essential element of political irrationality is a willful political gullibility. People are extremely willing to adopt the beliefs of their peers, even
if it means swallowing some bizarre premises. Where does this gullibility
come from? In order to understand political gullibility, we need to understand the evolutionary significance of deception and self-deception.

Humans, like other primates, are fundamentally social animals — constantly working together and cooperating. Whenever two individuals work
together, there is the possibility that one will do more of the work while the
other will reap more of the rewards (free-riding, or even worse, cheating).
Consequently, social animals have evolved an innate sense of fairness in social situations, a kind of *ur*-morality.

When capuchin monkeys are trained to perform an exercise in a cage
next to a fellow capuchin, they carefully observe the reward that their neighbor is getting for the same work. Capuchins greatly prefer grapes to cucumber slices. When a capuchin gets paid with a lousy cucumber slice for a
task that earned his neighbor a juicy grape, his outrage can be so extreme
that he will throw the food away. Capuchins, like humans, are liable to react
to unfairness with violent anger.

While social animals have evolved innate rules of fairness, they have
also resorted to deception as a strategy for cheating those rules. We all want
to have our social cake and eat it, too. We'd like the benefits of society, but
without the costs. Deception — and self-deception — are consequently fundamental social strategies.

Consider one of De Waal's stories about the wily alpha chimpanzee,
Yeroen. Chimpanzees observe a social duty to share large fruit. The prima-
tologists observing Yeroen's colony did an experiment in which they hid ba-
nanas throughout the animal compound while the chimpanzees were inside
their cages. When the chimps were let out, Yeroen walked past a spot where
a banana was hidden, though he had probably noticed it. Later, when the
colony was dispersed and sleeping, Yeroen returned to the spot and enjoyed
the banana in solitary gluttony. By pretending not to notice the hiding spot,
Yeroen had gotten around the tiresome expectation of sharing one's fruit.[44]

Evolutionary theory predicts that individuals should engage in this kind of deception whenever they can get away with it. This may provide an evolutionary perspective for the almost-universal human behavior of lying (excepting you and me, dear reader). It also makes evolutionary sense for one's neighbors to evolve ever-more sophisticated ways of detecting cheating (not to mention legal and cultural codes which prohibit it). Thus, although humans lie regularly in their everyday lives, our fellow humans are pretty good at detecting those lies. The best lie detector in the world is still an alert person with narrowed eyes. Our internal lie-detection mechanism is an exceedingly sensitive one, because it has been developed over hundreds of thousands of years. When you suspect that someone is lying to you, you are probably right.[45]

In the evolutionary cat-and-mouse game between liars and human lie-detectors, self-deception arose as a cunning new trick by the liars. The most convincing liar is the one who believes his own story. Consequently, it would be evolutionarily helpful for individuals to be able to lie to themselves, so as to be better able to deceive their neighbors. That self-deception is the technique of the good liar is confirmed by the habit of professional film actors who remain "in character" between takes. Similarly, salesmen are indoctrinated to believe in the value of their product — if they believe it themselves, the consumer is more likely to be convinced.

Likewise, any political candidate who fails to exhibit strong belief in his own policies is doomed. Belief is extremely convincing, and therefore was probably evolutionarily adaptive for social animals. The communicative power of belief had already been noted centuries ago by that keen observer of political cant, Jonathan Swift: "Positiveness is a good quality for preachers and orators, because he that would obtrude his thoughts upon a multitude, will convince others the more, as he appears convinced himself."

Evolution has programmed us to believe our own bullshit. Fortunately for society, however, we do not necessarily have to believe our neighbor's. In this sense, we are all our brother's keeper — we help our fellow citizens "keep it real," just as they do for us.

Political belief is often just a matter of self-deception at the group level. We deceive ourselves that our beliefs are logical, when in reality they are principally group-markers.

The Evolution of the Gender Gap

The most controversial subject matter in evolutionary psychology is the study of differences between male and female behavior. In a series of ground-breaking papers published in the early 1970s while he was still a graduate student at Harvard, Robert Trivers shook the world of gender relations when he proposed an evolutionary explanation for male promiscuity.[46]

Applying evolutionary theory, Trivers reasoned that men and women should have developed divergent reproductive strategies because the relative investments of the two genders in child-rearing are not symmetrical. While a male is able to reproduce merely by inseminating a female, a female can only reproduce by going through a long pregnancy, stressful childbirth, and draining child-rearing. Since the man's investment is relatively trivial and the po-tential payoff so great, it would make evolutionary sense for men to "invest" as often as possible, i.e., by being promiscuous. For women, conversely, promiscuity is of no reproductive benefit. A woman can only get pregnant once at a time. As a result, evolutionary theory would predict that men would be relatively more promiscuous, and in general more sex-driven, than women.

The theory also predicts that women would be more choosy in engag-ing in sexual relations, because with each pregnancy they are making such a large life-investment. Since a female is likely to be presented with various alternatives for mating, given the compulsive sexuality of males, it would make sense to be careful and discriminating in choosing the one with the best genetic potential. Note that this theory does not imply any moral validity to male promiscuity (nor to female reticence), though the accusation is often made. Feminists sometimes attack the theory on grounds that it represents an attempt by male researchers to justify male patriarchy, but the force of the critique is somewhat diminished when one considers that many evolutionary psychologists are women (Lena Cosmides and Sarah Hrdy, to take just two prominent examples).

Has the observation that men actually are more promiscuous than women been confirmed experimentally? Indeed, it has, though some would question the need to test a principle so self-evident. That men are relatively more sexually-obsessed than women is no surprise in many parts of the world, though the assertion still produces discomfiture at American universities.

In one experiment, a young man and young woman are given the following assignment. Each researcher is instructed to walk up to a number of randomly-selected members of the opposite sex and make the following offer: "I've been watching you and am very attracted to you. Would you like to come back to my room to have sex with me?" I often ask audiences to guess which of the two researchers is more successful — the young man or the young woman.

The young woman is successful in approximately three-quarters of encounters, while the young man is never successful (I guess they're not using Brad Pitt). If this were due to culture and socialization, we would expect to see some cross-cultural variation, but there is no country in which the females are as open as males to sex with random strangers. If there were such a country, it would soon be overrun by drooling male immigrants.

The differences in reproductive strategies between men and women are relevant for politics because they have left men and women with differing innate motivations. There is evidence that the best way for men to indulge their sex drive is to achieve high social status. In hunter-gatherer societies, just as in the societies of our primate cousins, males of higher status reproduce at a higher frequency. Many studies show modern women as well are attracted to men of high status, reflecting an evolutionary imperative observed in other primate species. How else could Donald Trump get a date?

Evolutionary psychology infers that males will be hard-wired to seek social status at any cost. Achieving political power is the classic way to that status. It thus makes sound evolutionary sense for men to be obsessed by politics — it is the royal road to sex. Indeed, surveys show that twice as many men as women respond affirmatively to the question, "Are you extremely interested in politics?" In virtually all countries studied (there are exceptions), men report a greater interest than women in politics. Men usually know more about politics than women do, a superiority which may account for a certain number of divorces. The male obsession with politics would help explain the persistence of patriarchy throughout history as well as today's gender gap in political representation.

Critics of Trivers' promiscuity theory have pointed out that the reproductive sex act requires the participation of both genders. Who can the promiscuous males have sex with, if not with equal numbers of equally promiscuous females? The answer has been provided by recent DNA techniques which allow scientists to study the separate evolution of male and male DNA lineages by measuring the rate of mutation in the male Y chromosome.

The DNA record shows that human history has significantly more female lineages than male lineages. Strangely, this means that we had more female ancestors than male ancestors. It now appears that throughout their evolution most humans were slightly polygynous, i.e., one man mated with more than one woman. This means that a lot of men got left out in the evolutionary cold, losers in the worst possible way — genetically. Less than half of all men who ever lived were successful in reproducing, while approximately 80% of all females were able to reproduce.[47]

Thus, throughout evolution one man's promiscuity could only be satisfied at the cost of his neighbor's reluctant celibacy. Since the odds against reproducing for any given male were daunting, it made sense for young males to take risks in order to reproduce. Whether it meant battling a larger rival, hunting dangerous game, or engaging in war-like raids against a neighboring tribe, the risk was worth it if it helped overcome the long odds against reproduction. Today, a taste for risk is much more marked among males than among females. Participation in extreme sports or dangerous professions is overwhelmingly male. We see the most concrete proof in our driver insurance premiums, which are much higher for young males.

The gender difference in risk appetite has strong implications for politics, especially as regards the most classic and enduring of all political dilemmas, the decision to go to war. War is the riskiest, most hazardous activity any person or society can embark upon, yet throughout history men have willingly and even eagerly marched off to battle while wives and mothers stayed behind. After the 2003 invasion, U.S. support for the Iraq War was marked by a clear gender gap, with more men than women supporting the war effort. Indeed, the first recorded evidence of the gender gap occurred in the 1968 presidential election in which Richard Nixon received 7% greater support among men than among women. The disparity was popularly attributed to the relatively more "dove-ish" sentiment among women voters as regarded the Vietnam War. Ever since that period, the Democrats have enjoyed a slight but consistent edge among female voters, attributed to women's lower support for military spending, a perennial plank of the Republican platform.

Evolutionary theory provides an explanation for the disparity in military attitudes. Although it has left humanity with a troubling genetic legacy, war and murder provided our male ancestors with an evolutionarily sound strategy for eliminating male rivals and gaining sexual access to females. Our female ancestors, conversely, received no benefit from war. Even in the best case (victory), war merely diverted the energies of males; in the worst case it meant defeat, rape or the death of one's children. Although females did not benefit from war, they nonetheless suffered a somewhat lesser risk from violent conflict (they had a lower chance of being killed in battle). Females would have been less likely to evolve an emotional response to threats of aggression. When our male ancestors found themselves threatened by a warlike neighbor, the stakes they faced was their own prompt and violent extinction (which explains why men can follow sports — a modern symbolic substitute for war — with such insane fervor). Thus, many of the great wars have sprung from an uncontrollable escalation of threats and counter-threats between male leaders. If we want world peace, evolutionary theory suggests that electing more female leaders would be a good place to start.

Immigration is another example of a policy area that may reveal male-female differences due to evolutionary pressures. Humans probably evolved as a "patrilocal" species, meaning that at sexual maturity males remain with the family unit while females migrate to other family units. We find an expression of patrilocality in the traditional cultural practice according to which a young man brought his bride to live with him in his family's house, while a young bride was expected to leave her family and join her husband's household. Since human females migrate to other family groups, one would expect evolutionary pressure for females to be somewhat more open to out-groups than males. Correspondingly, males should be expected to be somewhat more suspicious of immigrant groups, particularly if those groups are predominantly composed of impoverished, sex-starved males (annoying competition).

We see a humorous expression of the potential gender bias in immigration policy in the silly Sacha Baron Cohen film, "Ali G Indahouse." In this movie, the comical Ali G character ends up as Prime Minister, where his absurd policies prove surprisingly popular. He proposes that U.K. immigration policies be reformed so as to allow legal entry to all "fit" young women. U.K. men express their hearty support. The comic premise here makes a sound evolutionary point: men are receptive to Ali G's preposterous proposal because evolution would not have wired men to reject a sudden influx of nubile, exotic young women. When you see American men on the street protesting against illegal immigration, it is more likely that their ire was inspired by virile Mexican gardeners than by fit Swedish nannies.

Let us try to summarize the limited contribution of biology to the politics of gender differences. No serious evolutionary psychologist would assert that gender differences in politics are universal or that they mechanically issue from "different genes." The pathway from genetic predisposition to social trait is undoubtedly very complex and subject to a strong cultural influence.

No one would argue that all women are more dove-ish than all men, nor that all women will favor pro-immigration policies, etc. Moreover, it would make no sense to say that a particular woman is against military intervention "because" she is a woman. Rather, what is asserted here is that on a large scale — the scale of populations — we can detect the presence of a significant biological influence on political behavior, and we can better explain that behavior by understanding the evolutionary role it might have once served. On average, the genders react to politics in slightly different ways. The argument here has been that evolutionary theory predicts such a difference.

It has long been accepted that culture, personality, family history, and education play a role in the development of political behavior. To that list of factors we must now add biology. The value of the evolutionary perspective is that it allows us to explain phenomena — such as partisanship, and the gender gap — which would otherwise remain puzzling and obscure.

Evolution of the Generation Gap

> When a nation's young men are
> conservative, its funeral bell is already rung.
> — Henry Ward Beecher,
> *Proverbs from the Plymouth Pulpit*

> A mellowing rigorist is always a much
> pleasanter object to contemplate than
> a tightening liberal, as a cold day warming
> up… is much more agreeable than a
> warm one chilling down.
> — Oliver Wendell Holmes,
> *The Poet at the Breakfast Table*

In the 2008 Democratic presidential primaries, Hillary Clinton and Barack Obama cleaved the liberal electorate along a number of demographic lines. A generation gap appeared. Young voters overwhelmingly favored Obama, while their parents and grandparents just as strongly supported Clinton. Was there an underlying biological dynamic at play?

It is part of our received folk wisdom in politics that people become more conservative as they age. Thus it is a *cliché* to associate radical left-wing politics with the young, while in Hollywood films the role of Republican CEO is invariably given to a gray-haired white man. Is there any evidence of a correlation between aging and conservatism; and if so, does an evolutionary mechanism play a role?

American political scientists have *not* found that citizens become more conservative as they age. Rather, it seems that the most typical behavior is *persistence* – whatever people believed in young adulthood is what they continue to believe for the rest of their lives. Some people's attitudes may become more pronounced with age, so that staunch liberals and conservatives become ever more set in their ways. That finding would comport well with the theory that the confirmation bias plays a key role in politics. The widespread perception that people become more conservative as they age might have been caused primarily by those who were conservative to begin with.

However, while aging may not affect party loyalty, it is hard to believe that it does not affect political behavior in other important ways. There is so much anecdotal history that young people have different interests and motivations from those of older people. Consider the famous, bitingly-sharp distinction that Aristotle drew between the characters of young and old men:

> *Young men* have strong passions, and tend to gratify them indiscriminately.... They are changeable and fickle in their desires, which are violent while they last, but quickly over: their impulses are keen but not deep-rooted, and are like sick people's attacks of hunger and thirst. They are hot-tempered, and quick-tempered, and apt to give way to their anger; bad temper often gets the better of them, for owing to their love of honour they cannot bear being slighted, and are indignant if they imagine themselves unfairly treated. While they love honour, they love victory still more; for youth is eager for superiority over others, and victory is one form of this.

Elderly Men — men who are past their prime... have often been taken in, and often made mistakes; and life on the whole is a bad business....They are cynical; that is, they tend to put the worse construction on everything. Further, their experience makes them distrustful and therefore suspicious of evil.... They are small-minded, because they have been humbled by life: their desires are set upon nothing more exalted or unusual than what will help them to keep alive. They are not generous, because money is one of the things they must have, and at the same time their experience has taught them how hard it is to get and how easy to lose.[48]

In modern biology, the theory that organisms change their life-strategies as they age is known as Life History Theory (LHT).[49] LHT helps to explain generational conflicts, such as those between parents and children. One age-dependent trait that is clearly relevant for politics is the appetite for risk. Young people are in general more open to social innovations than older people, who are more likely to perceive such innovations as risky.

Small bands of humans left Africa about one hundred thousand years ago. Since then, the species has spread to a dizzying variety of habitats, occupying terrain from Norway to Tierra del Fuego. This suggests a restless species, often on the move. As little bands of our ancestors trudged, barefoot and half-naked, over mountain ranges, across deserts and through jungles, the going must often have been rough. The elderly, sick, infantile, or child-rearing members of society must often have shared a common interest in staying put, while adult males and childless females may have been more willing to take risks in order to explore fresh hunting and feeding grounds. In other words, at crucial times the different human generations may have faced opposing incentives. The generation gap in politics is probably a very ancient phenomenon.

One interesting aspect of the Clinton-Obama rivalry was that Clinton was, if anything, the more radical of the two candidates, but she was supported by older voters. Was this because the older voters had become increasingly radicalized after a lifetime of liberalism, continually-reinforced by the confirmation bias? I don't think so.

In our ancient inter-generational conflicts, it probably made sense, all else being equal, to support leaders who were closest to one's own age. Same-age leaders could best be counted on to follow a life-history strategy that would be most congruent with one's own. Recall that the Implicit Attitudes Tests revealed that most people have an anti-elderly bias. It made sense, from an evolutionary perspective, for humans to be able to detect the ages of prospective leaders (as by signals such as balding and gray hair), so as to be able to express a preference for those candidates closest to one's own age.

Long before tattoos, nose-rings and text-messaging were invented, evolution had developed ways for humans to clearly mark their generational divides.

Anthropology vs. Biology

Let us finally consider the long-standing critique of evolutionary theory that comes from cultural anthropology. In the late 1880's Franz Boas helped create the modern science of anthropology with his ethnographic studies of the Inuits. Boas was highly skeptical of Darwinian explanations for human behavior. In Boas' view, if human behavior were biologically-determined, it should be universal, e.g., everywhere the same. However, Boas' experience amongst the Inuits had taught him that human societies around the world were extremely different. Boas postulated that the existence of human culture interposed a crucial difference between men and animals. Humans could not be comprehended in terms of bare evolutionary theory because culture added an unpredictable, variable element. Boas asserted that human culture was infinitely malleable, thereby discrediting the evolutionary perspective. Boas' most famous graduate student helped convince the world of the anti-Darwinian case with a single book, one of the greatest scientific best-sellers of all time.

In 1928 Margaret Mead published *Coming of Age in Samoa*. Based on several months of close observation of the native population of a small Polynesian island, *Coming of Age* recounted and analyzed the experiences of adolescent females. Mead observed that Samoan females were extremely relaxed about their entry into puberty and sexual life. From this, she deduced that culture was actually a more important determinant of human behavior than biology. If biology were all-controlling, Mead reasoned (following Boas), we would expect to see universal behavior in puberty and adolescence — all cultures would share similar practices. In the West, however, it was observed that sexual coming of age was associated with stress and anxiety. The relative freedom from sexual anxiety of Samoan teen-agers was taken by Mead to disprove the universality of human adolescent experience. Basing a breathtakingly broad argument on slender evidence, Mead concluded that the difference between Samoan and American experiences in puberty was sufficient to prove that culture trumped biology. Helped by its titillating revelations of sexual promiscuity among the teen-age natives (and slyly prurient cover art), the book enjoyed colossal sales. Anthropologists rejoiced in their victory over the Darwinian orthodoxy. In the tug of war between nature and nurture, nurture was ascendant for several decades, thanks in no small measure to Margaret Mead.

Today, however, Mead's research has been discredited. Subsequent studies, published to controversy in the 1980s, revealed that many of the teen-agers that she reported on were making up stories to have fun with her. Moreover, she failed to detect social patterns in Samoa that should have been obvious to any professional anthropologist (but which would have contradicted her overall thesis). Later anthropologists, notably Donald Brown, refuted Mead with extensive cross-cultural research that pointed to a contrary conclusion: human culture around the world is indeed marked by a striking number of universal practices.[50]

Despite the vertiginous decline in Margaret Mead's reputation, it is necessary to understand the immense popularity that her work recently enjoyed, because it helped to firmly entrench an anti-Darwinian school of thought that remains robust. For an example of the power of the anti-Darwinian lobby, consider the affair of Larry Summers, chief economic advisor to President Barack Obama.

In 2005, Summers was weathering a controversial term as president of Harvard University. He had already offended a number of Harvard faculty members with his aggressive manner when he sealed his doom with a presentation on the topic of female academics in the sciences. It is a widely-bemoaned fact that only a very small percentage of tenured professors in the hard sciences are women. Summers was discussing possible origins of the problem. Amongst other causes, he mentioned the possibility of a biological link, which is suggested by evolutionary theory. Studies have confirmed that there is a greater genetic variability amongst males than amongst females. Thus, for example, three times as many boys as girls are diagnosed as autistic. Extremely high IQs are more common amongst boys, as are extremely low IQs. Summers conjectured, qualifying his statements carefully, that there was a possible biological source to the observed greater variability in male performance in scientific and mathematical performance, but only as a minor factor to be considered along with other social factors.

This statement provoked great horror, not to mention immediate symptoms of nausea. Nancy Hopworth, an M.I.T. professor listening to the presentation, had to rush outside, she said, to keep herself from vomiting. The press soon reported that the president of Harvard University was being criticized for saying that little girls shouldn't go into science because they weren't as smart as boys. Summers recanted, back-tracked and apologized as quickly and profusely as humiliated public figures are expected to nowadays. It was not enough.

Summers was thrown out on his tin ear. The Harvard faculty promptly issued a vote of no confidence in its gaffe-prone president and Summers meekly resigned soon after. What is remarkable about this incident for evolutionary psychologists is the fact that Summers was drawn-and-quartered for stating a plausible (if controversial) hypothesis. For evolutionary psychologists, differences between men and women are to be expected and such differences do not necessarily carry any great moral significance. All serious evolutionary psychologists agree that women must be accorded the same rights and privileges as men, and further all agree that the average professional aptitude of women is at least as great as that of men. However, evolutionary psychologists also accept it as commonplace that there are numerous physical and behavioral differences between the human sexes, just as there are between the genders of all the higher animals. This is not necessarily something to vomit about (it all depends where you ate for lunch).

Consider the viewpoint of Louann Brizendine, a neuropsychiatrist and author of the book, *The Female Brain*. Brizendine argued that Summers' argument was misguided because there is no evidence that women lack the requisite scientific aptitude to become science professors. However, Brizendine herself ascribes to a very dichotomous view of the male and female brains. For Brizendine, the two brains are quite different in every way and the advantage goes clearly to the female brain. Brizendine's research suggests that the male brain is just a stunted version of the female brain.[51]

All brains start out as female brains. Shortly after conception, though, those of us unlucky enough to possess "Y" chromosomes receive a harsh blast of fetal testosterone, turning us into little embryonic Beavises and Buttheads. The cognitive effects of that first testosterone shock can be observed in childhood. Boys are dumber, slower, more impulsive, aggressive and anti-social. Meanwhile the female brain, not similarly brutalized *in utero*, is allowed to flourish through childhood and is then further enriched by nourishing baths of adolescent estrogen. Women's hormonally souped-up brains are capable of a much richer emotional life than men's, and we can actually see this at the neuronal level, where there is a greater proportion of connective tissue. Women have more empathy and are more collaborative. All of this naturally leads to different *interests*.

Imagine that a young person is described to you as "intelligent, popular, and sociable," and that you are asked to suggest a career for such a person. What would be the first career option that would pop into your head? *Theoretical physics*?

It is impossible to be equally interested in everything, and it thus seems plausible that women would be less interested than men in certain disciplines. As Brizendine suggests, these different interests may well be rooted in biological superiority, not inferiority. If one manifestation of this difference in interests is that fewer women than men are interested in becoming physics professors, one returns to a biological explanation. Even if the pathway from biology is a complex one, mediated by culture, and ending only in a generalized difference of interests, that is enough to produce asymmetrical social results.

It is unfortunate that the president of America's most prestigious university could be forced out for uttering a scientific conjecture that would be commonplace in Evolutionary Psychology 101. However, Summer's experience should be instructive for the rest of us. In a book which deals with the biological origins of human irrationality, it is prudent to note that biological explanations of human behavior themselves tend to provoke irrationality, not to mention dyspepsia.

Having now repulsed the attacks of the cultural determinists, we must conclude a peace — by opening our gates to them. As we will see in the next chapter, they have something very important to teach us.

CHAPTER 6

Culture and Political Irrationality

> Because they were acquired so early in our lives, cultural values remain unconscious to those who hold them. Therefore, they cannot be discussed, nor can they be directly observed by outsiders. They can only be inferred from the way people act under various circumstances. If one asks why they act as they do, people may say they just "know" or "feel" how to do the right thing. Their heart or conscience tells them.
> — Geert Hofstede, *Cultures and Organizations*

DARK TRUTH #6
There is a map of the culture war. It was drawn by anthropologists.

Red Deserts vs. Blue Forests:
The Bio-Cultural Origins of Partisanship

As we have seen, evolutionary biology has greatly informed our understanding of political behavior. To appreciate the role of biology, we first had to topple the reigning paradigm of cultural determinism, which held that human nature was a blank slate for culture to write upon. Human nature is most emphatically *not* a blank slate. Humans come into this world equipped with a full suite of mental programs and sub-routines, ready to begin the strange business of being a human.

Now we must return to the concept of culture. Culture is not everything, but it is not irrelevant, either. *Cultural anthropology* is the science of human culture. Built upon the fieldwork and ethnographic studies of pioneers such as Bronislaw Malinowski, Franz Boas, Ruth Benedict and Margaret Mead, cultural anthropology in the 20th century was a vast, global enterprise of cultural analysis, as armies of anthropologists sought to chart the entire social world. Anthropologists insinuated themselves into thousands of micro-cultures around the planet, from primitive villages to boardrooms and bureaucracies. They carefully observed and meticulously recorded the rituals, customs and habits of each society.

Eventually, enormous databases of human behavior were assembled for comparative analysis. In the mid-1960s, Stanford anthropologist Robert Textor gathered information on 400-plus societies around the world and classified them according to nearly 500 traits. He then fed all this information into a computer which cross-correlated all the data. Textor's mammoth "Cross Cultural Summary" is the 3,000 page record of the most significant correlations.[54]

At the broadest scale, Textor discovered that most cultures could be classified as belonging to one of two large groups, desert cultures or forest cultures. Desert cultures tended to be monotheistic, hierarchical, sexist and warlike. Forest cultures, conversely, tended to be polytheistic, egalitarian, gender-neutral and peace-loving.

The cultural differences can be traced to the different demands of each environment. The desert is a harsh, unforgiving environment ruled by the law of scarcity. Human groups living in the desert operate on a tighter margin of error than groups in luxuriant environments. Rules are more tightly enforced and cohesion is more important. A solitary human may survive a while in the forest, but not in the desert. Far-flung groups of male goat and camel herders may have been the original warrior castes. In the desolate landscapes of the desert, the alternating dominance of sun and moon led naturally to monotheistic or dualistic religions.

In the forest, by contrast, food is plentiful and there are myriad forms of plant and animal life that can be either helpful or dangerous. In such a chaotic, teeming profusion, polytheistic religions arise. Simple rules are not as helpful as an appreciation of complexity. Since the danger of ostracism from the group is lower, group cohesion and respect for hierarchy is less important. The greater abundance of food permits a lower intensity of work and therefore less need for separation of labor, so that the sexes more often work and live together.

Which culture would you prefer to live in? At least one biologist, Stanford's Robert Sapolsky, has bemoaned the relative success of desert cultures:

> Desert cultures, with their militarism, stratification, mistreatment of women, uptightness about child-rearing and sexuality, seem pretty unappealing. And yet ours is a planet dominated by the cultural descendants of the desert dwellers. At various points, the desert dwellers have poured out of the Middle East and have defined large parts of Eurasian cultures. Such cultures, in turn, have passed the last five hundred years subjugating the native populations of the Americas, Africa, and Australia. As a result, ours is a Judeo-Christian/Muslim world, not a Mbuti-Carib/Trobriand one.[52]

In Sapolsky's view, the original red vs. blue divide was between desert cultures (conservatives) and forest cultures (liberals) — and the desert cultures won. Sapolsky, a bushy-bearded professor from San Francisco who likes to hang out in jungles watching baboons, leaves no doubt as to his preference (forest). He finds the enforced conformity of desert culture appalling: "Only one way to think, to do, to be. Crusades and *jihads, fatwas* and inquisitions, hellfire and damnation."[53] Presumably, Dr. Sapolsky will not be moving to Tucson anytime soon, nor voting Republican. He's a forest man through and through.

In this chapter I will argue that cultural characteristics — such as a tendency toward conservatism or liberalism — emerge from biological sources. As populations of humans spread across the planet, they encountered radically different ecological conditions. The evolutionary pressure of prolonged exposure to different conditions led to populations with different behavioral characteristics. The twin-based research we looked at earlier demonstrated that humans inherit political predispositions ranging from conservative to liberal. Textor shows us what happens when this human variability is allowed to play out over time in different environments. Certain types of individuals will tend to do better in certain kinds of environments. The tough-minded did well in harsh environments, and their proportion of the population increased. The soft-hearted did well in luxuriant environments and the proportion of like individuals increased over time. Eventually, human cultures have diverged and stratified into the forms observed by Textor: desert cultures (red countries) and forest cultures (blue countries). Textor allows us to extend the red-blue metaphor to a global scale — conservative-liberal polarization is present both within societies and — globally — between countries.

Since America is composed of a native population mixed with immigrants from every country on the planet, America's cultural divide is a mirror of the world's cultural complexity. If we wish to negotiate a truce in our culture war we should first seek to understand how red cultures differ from blue cultures around the world.

Anthropologists have shown us the way, by providing a helpful framework which allows us to pinpoint the cultural differences underlying any social conflict. Before turning to that framework, let us summarize how biology and culture interact in the development of an individual's politics.

The Bio-Cultural Model of Partisan Development

Personal political growth is organic. The best analogy is to some kind of plant life, such as a tree. Any living tree represents the intersection of at least three factors: genetic (the seed); local (the soil); and environmental (the climate). From the same type of seed we could grow a great variety of different-looking trees by subjecting them to different environments, yet each tree would still recognizably belong to the same species. As trees (and humans) grow, they are shaped by local and environmental pressures so that they become progressively rigid, with only the top-most shoots and branches still showing flexibility.

The twin research on the heritability of ideology suggests that humans fall into two broad phenotypes that might be characterized as tough (red-state, desert culture) or soft (blue-state, forest culture). A particular individual might fit anywhere on the spectrum between tough and soft — i.e., we can inherit a hue anywhere from carnation red to cobalt blue. However, that is only the beginning of the story, as is indicated by the four-part structure of what I call the bio-cultural model of political development:

1. The biological foundation — As we observed above, the "ground floor" is biological. We are each born with a political predisposition that falls somewhere in the range from tough to soft.

2. The cultural environment — This is perhaps the most important layer, as it has the power to over-ride genetic predispositions. In the socialization process, we gradually acquire beliefs and values which shape our politics. Commonly, this heavy cultural layer reinforces biological tendencies, but sometimes it doesn't, which explains why some people suddenly "discover" their true political values only after they have left the home. Although we speak of a single culture, it would probably be more accurate to speak of layers of overlapping cultural influences. Every person really belongs to several cultures and also bears the influence of several cultures. Our first cultural influence is contributed by our family. The single greatest predictor of our political orientation is our parents' political orientation. Culture finishes writing on the biological slate when we are still young. Political change after age 25–30 is rare.

3. The framing layer — The framing layer is the point of contact between our inherited and socialized predispositions and the conventions and manipulations of the outside world. Political problems and issues are not inherently "liberal" or "conservative" — it is up to the politicians to create distinctions by reacting to problems in different ways.

The framing layer introduces a great deal of irrationality into the political sphere because the political parties successfully convince their members to follow platforms that are internally inconsistent. Thus, in America conservatives are against abortion and euthanasia because of the "sanctity of life," but they are also in favor of the death penalty and foreign military intervention. Liberals, conversely, believe in the universal rights of the weak, defenseless and underprivileged, but exclude human fetuses.

4. The rational surface — The individual's abstract capacity for logical analysis of issues, politicians and policies resides in the rational layer. Theoretically, we can ignore the influences from biology, culture and framing, by reaching decisions that are purely based on logic and evidence. It is my contention that this rarely happens. Although we do have a strong capacity for reason, our rationality is regrettably also further divided into sub-levels:

a) The defense lawyer — The defense lawyer is the mind's ability to develop logical arguments to support positions that are deeply rooted in the biological and cultural layers. The defense lawyer helps us engage in "motivated reasoning": logic at the service of an argument.

b) The neutral arbiter — This refers to the mind's capacity to arrive at a rational, disinterested conclusion. By common convention, we pretend to make political decisions at this level. However, it is really the least important from a practical perspective. It exists theoretically but is rarely (if ever) observed in nature.

During the process of political growth, there is a certain amount of potential flexibility. Unlike trees permanently rooted to one spot in the forest, humans are frequently transplanted into different environments. A person may move from one culture to another during his or her life, disrupting the gradual political calcification. However, the likelihood of major shifts diminishes rapidly with age. Once an opinion gets locked in by the first three layers, the mind's inner "defense lawyer" ensures that no contrary opinion will ever be granted a fair hearing.

Thus, we should not overly indulge the hope that we will convert our political rivals. Their political orientation took decades to grow and solidify, and is solidly-rooted in genetic and cultural programming. Our political rivals, like our spouses, are people we should give up trying to change. There is hope, however, for a better life in mutual comprehension and tolerance (in politics, at least).

Red Culture vs. Blue Culture: or, How to Dance the Bubble Tango

Each of us has an invisible "bubble" of space around us, a sort of natural comfort zone. When a stranger gets inside of that space we feel disturbed. However, from country to country the size of the bubble varies enormously. The warm and empathic Brazilians have virtually no bubble at all — they love to stand close and even touch their interlocutors as they talk. Relating warmly and physically to others is an unspoken positive value in Brazilian culture. The Finns, like other Scandinavians and northern Europeans in general, are more reserved and prefer to keep a distance of at least

18 to 24 inches between themselves and any person who is not a close friend or family member. Scandinavians place more of a positive value on privacy and independence.

Imagine a Finn and a Brazilian talking at a cocktail party. The two speakers will engage in a funny dance — the Brazilian constantly moving in to make a point, the Finn adroitly stepping back to a comfortable range. Depending on the size of the venue, the Brazilian may gradually chase the Finn across the room and back again. We could call this the Bubble Tango. You can see a version of it happening at virtually any large international cocktail party, but it is often not perceived by the dancers themselves.

Afterwards, the Brazilian might remark that the Finn seemed "cold" or "aloof." The Finn might complain that the Brazilian had seemed "pushy" or "nosy." This is how cultural conflict begins: a clash of unseen values followed by discomfort, which both sides explain by making negative evaluations of the other. Of such insubstantial conflict are real, bloody wars born.

The study of cultural dimensions provide us with a much more productive way of reacting to cultural conflict. Instead of seizing upon each political dispute as fresh evidence of the evil stupidity of the other side, we can trace our discord to different positions on the cultural spectrum. Cultural understanding is the foundation for political peace.

The dean of the cultural dimensions school of cross-cultural studies is Geert Hofstede, a Dutch social psychologist who spent part of his professional career with I.B.M.[54] Building upon a framework provided by cultural anthropologists, Hofstede marshaled survey data from over seventy countries to show that societies differ according to a set of five "cultural dimensions":

1) POWER DISTANCE — acceptance or rejection of inequality;

2) INDIVIDUALISM — preference for individualism or group membership ("collectivism");

3) MASCULINITY / FEMININITY — tendency toward assertiveness or nurturing;

4) UNCERTAINTY AVOIDANCE — preference for tradition or innovation,

5) TIME ORIENTATION — long-term or short-term perspective.

In Hofstede's view, when people from different cultures fail to work effectively together, it is generally because their implicit values conflict along one of these dimensions.

The unspoken and invisible nature of cultural conflict is one of its most frustrating aspects. It is impossible to get people to work together if they cannot see why they are clashing, but cultural conflict is frequently subterranean and unconscious.

The Dimensions of Difference: Mapping the Cultural Fault Line

> The world is like a map of antipathies,
> almost of hates, in which everyone picks
> the symbolic color of his difference.
> — Juan Ramon Jiménez, *Heroic Reason*

Cultural dimensions allow us to map the contours of the cultural divide between the red states and blue states. Below, let us review the common cultural stereotypes of conservatives (authoritarian, community-minded, tradition-oriented and masculine) and liberals (egalitarian, individualistic, future-oriented and feminine), from the perspective of international survey data on cultural dimensions:

RED-STATE / CONSERVATIVE STEREOTYPE

People from tough cultures are deferential to authority and tradition,
suspicious of individualists and outsiders, are relatively sexist,
and place great value on the acquisition of social status.

BLUE-STATE / LIBERAL STEREOTYPE

People from soft cultures are more egalitarian and individualistic,
less attached to traditions and gender roles, and less materialistic.

Individualism

In individualistic countries, the individual's interests are allowed to prevail over the group's. Individuals are allowed to choose their own life paths, even if they are not approved of by the group. In countries that rank low on individualism (Hofstede calls them collectivist), the group's values are considered supreme.

The U.S. ranks number one in Hofstede's studies on individualism, beating out 73 other countries in the study. Although we are the champions, other individualistic countries include Australia, Great Britain, the Netherlands, Italy and France.

On the collectivist side, where conformity to the group's wishes is more important, we find Ecuador, Pakistan, China, Mexico and Greece.

In the U.S., the blue states are individualist while the red states are collectivist. Citizens of the blue states insist on protection of individual freedoms, whether they include a woman's right to choose, a gay couple's right to marry, or a protestor's right to burn the flag. Citizens of red states lament the decline of small-town, communitarian values, where neighbors could count on each other. Red state residents view the individualism of the blue states as being reckless, selfish and unpatriotic. For red-state culture, the ultimate act of citizenship is to give up one's life for one's country in military service. For blue-staters, in contrast, a brave protest against repressive laws is more heroic and admirable.

For several of the cultural dimensions listed below we only have international comparative data, with nothing to allow us to compare the U.S. states internally. However, when it comes to the culture of individualism, we do have an additional set of helpful data from social psychologist Robert Levine, presented in his highly-readable book *A Geography of Time*.[55]

Levine's international travels left him with the conviction that there is a relationship between a culture's health and its pace. He sought to measure this relationship by establishing a number of simple metrics for social health. These involved the willingness to perform a small act of altruism, such as helping a blind person cross the street, or helping return a lost letter. When people are too rushed and pressed for time, Levine reasoned, they start to abandon traditional altruistic practices, and become more selfish.

Levine's data suggests that blue states, and blue cities in particular, are individualistic (selfish) while red states are collectivist (helpful).

Amongst the most individualistic cities were New York, Los Angeles, San Francisco, Chicago and Philadelphia. Amongst the most helpful cities were Rochester, Nashville, Memphis, Houston and Kansas City.

Power Distance

This dimension measures how accepting a culture is of inequality. In the U.S., red states are high in power distance, blue states are low.

Thus, conservatives tend to respect authority, while liberals are suspicious of power. This explains the emotional reaction from the red states when liberals criticize a conservative president—from the perspective of high power distance culture, it is simply wrong to challenge one's leaders. When a liberal administration is in power, however, conservatives self-servingly forget the importance of respecting one's leaders.

Countries that rank high in power distance, such as Russia, Mexico, China, the Philippines, and India, have a tradition of autocratic government and strong class divisions.

Countries that rank low in power distance, such as Denmark, New Zealand, Ireland, Great Britain and Germany, prefer social structures based on equality.

Interestingly, Hofstede discovered a rough correlation between power distance and latitude. Tropical countries tend to have high power distance, while countries in the temperate latitudes tend to be more egalitarian. In the U.S., similarly, conservatism historically was more associated with the South than with the North.

Masculinity / Femininity

Hofstede came to the somewhat controversial conclusion that some societies are relatively "masculine," others "feminine." Masculine societies are marked by a tough, competitive work-place, where men battle for material signs of success, while women manage the home and child-rearing. In feminine societies, work roles are not gender based, and material success is considered less important than having successful relationships in one's family and community.

Masculine societies include Japan, Austria, Italy, Mexico, China and Germany, while feminine societies can be found in Sweden, Slovenia, Costa Rica, Portugal and Thailand.

In the U.S., the red states are masculine while the blue states are feminine. Indeed, Republicans are from Mars, while Democrats are from Venus.

When arch-conservative Ann Coulter wants to insult the Democrats, she accuses them of "female whining." Not surprisingly, Democrats are always worried that their leaders are acting like "wimps" (or in the California Governator's classic formulation, "girlie-men").

Uncertainty Avoidance

This dimension measures the strength of a culture's attachment to traditions, rules and customs. Countries that are high in uncertainty avoidance would prefer life to stay the same, and they look at social innovation with suspicion; examples include Greece, Portugal, Uruguay and Russia. Countries that are low in uncertainty avoidance welcome change and innovation; examples include Singapore, Denmark, Vietnam and Ireland.

In the U.S. the red states are high in uncertainty avoidance (preference for tradition), while the blue states are low (acceptance of change). This is another way of stating the old story of politics — liberals view change as positive and associate it with "progress," while conservatives view change as dangerous and inimical to valuable "traditions."

Time Orientation

Some cultures take a long perspective on time and history (China and Japan), while others are focused on the here and now (Canada and Spain).

In the U.S., the red states have a long-term time orientation, while the blue states have a short-term perspective. Studies have established a correlation between population density and perception of time. As we move from the country to the city, we can observe a gradual increase in tempo, and a corresponding decrease in civility. Country folk take the time to stop and say howdy, while city slickers bump you as they race by to steal a cab from someone else. Blue-state residents want social change to happen right away, while red-state residents are suspicious of anything done in a rush.

Robert Levine provides us with some additional data. He measured the pace of life in cities around the U.S. using a few ingenious and simple

---

* Several of my Irish students have speculated that the Irish data was probably tainted as obtained in too close proximity to a pub.

metrics. For example, he measured the average walking speed of pedestrians in the street. He found that speed of walking is proportional to population density. As they approach a city, people speed up. People walked especially fast in Ireland, Holland and Switzerland, while they dawdled in Brazil, Indonesia and Mexico.

Levine also measured a culture's respect for punctuality by recording the time on public clocks and then comparing it to the exact time as determined by a chronometer. Internationally it was Switzerland, not surprisingly, that had the most accurate clocks (an average deviation from perfect of seventeen seconds). El Salvador's clocks were either very, very far off the correct time, or they were all broken.

Within the U.S., an overall fast pace of life appeared to correlate roughly with blue-state politics. Thus, Boston, New York and Providence ranked as the speediest cities (blue), while Sacramento, Shreveport and Memphis were at the slow end (red).

Bridging the Cultural Divide

How does Hofstede suggest that we bridge the inevitable cultural divide when individuals work together with individuals from different backgrounds? How can we get over our habitual red vs. blue conflict?

The key lies in realizing that your own values are not universally correct — there is no "right" culture. Knowledge of cultural dimensions is helpful because it allows us to spot the cultural tension underlying many political issues. Applying a modicum of cultural savvy we might realize, for example, that a given political dispute arose because citizens had different cultural attitudes toward power and authority. As we have seen, some cultures have a tradition of great respect for authority, while others have the opposite tradition — it is impossible to say that one way is right and the other wrong.

If we wish to discuss such issues productively, we must begin with a basic respect for the validity of the different perspectives that arise at each end of the cultural spectrum. The great contribution of cultural anthropology has been to teach us that each perspective, whether red-state or blue, is internally justifiable. Everyone is "right" from the perspective of his or her own culture.

The ability to tolerate fundamental differences in values is difficult for people who lack experience with other cultures. Since Americans prefer increasingly to socialize with people of similar politics, many of us do not get the opportunity to realize that cultural values which are different from ours are not necessarily wrong.

Parental Culture: Mommy Democrats, Daddy Republicans

George Lakoff, a professor of cognitive linguistics at the University of California, Berkeley, maintains that political polarization stems from a clash of different "worldviews." Worldviews are ethical and moral frameworks learned principally from the family. The problem, for Lakoff, is that there are two completely different kinds of families.

Thus, some people grow up in families that posit the "tough daddy" or "strict father" as the guiding social archetype. In such families, the father has primary responsibility for "bringing home the bacon," while the mother takes care of the house and raises the children. The tough daddy provides safety in an uncertain world, sets and enforces a strict code of authority, and expects the children to acquire self-discipline and self-reliance. People who grow up in these families place great value on these concepts: *character, discipline, self-reliance, personal responsibility*, and *hard work*. Tough-daddy families tend to produce conservatives, who will find it natural to support and vote for the Republican Party.

In another kind of family, a "loving mommy" or "nurturant parent" provides love, empathy and understanding. In such a family, children become responsible through being cared for and through caring for others. Obedience is not compelled but derives from love and respect. The goal of nurturance is to create autonomous, happy adults. People who grow up in these families place great value on these concepts: *social responsibility, free expression, equality, human rights, empathy*, and *health*. Loving-mommy families will tend to produce liberals, who will support the Democratic Party.

Republicans and Democrats clash, in Lakoff's view, because they attach radically-different connotations to the same words. The two sides "frame" issues distinctly, depending on their backgrounds. Thus, if you grew up in a tough-daddy family, the words "big government" may evoke connotations that a "stranger" is going to "meddle" with your "independence" and "freedom" and take away "your money." If you grew up in a loving-mommy family, the words "big government" might connote a "helpful" or "caring" "neighbor" who can provide "equality," "human rights" and "social welfare."

Lakoff does not hide his preference for the mommies. He achieved celebrity status among Democratic strategists by providing specific advice on how to frame public issues so that liberal viewpoints were more palatable to voters. For example, Lakoff observed with grudging admiration that the Republicans always referred to their tax cuts as "tax relief." Lakoff believed this to be an effective strategy because the phrase conveyed the impression that taxes were *already* oppressive. By getting the media and citizenry to discuss tax cuts in the terminology proposed by Republicans ("relief" is so soothing), the battle was already half-won for conservatives. Lakoff argued the Democrats should follow suit, applying a kind of linguistic judo to each political occasion. When the Republicans referred to their proposed restrictions on civil law judgments as "Tort Reform," Lakoff advised the Democrats to counter by referring to the draft bill as "The Corporate Immunity Act."

Such pragmatic advice may well be useful to political candidates engaged in the rough-and-tumble of political combat. However, for voters on the quest for truth and rationality, Lakoff is of little use. Conservatives, especially, will enjoy reading Lakoff's books about as much as liberals enjoy listening to Rush Limbaugh. The main flaw in Lakoff's theory is that he assumes that readers will agree with him that the loving-mommy family is better than the tough-daddy family. It is no surprise, from Lakoff's perspective, that Democrats currently hold a substantial lead over Republicans amongst women voters. However, by simply assuming that all his readers are liberals, Lakoff avoids fully engaging the question of conservatism. How is it that in all cultures and times some extremely intelligent people been conservative, and have given a reasonably coherent account for their being so? Lakoff does not say.

Lakoff is entirely dismissive of conservatives (not to mention, men), although the bio-cultural model suggests that half the population will remain relatively conservative (and half will always be male). His explanation of why conservatives are wrong is gnomic: "Strict Father morality is not just out of touch with the realities of raising children.... It is out of touch with the realities of the human mind."56 For Lakoff, the application of absolute moral rules (strict-father morality) is illogical in a multi-cultural society. Conservatives, by Lakoff's less-than-neutral definition, are people who fail to accept cultural diversity; hence, they should lose elections.

This is a paradoxically intolerant point of view. As we have seen from Geert Hofstede's cross-cultural research, many cultures around the world are deeply rooted in a tough-daddy morality, so actually Lakoff can also be accused of cultural intolerance. When Lakoff condemns conservative culture, he is condemning half the world. He may well be right to do so, but he needs to give us better reasons.

According to Hofstede's data, countries that rank high in uncertainty avoidance are: Greece, Portugal, Uruguay, Belgium, Russia, Poland and Japan. That's rather a lot of people to condemn as being "out of touch with the realities of the human mind."

Understandably, Lakoff (a Berkeley professor, after all) would be more comfortable in low power distance countries like Jamaica, Denmark, Sweden, Vietnam or Ireland. I don't blame him; those are nice countries. But Lakoff would like those cultures better because they are more congruent with Lakoff's own bio-cultural profile, not because they are somehow intrinsically *better*.

What would happen if Lakoff's framing strategies were so successful that the entire populace voted Democratic and the Republican party went extinct? Would we live happily ever after in liberal uniformity? I fear that any utopian unity would be short-lived, as the Democratic Party would promptly split into two factions, one conservative and one liberal. After a while, the conservatives would re-name themselves the Republicans, and we would be back to square one. Lakoff does not confront the reality that populations of humans will always fall along a normal distribution on a left-to-right ideological scale. Frames will not abolish human differences. As the twin studies, not to mention, history, have confirmed: we have always had conservatives, and always will.

Lakoff claims that child developmental psychology has established that tough daddy child-rearing practices harm children, while nurturant parent practices result in healthy adults. This is arguable. How does Lakoff explain the surveys which show that conservatives are happier than liberals? Moreover, how does he explain the research of Judith Rich Harris, the independent scholar who infuriated child psychologists by proving that even very bad parenting has little effect on the psychological health of adults? If we remember the case of the twin Jims, we will recall that the twins were brought up by different parents, but developed very similar behavioral traits. It seems that for most people our genetic programming is resilient enough to withstand some pretty terrible parents. This research may be disappointing to you if you have been an incredibly conscientious parent, but on the other hand, it should be a bit of a relief if you haven't.

Young boys often compete by boasting of the strictness of their fathers; many continue to do so for the rest of their lives, with increasing nostalgia. To be sure, nobody has fond memories of an abusive parent, but an extremely strict but loving father is remembered with respect and gratitude. For people with memories of such fathers, Lakoff is barking up the wrong tree. Regardless of one's own tastes or bio-cultural background, one must accept that America will always have its share of tough daddies. It is wishful thinking to believe that we can make them go away, but maybe we can keep the family together by following a political version of John Gray's marital advice. Mars and Venus must learn to get along.

Like any healthy family, America needs both its parents, tough daddies and loving mommies, to work together.

CHAPTER 7

Irrational Partisanship

DARK TRUTH #7
Irrationality is proportional to partisanship.

Blue Books, Red Blood

American elections are now framed as a contest between red and blue, between Republicans and Democrats. The red vs. blue metaphor has so thoroughly permeated our social consciousness that we can instantly categorize any aspect of our lives through a simple blue/red reference. A friend of mine, showing me around his home city of Seattle, referred to certain neighborhoods as "red-state parts of town." If we take the popular media as any guide, we would have to conclude that there is a big difference between the red state and blue state parts of town, and further that the red-staters and blue-staters don't get along. Indeed, statistics show that increasingly, liberal Americans move into blue-state parts of town, and conservatives do the opposite. Over time, our ideological polarization leads to a crazy-quilt political map, as America separates into red-or-blue enclaves.

A visit to our local chain bookstore confirms that America has divided into red and blue publishing markets. Barnes & Noble now commonly has a table which is marked "Red" on one side and "Blue" on the other, making it easy to shop for your prejudice (one can imagine quite a few interesting glances being tossed across the top of that book table at your local B & N).

If you are conservative, and shopping on the "Red" side, publishers are hoping that the following book titles will whet your political curiosity:

Treason: Liberal Treachery from the Cold War to the War on Terrorism

Deliver us from Evil: Defeating Terrorism, Despotism and Liberalism

Why the Left Hates America: Exposing the Lies that Have Obscured Our Nation's Greatness

The War on Christmas: How the Liberal Plot to Ban the Sacred Christian Holiday is Worse than You Thought

Of course, if you are a liberal, the above books might not be entirely to your liking. Not only will you refrain from buying such books, if given one as a present, you will subject it to creative forms of mutilation before recycling it in the fireplace. Therefore, the same publishing industry that brought you the above titles has also been careful to provide a fair and balanced counterpoint for the "Blue" side:

Bloodthirsty Bitches and Pious Pimps of Power: The Rise and the Risk of the New Conservative Hate Culture

The I Hate Republicans Reader: Why the GOP Is Totally Wrong About Everything

The Bush-Hater's Handbook: A Guide to the Most Appalling Presidency of the Past 100 Years

Fraud: The Strategy Behind the Bush Lies and Why the Media Didn't Tell You

The lesson of the confirmation bias, introduced in Chapter 2, is that conservatives will seek to acquire political information by reading books from the first list, while liberals will rely only on the second. We should not be so surprised at the existence of an escalating culture war.

Some commentators fear that the American cultural divide threatens our government's very ability to face the future. Thus, conservative political scientist James Q. Wilson warned in a 2006 *Commentary* essay:

> The steep decline in popular approval of our national officials has many causes, but surely one of them is that ordinary voters agree among themselves more than political elites agree with each other.... Sharpened debate is arguably helpful with respect to domestic issues, but not for the management of important foreign and military matters. The U.S., an unrivaled superpower with unparalleled responsibilities ...is now forced to discharge those duties with its own political house in disarray.... A divided America encourages our enemies, disheartens our allies, and saps our resolve — potentially to fatal effect.... Polarization is a force that can defeat us.[29]

Is polarization a "force that can defeat us"? Perhaps; but polarization is also a force that explains us. As we have seen in earlier chapters, humans are predisposed to partisan bias. Large societies are therefore always susceptible to polarization. It is not only for the sake of our country, therefore, but for the sake of the entire world, that we must come to grips with this quintessentially human — but potentially diabolical — tendency. To say that partisan bias has been a problem in history is a sad understatement. In our own era, which is occurring after the anticipated "end of history," we have witnessed the Rwandan genocide, the chaos of the former Yugoslavia, endemic civil war in Sri Lanka and Colombia, mass murder in Darfur, and most recently, the blood feud between Sunni and Shia in Iraq.

This is nothing new. From earliest history, the story of humankind has been a recitation of xenophobia and warfare. The only difference is that now we understand why.

What's the Matter with Sausalito?
Why There Will Be No Final Victory (or Defeat)

> *What's the Matter with Kansas?*
> — Title of book by Thomas Frank

> The two parties that divide the state,
> the party of Conservatism and that
> of Innovation, are very old, and have
> disputed the possession of the world ever
> since it was made.
>
> — Ralph Waldo Emerson,
> *The Conservative*

There is nothing wrong with Kansas, despite the plausible central argument in Thomas Frank's best-seller. Frank argued that poor and middle-class Americans (represented by the typical Kansan) are illogically voting against their own economic interests when they vote Republican, because Democratic policies would be more favorable for them.[57] The Kansans may well be guilty of illogical political analysis, but this apparent self-contradiction should not be surprising to the reader of this book, given the existence of innate political irrationality.

One implication of the bio-cultural model is that each political party can always count on solid support from about half the voting public, *regardless* of whether that party's policies are actually good for its supporters. Biology and culture make sure that most citizens are tilted either to the left or to the right — and cognitive bias guarantees that we stay that way.

The Republicans in Kansas are going to remain Republican, regardless of the success of policies adopted or implemented by the Republican leadership. If the Kansas Republicans should ever be confronted by evidence that their party is acting against their interests, it is likely that they would filter such evidence through their own confirmation bias until they reached an even greater conservative militancy, as we have seen from Drew Westen's brain scan research. The stronger the opposing arguments a partisan faces, the more thoroughly the partisan reinforces his biases.

Frank is thus hoping for an impossibility: that the great mass of people will suddenly decide to use their reason to over-ride their bio-cultural programming. It is not going to happen. In 2008, as in previous elections, Kansas remained in the red column.

By defining economic self-interest as the primary test of voter rationality, Frank wants to expose the illogic of Kansas's working-class Republicans, but he does not seem to realize that he is opening up wealthy liberals to the same logical attack. If poor people "should" be Democrats, then rich people "should" be Republican. Yet there are many wealthy liberals, proving that, at least for wealthy people, choice of political affiliation is not purely a matter of finance. Why should we not allow poor people the same dignity of choice?

Frank's book is interesting as an example of the almost invariably red-or-blue tint to popular political books. Virtually all our popular pundits follow a similar line of reasoning, beautifully exemplified by the title of a James Carville book: *We're Right, and They're Wrong!* Popular political books, whether written by Franken, Limbaugh, Coulter, Huffington or whoever else, follow the same script. These pundits are all peddling a childish form of wishful thinking — that ultimate victory is almost in sight.

"If only the other side will just learn to see things our way, they will give up," seems to be the underlying premise. Arch-conservative Ann Coulter suggests that Democrats are a sort of vile disease, kind of like a social form of gonorrhea, of which the homeland could be cured by application of enough conservative penicillin. Liberals also perennially succumb to fantasies of Republican extinction.

Partisan screeds conintue to roll off the presses at a lively clip. As I worked on this section, a new one, written by Peter Beinart, arrived to much fanfare: *The Good Fight: Why Liberals — and Only Liberals — Can Win the War on Terror and Make America Great Again*. There will be another one out next week. These books are the romance novels of the political class: Harlequin plots in which everything comes out all right in the end.

These pundits are hoping for an impossibility (which, if it arrived, would put them out of business anyway, since they are all fundamentally profiteers from political polarization). The natural distribution of human political leanings across a broad left-right spectrum ensures that we will always have liberals and conservatives. We will never have a country indefinitely governed only by "tough daddies" or only by "loving mommies."

Given its current structure, the American polity is destined to remain governed by a rough average of Democratic and Republican administrations, as Ralph Nader has pointed out repeatedly to unfair derision. Half the populace will tend conservative, half will tend liberal, and political machinations and skullduggery will determine who pulls the swing voters in any given election. Each party will win some, then lose some. The political winners will always get cocky, bogged down in scandal, and then lose their majority, as we have already seen a dozen times in our history. The political tables will turn, then turn again. Rock, paper, scissors.

In the ebb and flow of American political tides, there can be no final victory or defeat.

Understanding Polarization

> Party is the madness of many for the gain of a few.
> — Jonathan Swift, *Thoughts on Various Subjects* (1711)

> The beating of drums, which delights young writers
> who serve a party, sounds to him who does not
> belong to the party like a rattling of chains, and
> excites sympathy rather than admiration.
> — Nietzsche, *Miscellaneous Maxims and Opinions*

In *The Myth of the Culture War* (2004), Stanford political scientist Morris Fiorina argued that our so-called polarization is an illusion, that in fact Americans are not that far apart when it comes to politics. Using poll data from the Pew Research Center, Fiorina demonstrated that Americans, whether they live in red or blue states, actually differ very little in their political views (though they think they do).[58] In Fiorina's view, it is political parties that grow progressively more polarized for competitive reasons, while the citizens stay the same. The media like to take the politicians' partisan battles as evidence of a culture war because the culture war is a good story that sells papers and gets ratings. Out of self-interest, the media prefer to ignore the overwhelming evidence of consensus amongst Americans.

If we plot out a bell curve to represent American voters on a liberal-to-conservative scale, it would probably look like this (Figure 1):

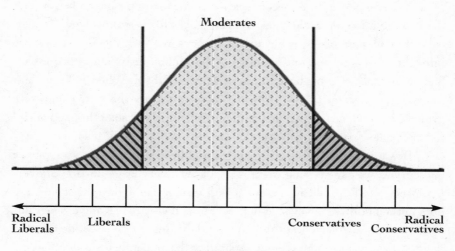

Moderates

Radical Liberals — Liberals — Conservatives — Radical Conservatives

Figure 1 — What Culture War?

Surveys suggest a great deal of consensus on most political issues — and that the largest group of voters is the one in the middle of the political spectrum.

The core section of moderate voters represents the largest group in the country. It would appear to be more logical to have a political system with three parties, one far-left, one far-right, and one in the middle. That middle party would be formidable. Unfortunately, most political scientists doubt that such a system could survive for long. Game theory tells us that there would be too much incentive for two parties to join together, bringing us back to a two-party system. Thus, even in countries with many parties due to proportional voting, the presidential elections still devolve into one-on-one contests between a liberal and a conservative.

The moderate majority does not disagree much internally. However, our modern political party system is based on its ability to cut the moderate majority in half, with each party claiming their half. The parties are then able to drive the two halves of the citizenry further apart. Both parties take advantage of our animosity for opposition public figures. It is enough for us to hate one of the candidates for us to be driven into the welcoming arms of the party that opposes him or her. In the 1990s Republicans voted against Clinton, not for Bush or Dole. In 2000 and 2004, Democrats voted against Bush, not for Gore or Kerry. In 2008, once again, Republicans were more motivated by distaste for Democratic leaders than by love of their own.

The two parties have become expert in the use of propaganda based on the manipulation of subtle clues and references to the cultural and biological differences amongst the electorate. George W. Bush's tendency to lapse into Christian code was one example of this technique, which was quite effective in reassuring his base that he was one of them. When Hillary Clinton famously became teary-eyed while campaigning for the New Hampshire primary in 2008, her display of emotion communicated something powerful to her female base while it befuddled pundits and Republicans alike.

If we map the Democratic and Republican populations as separate bell curves, we can see that there is probably a very large portion of overlap. Moderate Republicans and centrist Democrats fall into the same large pool in the middle. However, at both extremes there are real and obvious differences. Far-left Democrats and and far-right Republicans will tend to tug their parties away from the center, separating the moderate majority. Figure 2 explains why Americans appear to be polarized, though the majority of us are really in agreement.

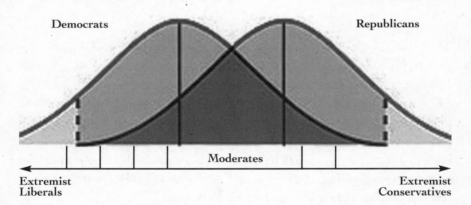

Figure 2 — Democrats and Republicans as Overlapping Bell Curves

There is a good amount of agreement amongst moderates toward the middle, but at the extremes partisans tend to pull the parties further apart.

Polarization is often presented by the media as a sort of unmitigated evil with virtually no support from the public, a display of bad manners indulged in only by politicians and activists. However, this is naïve. We should expect that the nation will at regular intervals be confronted with challenging policy debates that will necessarily polarize the citizenry. The revolution against England was the first of these critical junctures, the end of slavery another, and there have been a dozen since then. When the U.S. finally begins to implement universal health care for all its citizens, the means for doing so will doubtless be the subject of general debate and polarization. But is that not as it should be? Aren't there some arguments that are so important that we should expect heated public opinion upon them? Why, then, are we so intolerant of, and surprised by, polarization?

There is substantial historical evidence, for example, that the degree of polarization is directly related to fluctuations in social inequality.[59] As the American economy has evolved over the past two centuries, it became at times progressively more egalitarian (for example, from about 1930 to about 1980), while at other times it became more stratified and unequal. During times of increasing economic inequality, the political sphere becomes tense and marked by polarization.

In other words, our polarization is usually about something, or at least signals something — even when we agree broadly on most political issues. If we perceive increasing polarization today, it is because society is undergoing economic stress that threatens to change our social contract.

Inequality and immigration are currently two of the main drivers of polarization. The failure of our government to integrate 12 million undocumented workers has created an enormous underclass with no political voice. At the same time, growth in the economy for the past twenty years has disproportionately benefited the upper classes, and in particular the rarefied top 1%. The result is a society under pressure from economic stratification.

While working-class Americans have seen their incomes stagnate, the success of the upper-class Americans has increased the overall average income. From 1980 to 2008 the Republicans benefited from this trend because there is a rough correlation between income and party. Make a group of middle-class Americans suddenly richer and quite a few of them, though certainly not all, will wake up the next morning as newly-minted Republicans. Buoyed by their newly-affluent reinforcements, the Republicans moved sharply to the right in the 1980s and 1990s, most notably with Newt Gingrich's "Contract With America" in 1994. The Democrats found themselves pulled reluctantly toward an American political center that was drifting steadily to the right.

As in all previous periods of economic stress and transformation, political debate and disagreement has intensified. Given the intensity of the economic upheaval of 2008–2009, that may be a good thing, or at least, a necessary one. We do have things to talk about. If we can learn to discuss these issues without allowing our discourse to degenerate into hatred or violence, we may well profit from vigorous social debates in the coming years.

Why do people react so emotionally to political figures?

Why do opposing political leaders irritate us so much? The study of "social cognition" has demonstrated that humans can rapidly detect through a variety of subtle clues whether another person has a similar bio-cultural background. We tend to like people more when they are similar to us. Most of us choose friends who are relatively similar in cultural background, socioeconomic status, profession, and even age, height, attractiveness, intelligence, and wealth.

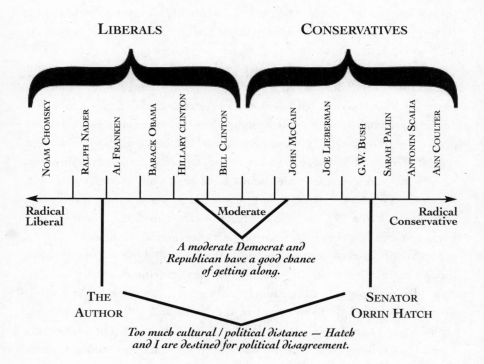

Figure 3 — The Theory of Political Distance

The further we are apart from someone on this political left–right spectrum, the more likely it is that we will feel negative emotions in their presence.

When two strangers meet and there is a very great disparity in backgrounds or capabilities, an unspoken tension fills the air. Senator Hatch made my hackles rise because I could feel, by looking at him and listening to the sound of his voice, that his bio-cultural programming was diametrically opposed to mine, and that he would therefore probably hold a number of values completely opposed to mine.

Look at Figure 3 for a sketch of the principle suggested here — when people occupy positions on the political spectrum that are very far from ours, we feel a proportionally strong discomfort in their presence. This explains why extremist candidates have such difficulty in getting elected. Regardless of their personal brilliance, too many of the voters will take an instinctive disliking to them. Genetic similarity theory predicts that candidates will do best when they exhibit genetic traits that are close to the median for their constituencies.

In politics, average can be much better than excellent.

Confronting Our Own Irrationality

> A sect or party is an elegant incognito
> devised to save man from the vexation
> of thinking. — Emerson, *Journals*, 1831

Today, most Americans identify themselves with one of the two main political parties and prefer to socialize with people of similar politics.* When Democrats talk politics with Democrats, they express their frustration at the idiocy and corruption of the Republicans. When Republicans socialize with Republicans, the political insights expressed are similarly one-sided.* Over

---

* What about the so-called "purple babies"? Aren't they the ones that polls classify as a growing class of "independents"? Where do they fit in? Actually, into this footnote. Although increasing numbers of people claim to be neutral or independent, research shows that in the end about 90% of these putative independents end up consistently supporting one party more than the other (revealed in *The Myth of the Independent Voter*, by Bruce E. Keith, et. al.). However, there are probably some true independents. According to the normal distribution suggested by bio-cultural model (Fig. 1) there will be a small number of people who sit precisely on the fence between the two parties. These poor people are especially in need of this book, as it will explain why so many of their fellow citizens seem to have fallen under the spell of a bizarre partisan enchantment.

the years, those of us who participate in this game are forced to seek an explanation for the strangely persistent stupidity of the other political party.

"How can they possibly be so dumb?" we ask ourselves in astonishment. "Are they doing it on purpose?" The other party seems to get everything wrong — whenever a new issue comes up, they predictably take the wrong approach. Time after time, they always do the wrong thing. "At least they're consistent," we conclude, shaking our heads.

Both sides seek explanations for the habitual erroneousness of their opponents, and find it in the other's self-deception. Democrats observe that the Republicans refuse to admit that they represent wealthy corporate interests to the detriment of the whole community, that their campaigns appeal to closet racists, that they're too cheap to cough up the taxes that build schools and hospitals, etc. Republicans, conversely, assert: Democrats refuse to confess that they're not patriotic and that they want to tax all our money and spend it on things like midnight basketball for illegal immigrant crack addicts.

Apples arguing with oranges, dogs debating with cats — upon this curious custom have we founded the edifice of our republic. After each political debate, we come away with renewed respect for the intelligence and wisdom of those who share our views, just as we are once again discouraged by the stubbornness of the fools on the other side. Like a perpetually-feuding husband and wife in need of marital counseling, bi-partisan America is a couple that cannot get along because the two sides do not know how to listen to each other. The bio-cultural model tells us what to listen for: deep underlying predispositions that are almost impossible to change.

The scientific research cited in the book suggests that political beliefs are the outward manifestation of cultural and hereditary biases, and are therefore not accessible to arguments based on logic or facts. Over time, our inherited tendencies become petrified by reinforcement from family and work environments, and then are further hardened by lifetime habits of biased perception.

If you consider that the bio-cultural model also applies to you (yes, I'm talking about thee, gentle reader), then you must face the disheartening possibility that your own political views are not necessarily the fruit of logic, research and deliberation, but are to some extent an accident of birth or affiliation, like your pretty blue eyes or the prestige of your home address — attributes which you may be proud of but hopefully don't take too seriously.

If we accept that Democrats and Republicans have been shaped by biology and culture to become fundamentally different kinds of people, and if we follow this concept to its logical conclusion, we will arrive eventually at a surprising humility. We realize that we have become accustomed to artificially boosting our vanity through partisanship. It is human nature to flatter ourselves when we feel superior to someone else because they are of the "wrong" political party, but if we are all just born or brainwashed into one political orientation or another, such self-flattery is not only misplaced and unjustified, it is a tiny bit ridiculous.

A lot of Americans really should come down off their high horses, politically speaking. Our preference for the Democrats or Republicans deserves no greater intellectual respect than our children's preference for vanilla over chocolate:

> REPUBLICAN CHILD: Why will the Democratic children of this family never understand that chocolate was the only ice cream envisaged by the drafters of the U.S. Constitution? Vanilla is expensive and wasteful, betrays a lack of personal responsibility. Worst of all, it is often French!

> DEMOCRATIC CHILD: I hope our parents will understand that the rich and powerful elder siblings of this family want to force us to eat their disgusting expensive premium imported chocolate, but the hardworking junior siblings of this family, who have already done their homework, know that honest vanilla is the only way to crown an American child's apple pie!

Before I immersed myself in the research that led to this book, I used to spend time with Democrats griping about Republicans. But now when this goes on too long I feel like we're sitting around vituperating vanilla or chocolate, and I start to feel silly. We are all dupes of an oligarchic system, anyway, both Republicans and Democrats, as I will explain in the following chapters. Today, there are really only two kinds of Americans, red sheep and blue sheep. It's the sheep part that should concern us more than the red-or-blue part. However, this requires us to wake up to the biases underlying our own partisan outlook. From my own experience I will tell you — this is extremely difficult for most people, and for many others... impossible.

We are not the only nation stuck in a red-blue stalemate. Political systems around the world are mired in the trench warfare of partisanship (Iraq and Kenya are two contemporary examples). These unproductive partisan feuds hinder our societies in their efforts to negotiate an increasingly complex, global society, and to fight looming global catastrophes, like the threat of global epidemics or nuclear terrorism. However, if we can reveal to voters around the world the illogical underpinnings of partisan wars, we can hope for an eventual diminishment in hostility, and a loosening of political log-jams.

Tips On Avoiding Partisan Irrationality

1. Avoid political arguments.

Political opinons are only partially based on reason, logic, or facts, so you generally can't win a political argument with reasonable arguments or factual evidence. However, you can lose friends, alienate co-workers, and irritate your spouse, children, parents and siblings.

2. Don't disparage people of different political leanings.

You have little reason to feel superior to people who support the other political party. The odds are that you arrived at your own political opinions through accidents of birth and social environment rather than as the fruit of rational analysis, so you have nothing to feel especially proud of. There are no persuasive studies that correlate IQ or general intelligence with political persuasion. There are smart, honest, and sincere people on both sides. Even if you are absolutely certain that your party is correct on a particular issue, at least try to appreciate how deeply-rooted and emotional the other side's views are, and you won't expect them to change on the spot.

3. Research the facts by looking for information from both sides.

The odds are that many of your political beliefs are held with pretty flimsy evidence (but strong feelings) to support them. Stop assuming that your political side is always right. If you want to develop a rationally-based opinion on a particular political issue, do some research on your own and try to obtain information and arguments presented by proponents from the other side. Understand that your views have been formed over a lifetime of filtered perceptions. You may find you are not always "loyal" to your "team," but you will become a more rational and knowledgeable citizen.

4. If you must talk about politics,
respect the constraints of biology and culture.

There are two unproductive ways to talk about politics and one productive way. Most people rely exclusively on the first two:

1) Mutual Self-Congratulation: this is where we sit around and congratulate ourselves on our superior intelligence to the morons who support the other political party;

2) The Emotional Political Argument: when confronted by an opposing political viewpoint, we react emotionally. Both sides only resort to logic as a weapon intended to secure victory, rather than to locate and define the truth.

Theoretically, there is a "right way" to talk about politics, though in practice we rarely see this method used by actual living, breathing human beings. This is the right way to debate politics:

1) Begin any political discussion by acknowledging you have partisan biases or leanings;

2) Understand that your interlocutor also is constrained by his or her partisan point of view — so you are not going to "win." I believe that it is actually impolite to even try to win a political argument;

3) Accept that if there is a disagreement at all it is probably because you are different kinds of people with different backgrounds and therefore have fundamentally different perceptions of the nature of political life. In such a context, the right thing to do is to try to explore and define the nature of one's differences, rather than convince or persuade the other side of their error. The end of this type of political discussion comes when you have agreed on a definition of your disagreement and on the kinds of data that might be found to help prove or disprove either side.

A final hint: listen to your heartbeat. When you can feel your chest pounding or your face flushing, constructive political discussion is no longer possible. I recommend that you follow Monty Python's military strategy: Run away! Try again later, when both of you have cooled down.

CHAPTER 8

Voting and Political Irrationality

Vote or die. — Campaign slogan, 2004

Elections are the opiate of the masses.
— Guillermo C. Jiménez

DARK TRUTH #8
*It doesn't matter whether you vote or not
(but go ahead and vote anyway — it's fun).*

To Vote or Not to Vote

W hy do people vote? The answers are remarkably obscure. The logical puzzles underlying individual voting behavior were first explored in Anthony Downs' classic 1957 *An Economic Theory of Democracy*, one of the founding texts of the "rational choice" school. Downs began with the neo-classical assumption that voters, like consumers in the marketplace, are rational and self-interested.[60]

Downs found that his rationalist assumptions led to a frustrating paradox. Since voting is not a perfectly "free" activity for the individual, because it requires a minimum of time to actually vote, and requires even more time if one wants to be well-informed on the issues, it follows that rational voters must derive some significant benefit from voting. Otherwise they would not spend their valuable time on it. However, Downs found that it was strangely hard to identify what benefit rational people could expect from voting. In any electoral system in which only one candidate can win, the only way that your vote can change the outcome is if there is a tie vote and your vote either makes or breaks the tie. In all other cases, your vote was either superfluous for the winning side (they would have won anyway, whether you voted or not) or insufficient for the losing side (they would have lost anyway).

Since a single vote can have no possible effect on the outcome of an election unless there is a tie or one-vote victory, and since there has never been a tie or one-vote victory in any presidential election anywhere in the world at any time in history (to my knowledge), the likelihood that your vote will affect the outcome of a U.S. presidential election is actually (according to my own rough calculations), about one in fourteen trillion gazillion bazillion.* Unfortunately, as the contested 2000 U.S. presidential election demonstrated, the reality is actually worse than those semi-imaginary numbers indicate. If, by some freakish coincidence, the Democratic and Republican candidates actually did tie, and your vote was the deciding vote, there would inevitably be a recount and extended litigation until a final count would determine a winner with a margin of victory in the hundreds or thousands (hello again, Supreme Court). Therefore, I would argue that an individual voter's chances of affecting a U.S. national election are effectively zero. The election results will be the same whether you vote or not. The only difference is that if you vote, you must expend a minimal amount of effort, whereas if you don't vote, you save yourself that slight but unproductive effort.**

---

* OK, I'm guessing there. But I'm sure it's in the high bazillions.

** It actually is even worse than that: if the miracle happened and there was a tie vote and your vote broke the tie and there was a recount and once again your vote broke the tie (and assuming you weren't just experiencing a schizophrenic hallucination), it is still far from certain that you would have accomplished anything rational, because it is quite possible that your candidate would be so constrained by Congress or economic problems or unexpected issues (i.e., terrorism, a financial meltdown) that none of the policy objectives which you hoped for would come about. It is also possible

Strangely enough, though, people *do* vote. Lots of them! Thus we arrive at the so-called Voter's Paradox. Either people are not rational when they vote, which upsets our cherished assumptions about the citizenry, or there is some other mysterious explanation for voting.

Downs made a gallant attempt to find a loophole in the Voter's Paradox. Rational people vote, he proposed, because they are reasoning that if they did not, democracy would collapse. Each of us rationally prefers to sacrifice the small amount of time it takes to vote, because we wish to avoid the alternative of having no government at all. Although Downs' economic analysis of voting was a work of creative genius, this explanation begs more questions than it answers.

For one thing, Downs failed to address the issue of rational "free riding." If my fellow citizens say they are going to vote in order to sustain our form of government, and if I can predict with a good level of certainty that most of them actually will vote, then why can't I stay home?

"You don't really need me," the rational non-voter could point out, "You already have more than enough people to sustain democracy. Besides, you guys like voting, whereas I prefer baseball!"

Typically, we disdain free-riders as parasites. Most people consider free-riders as people who shirk the duties required by their communities. However, it does not have to be that way. I once knew a married husband who enjoyed washing dishes. For some peculiar reason he thought washing dishes was enormous fun. Although the family was well-off financially, he refused to buy a dishwasher because he enjoyed washing dishes so much (at first I

---

that your candidate would follow standard post-election procedure and promptly forget about all of his or her campaign promises. It is also quite possible that you are an ignorant, biased dope and that you have chosen the wrong candidate for the country. It is possible that you, like many other Americans, have so failed to keep up with political issues that you do not really know which candidate would be better for your own interests. Finally, if you voted in Florida, it's possible that the ballot was so confusing that you think you voted for one party but you actually voted for the other party. There is no longer space in this footnote to factor in the risk of stolen elections (rampant throughout US history), so I simply refer readers to the excellent book, *Steal This Vote* by Andrew Gumbel. Literally, when it comes to rational voting, only a miracle will keep you from wasting your time.

didn't believe it either). In such a family, is it reprehensible for the wife or children to forego their share of the dish-washing "chores"? Surely they can be free-riders on the husband's dish-washing passion, and so long as they help out elsewhere, the family is no worse for letting the husband do all the dish-washing. We could call this "harmless free-riding."

I would argue that most voter abstention falls into this category: harmless free-riding. Research indicates that most non-voters are apathetic and uninformed, so society is not losing a lot when they don't vote. Moreover, no democratic government in history has ever collapsed due to an absolute failure of voters to turn out at a national election, so it does not seem that free-riding is threatening any imminent social catastrophe. Quite the contrary, even in Switzerland, where the inhabitants are subjected to a never-ending barrage of time-consuming direct elections, a third of the populace resolutely turns out. In most other industrialized republics, the turnout is at least one-half of the voting public, and often runs as high as three-fourths. There seems to be no danger that the remaining staunch voters will suddenly stop voting.

If the abstention of non-voters is harmless, then it is also rational. Surprisingly, it is much harder to figure out what is going on in the heads of the voters. Despite the befuddlement of Nobel prize-winning economists, millions of voters keep showing up at the polls, election after election, rationally or not. How can we explain their stubborn behavior? Surely it can't just be a matter of all these people over-estimating their chances of breaking a bizarre tie vote?

Why Do They Do It?

A generation of rational choice theorists has taken a crack at solving the Voter's Paradox.

Political scientist William Riker built on Downs' framework by suggesting that a voter's sense of duty made up for the low odds that any single vote could affect the outcome of a national election. In Riker's formula, the fact that the costs of voting (COST) usually outweigh the likely benefits (which is the probability of making or breaking a tie times the policy difference between the candidates, or POLICY BENEFITS), is made up for by a positive "DUTY" term: POLICY BENEFITS – COST + DUTY = VOTING. This is an economist's inimitably nerdy way of saying that people vote because they feel they "oughta," which seems sensible, but leaves us with the same old questions.

How can it rationally be your duty to do something that can have no possible effect (since your chances of determining the election are zero, so are the Policy Benefits)? Moreover, why can't society simply rely on one-half of its citizens to feel that sense of duty, while the others don't feel it? Even if the sense-of-duty approach explains why some people vote, it does not explain why we condemn the others, as it utterly fails to address harmless free-riding.[61]

Subsequent writers felt that Riker's formula was essentially correct but that the variable "D" term should not be interpreted in terms of duty, but rather in terms of expressive enjoyment. Voting is not a logic-driven act of investment (e.g.,"I expend twenty minutes of my time voting in order to obtain 'X' units of value") but is rather an act of expression, like attendance at a football game ("I like going to the game and cheering for my team even if my individual cheering alone is not likely to help them win"). No one buys a ticket to a football game as an investment in the likelihood that his or her team will win. We go for the thrill of the game. We want our team to win and we cheer lustily throughout the combat, but not because we believe that our personal cheering is going to bring the team to victory.

Voters vote because it's fun, in this view, but they don't really believe that they are going to influence the outcome of the election. This comports well with the observation that there is often a jovial, public-spirited ambiance at the polling booths. People are feeling good about themselves and their country, and they are feeling empowered. Every major election has a bit of the small-town July 4th parade about it. As we wait in line to cast our ballots we could be posing for a heart-warming Norman Rockwell depiction of American democracy at work.

Still, there are problems with the expressive enjoyment theory. For one thing, harmless free-riding is unscathed by the enjoyment perspective. If the only rational justification for voting is that it is fun, there is no reason to condemn those who do not find it fun. The "get out and vote" exhortations that rain on us from all quarters prior to elections become absurd. It surely cannot be a *duty* to have fun, even in this most hedonic of republics. On the other hand, this view suggests that those who are concerned about a possible decline in voter participation might want to look more closely at the pleasurable aspects of elections. If voting could be made even more enjoyable, more people would probably vote. Personally, I like the idea of a state lottery or raffle in which all voters would be automatically entered. If each citizen had a chance of becoming a millionaire through voting, we'd have no more problems with turnout.

The voting process should also be easy and fun. It should be more like going to a football game, and less like going to the Department of Motor Vehicles. You don't necessarily have to provide free margaritas and neck massages at the polling booths, but at the very least the major fun-killers should be eliminated. Residents of Ohio will remember the 2004 election, when voters had to wait for hours in the freezing rain to cast their ballots. I would wager there weren't too many rational-choice theorists in those long lines. Both Republicans and Democrats will agree that waiting for hours in the rain is not an especially fun way to express their support for democracy.

Voting So Our Friends Won't Bug Us

Part of the difficulty that the rational-choice school encountered in solving the Voter's Paradox was due to their atomistic focus on the individual voter. However, no one votes in a vacuum — we all take cues from our environment. In real life, human beings are always embedded in social networks. Regardless of any internal mathematical calculations we might make about the efficacy of voting, there is evidence that we are more strongly influenced by peer pressure than we are by logic.

We are badgered on all sides to vote. Every election cycle features endless advertisements from admired celebrities urging us to participate. The candidates themselves repeatedly ask, cajole and even beg for our vote. Before the election, our friends and neighbors quiz us to find out who we'll vote for, and afterwards, reproach us bitterly and vehemently if we are foolish enough to admit that we didn't vote. Why do we care so much about the opinions of all these other people?

Harvard political scientist Samuel Abrams* proposes an ingenious "social-embeddedness" explanation:

---

* For convenience I refer here to Abrams, though his colleagues Torben Iversen and David Soskice co-authored the paper on social embeddedness which I am citing.

> People get involved in politics because they have a desire to be
> valued members of the groups or networks to which they belong….
> Humans are social animals who crave the approval and respect of
> other people. To achieve this people will sometimes go to great
> lengths in doing what is expected of them by the group. There is
> nothing irrational about voting…. When people vote and read about
> politics it is because this is sometimes a way to get respect from
> other people in their social networks. Politicians understand this
> and try to influence what groups discuss….[62]

Abrams' research provides evidence that the more "embedded" we are
in society, meaning the greater the number of our connections to the people
around us, the more likely we are to talk about politics, and the more likely
we are to vote. All of these factors also correlate positively with the length
of time that someone has lived in a particular neighborhood or worked at a
particular job. In short, the more socially-embedded we are, the more political we are. People are motivated to learn about politics in the same way that
baseball fans are motivated to memorize reams of statistics: it's a way to im-
press your fellow fans (and sometimes a way to compete with them). This is
similar to the argument that voters are motivated by enjoyment, but from
the perspective of social-embeddedness, voting becomes the manifestation of
something laudable and even necessary for a good society: the citizen's desire to belong, to be a part of something bigger.

Abrams contrasts the voters' motivations with the politicians':

> One of the most intriguing facts about voting is that the act it-
> self produces no tangible benefits to the individual, yet it is of great
> value to those who get to run the government…. [T]here is little
> reason for people to seek information about the candidates or… the
> issues…. By contrast, from the perspective of politicians, or the
> groups that stand to benefit from public policies, voting and politi-
> cal knowledge are of critical importance…. Because voting is such
> a trivial act for the individual but such a crucial one for politicians,
> the latter will invest heavily in convincing people that their vote re-
> ally does matter or that their expression of partisan allegiance is
> worth the trouble.[63]

Although Abrams believes it is in the interests of America's political elites to try to convince us to vote, he does not believe that we are simply fooled into voting by shrewd politicians. The most important reason for voting is that doing so is an integral part of the ongoing political conversation that people carry on with their families and co-workers.

Abrams' social-influences theory of voting is a valuable addition to the rational-choice model, but he crucially fails to address the issue of rational voter *intention*. Voters can only be considered rational in pursuing enhanced social relations through voting if that is in fact what they *intend*. But, do people really vote only so as to improve their ability to discuss politics with friends? I doubt it.

If Abrams had asked his research subjects why they voted, I conjecture that the following would have been the majority answer: "We vote to get our candidate elected. Duh!" As we now know, this is not a rational answer (at least from a rational-choice perspective), but that is what people will tell you.

Not many would answer along the lines of: "I believe it is my solemn duty to vote so that I will be able to shoot the bull with my buddies tomorrow after work while we're drinking beers and eating peanuts at Sam's Bar & Grill."

Despite the theory of social-embeddedness, I believe that the rational-choice school has been unable to save voting behavior from the charge of irrationality. The most convincing proof of this came to me through observation of my own irrationality in analyzing the issue of close elections. It had long seemed obvious to me that if my preferred candidate were forecast in the polls to be thirty points ahead on the eve of the election, it was okay to abstain. The victory was guaranteed. What's the point in voting when the election has already been decided in advance by the public (assuming you trust the polls to be accurate within thirty points, which I do)? However, in cases when the race was too close to call on the final days, it seemed cravenly to fail to show up to support the team. It took several days of reflection for me to realize that — from a rational point of view —close races are no different than lopsided ones. Your vote in a close presidential race is equivalent in value to your vote in a lopsided race: zero. Zero equals zero, depressing as that math may be to some of us.

We are understandably deceived by the drama that closely-contested races generate. Although our vote is equally ineffective in the close election, it is still quite true that you would probably feel guiltier having failed to vote if your candidate lost by a small margin. Even more importantly, you would have greater reason to fear the irrational wrath of your friends. The flip side of the coin of Abrams' social influences theory is that we vote partially out of fear of reproaches for not voting. You could argue that it is therefore rational to vote because it keeps our friends and family from nagging, harassing and criticizing us, but then we would have to ask if your friends and family are rational in nagging and harassing you, given that your vote can have no possible influence on the outcome of the election.

Voting is thus not adequately explained by any rational framework. Fortunately, we still have evolutionary biology.

Evolutionary Psychology:
Why We Really Believe in Voting

Why is the myth of individual voting efficacy so widespread? Why are citizens everywhere unwilling to believe that their individual vote does not matter? Evolutionary psychology provides answers where rational choice fails. As noted earlier, humans evolved for thousands of generations in groups of no larger than 150 (and usually much smaller than that), in which individual acts of expression (precursors of voting) could make a difference in group deliberations. The contrast between such societies and our modern nations is total. Our brains are not wired to comprehend how minuscule we are in comparison to our huge contemporary societies. As individual citizens, we are like single grains of sand on an enormous coastline. Although our society repeatedly tells us that a single individual can make a political difference, this is almost always not true (unless you become a politician or a billionaire). The harsh truth of modern society is that in a political sense, at least, a single individual does not matter. Depressing? That's why we don't believe it.

It wasn't always that way. Let us recall the example of the chimpanzee alpha-male contests observed by Frans de Waal, as an indicator of possible behavior in early proto-human tribes. In Chapter 5, we saw that alpha-male contenders used a combination of violence and strategy to defeat their opponents. Importantly, though, De Waal identified another crucial element to chimpanzee politics — partisan support from females. De Waal observed that it was difficult for the alpha male to achieve or maintain power without the support, or at least the non-interference, of the troop's leading females. Whenever a conflict between alpha-male pretenders would arise, the females would play a crucial role as chorus, hooting and stamping, and sometimes intervening physically, to indicate their preferences. It is clear that the males kept track of who supported them and who didn't, and punished defectors whenever possible.

There is a telling photograph of the chimp named Luit jumping up and down on top of a female — she had "betrayed" him politically by befriending his alpha rivals.[64] Vote or die, indeed! Thus, it seems plausible that members of proto-human troops would have evolved in such a way that individuals felt an evolutionary imperative to "vote" by hooting and stamping to indicate their support for one alpha-male candidate over another. In these contests, it would make sense for family members to support those males to whom they were most closely related. Thus, the evolutionary origin of political parties, and of partisan bias, can be traced to family-supported campaigns for tribal leadership. Those who "abstained" from voting not only failed to promote their own genetic interests (your own chances for reproductive success would be increased if your close relative became the tribal boss), they cost their families a valuable ally. If the analogy from chimp society to proto-human society holds true in this regard, it follows that humans would have evolved a hard-wired propensity to believe that our political input matters — because, for hundreds of thousands of years, it did. Equally important, we would have evolved a tendency to punish those lazy family members who refused to help out.

As we observed earlier, humans have a deeply-ingrained negative attitude towards shirking, the earliest form of free-riding. As Robert Trivers first theorized in the 1970s, it is likely that humans have developed exquisitely sensitive mechanisms for detecting cheaters and freeloaders. During the period when our brains were evolving in the long twilight of pre-history, if you chose to abstain during the dangerous part of the hunt, you were unlikely to receive a gift of meat from the intrepid hunters who went in for the kill. When tribal societies were engaged in a vital common enterprise, like hunting, migration or combat, anyone who shirked at a crucial moment could bring death and ruin to the entire tribe. Since earliest times, desertion of an army in time of war has been punishable by death. Deep in our genetic wiring, humans are programmed to hate shirkers. The problem today is that in modern societies it is sometimes difficult to distinguish between shirking and reasonable abstention. In Nazi Germany, teen-agers who refused to join the Nazi Youth were accused of shirking patriotic duties, but we now understand that they had good reasons.

Our biological impetus to take voting seriously has been reinforced by a number of historical and social factors. Consider the historical origins of modern republics, most of which were born in periods of turmoil or revolution, replacing hated monarchies or dictatorships. There is something special about any nation's first election. One only has to think of the first Iraqi election after the fall of the Saddam Hussein regime. Braving credible threats of bomb attacks, millions of voters turned out. It is doubtful that any of them had any clear understanding of what they were voting for. Any rational-choice professor could have written a whole book about how irrational they were being. Their country was in the midst of chaos which no one seemed able to calm, resolve or even understand. And yet, movingly, they came out by the millions.

Most modern republics went through this phase. At the beginning, every vote is a vote for democracy, a system which recognizes the individual's evolutionary imperative to be heard and counted. In a sense it doesn't matter who you vote for. Fortunately or unfortunately, that changes fast. When a so-called democracy has been around for fifty, one hundred, or two hundred years, you no longer vote out of relief for not having a king. And yet the semi-sacred aura of that first election still lingers over all subsequent elections, endowing them with a traditional solemnity that rational choice can do little to tarnish.

That individuals are hard-wired to vote is further confirmed by the modern media fascination with public voting contests and mechanisms, of which the television program "American Idol" is but one classic example. As with presidential voting, it is impossible that our vote will make a difference, but in the case of "American Idol," what possible "policy benefits" can we expect from voting? There are none.

Human beings simply enjoy voting, it is part of human nature. As with other evolutionary imperatives, we can deduce the existence of biological programming from the enjoyment we derive from a particular activity. The most important things we have to do from an evolutionary perspective are for that reason also the most fun (sex and food, for example). Voting comes not far behind. Voting makes people feel good.

Part of the existential anomie felt by members of modern society lies in the lurking suspicion that, in fact, our vote really does not matter at the national level. Psychologists have established that a primary element of a healthy personality is the belief that one can control one's environment. Albert Bandura developed his influential "self-efficacy" theory from research which showed that psychological well-being correlates strongly with a belief that one is in control of one's life. Depression, conversely, results from the conclusion that one is powerless in the grip of environmental factors. This suggests that voting may be good for us psychologically. Unfortunately, that may also require us to be a bit irrational and ignore some obvious truths about the power of a single vote.

We are thus left with a final taste of the voter's paradox: although citizens may be voting for the right reasons (psychological well-being, social bonding and symbolic self-expression), if asked why they vote, they will usually provide an illogical answer (it is an effective way to get your candidate elected).

"Rational Ignorance": Why Voters Don't Know Anything

Another key principle proposed by Anthony Downs is that of "rational ignorance." Downs contended that it actually made sense for the average voter to remain quite ignorant. If the individual voter's chances of affecting an election really are infinitesimal, then the voter has little incentive to acquire any information about the election. Instead, the voter should do the bare minimum that it takes to cast an intelligent ballot. What is the bare minimum? In America, if you want to play Political Trivial Pursuit at work or in the bar after work, all you have to know is whether you are a Democrat or a Republican. With that, your political sophistication is complete and sufficient for voting purposes.

Rational-choice theorists might argue that you would achieve higher stature in your local political network if you learned to discuss politics intelligently, but I suspect that's because most of them spend their time arguing with other professors. The rest of us don't need facts for our political discussions — propaganda, rumors, assorted slanders, scabrous jokes, preposterous lies and half-baked myths will do just fine. Moreover, our knowledge does not even have to be about the issues, it is enough if we are familiar with a few juicy facts about the candidates, or their relatives.

Just as teen-agers are able to sustain long conversations on the relative merits of the latest pop celebrities, political conversations can thrive on a steady stream of politico-celebrity gossip. Michelle Obama wore what? Dick

Cheney shot whom? Clinton was fellated where? Hillary cried, why? It is far more entertaining to discuss the foibles of our candidates than it is to discuss their policies. When Republicans got together before the 2004 election, the comparison of John Kerry's head to Herman Munster's was a more common topic than Kerry's position on social security. Democrats likewise were quick to share reports on the latest two-syllable word that President Bush had mispronounciated. Everyone remembers when George H.W. Bush expressed amazement at the modern supermarket scanner, or when Michael Dukakis rode around in a tank looking like a turtle on wheels — proving that these episodes were very widely discussed — but who remembers what the candidates' policy positions were at the time?

Should any of this make us doubt whether Americans citizens are well-informed enough to cast meaningful ballots? Are there any indications that the citizenry is "rationally ignorant," as rational-choice theory predicts?

Consider the following evidence:[65]

◆ Three-quarters of Americans admit they know little or nothing about the USA Patriot Act.

◆ As of 2006, three years after the Iraq invasion, 58 percent of Americans mistakenly believed that the Bush administration had explicitly stated that there was a direct connection between Saddam Hussein and the 9/11 attacks. Over 85 percent of soldiers fighting in Iraq believed in such a connection.

◆ In 1952, 1989, and 1994, at least one-fourth of Americans could not correctly name the vice president.

◆ Only one-fourth of Americans can correctly name their two senators and only one-third can name their representative.

◆ The average American thinks America is 32 percent black, 21 percent Hispanic, and 18 percent Jewish (the real figures are 12 percent, 13 percent, and 2 percent).

◆ Over half of Americans think that the nation is at least 30 percent black and a seventh of Americans think the nation is half black.

◆ Almost three-fourths of Americans believe that most new immigrants come into the country illegally, whereas in fact most enter legally then overstay their visas.

◆ A fifth of Americans think that the government spends the most money on foreign aid (actually less than 1 percent) and another fifth thinks the greatest expenditure is on welfare for the poor (actually less than 3 percent), while in reality defense and military spending is the largest part of the budget (ranging from 20 percent to 50 percent, depending on whom you believe).

◆ In 1985, almost a third of the Jews in one northern California region said that they did not believe that Gentiles would ever vote for a Jew for Congress. At the time they said this, all three of their elected Representatives in that area were Jewish.

◆ Americans do not have a clue what is in their own Constitution: one-third think it establishes English as America's official language, and another sixth believe it establishes America as a Christian nation; one-fourth can't name a single First Amendment right.

Americans spend a great deal of time talking about politics, but it does not appear that many of those discussions are grounded in those old-fashioned things called "facts."

Vote or Die, Truth or Lie?

If it is irrational for a single individual to vote, does that mean that all of the get-out-the-vote campaigns are absurd? Not necessarily. As Samuel Abrams pointed out, voting does not accomplish much for any given individual, but it is absolutely essential for the politicians. Therefore, get-out-the-vote campaigns make sense from a rational point of view, though not for the reasons that are usually given. They are vital for the politicians more than for the voters. If a get-out-the-vote drive can get an extra hundred thousand people to the polls, that might be enough to swing a victory.

There are problems with an inflexible get-out-the-vote philosophy. Since get-out-the-vote drives are aimed at marginal voters, who may have little knowledge and unclear or ambiguous political opinions, one of the potentially perverse effects of these drives is that they create even greater polarization, and they do so amongst the most ignorant voters. Voters are always more polarized than non-voters, so in the end all that get-out-the-vote drives accomplish is to create partisans out of ignoramuses. This may not be the finest starting ingredient for a healthy democracy.

Get-out-the-vote drives can backfire politically, because they are easily-copied strategies. The other party is monitoring your get-out-the-vote efforts and will endeavor to match them. It might be easier for wealthy white populations to organize get-out-the-vote drives than poor minority populations, so such drives might be more cost-effective in wealthy areas than in the poor ones. In other words, a get-out-the-vote drive on behalf of minorities might do nothing more than spur the wealthy to organize an even more successful drive at cheaper cost, thereby gaining an important tactical advantage. Get-out-the-vote drives might just be expensive ways of shooting yourself in the foot. They utterly failed to help the Democrats in 2000 and 2004, just as they failed Republicans in 1992, 1996 and 2008.

What if they Held Elections and Nobody Came?

The great puzzle at the heart of the Voter's Paradox is that people vote when we cannot identify any rational reason for them to do so. If people really were rational, the theory holds, they wouldn't vote at all. Should we, therefore, take cold comfort from the fact that so many millions of people turn out to vote in national elections? Is it encouraging that deep in the core of this vast, industrial beast there beats a resolutely democratic heart?

The stirring irrationality on display in national elections is not confirmed in local elections, where we find no trace of the Voter's Paradox. In many local elections, the voters display a disturbing level of rationality in the most concrete way: by staying home.

In the past decade we have seen the following turnouts at U.S. mayoral elections: 5 percent in Dallas, 6 percent in Charlotte, 7.5 percent in San Antonio, 7 percent in Austin. A Tennessee congressional primary attracted a full 7 percent of the state's voters, while a gubernatorial primary in Kentucky drew 6 percent. School board elections around the country have seen turnouts as low as 1 percent. In seven cities in Los Angeles County, California, elections for city council were canceled when no challengers emerged. Only 12 percent of eighteen to twenty-four year olds voted in the 1998 Congressional elections.[66] When it comes to local politics, Americans are either getting lazier or more rational, or both.

The "Who Cares?" Theory

> Non-voting is the way many
> contented people express
> passive consent. — George Will

In a future book I hope to marshal empirical evidence to support the following thesis: "People who are obsessed with politics often become unbearably boring and self-righteous when discussing politics."

People who are especially interested in politics seem to possess a genetic defect in their brains which prevents them from perceiving that not everyone else is similarly fascinated. They appear unable to appreciate the fundamental reality that society needs people with diverse interests — artists, firemen, female beach-volleyball players, etc. These other folks are fully-occupied with their own professions, and don't always have time to relish the latest absurd political debates. While political junkies derive enjoyment from endlessly rehashing elections, others regard such conversations with the dread of a dental appointment. If a person is utterly uninterested in politics, what benefit to them or to society from forcing them to argue about politics, or even vote?

Self-righteous voters tend to condemn a lack of interest in politics as "apathy," though it may simply signal that the person has rationally decided to accept the political status quo. The conservative columnist George Will has suggested that one of the reasons for declining voter turnout in the U.S. is that Americans are just too darn contented. These non-voters apparently hold a view along these lines: "Apparently someone is running the government, and as I'm on my way to the beach right now in my shiny new Prius, and as I've got a cooler full of ice-cold Coronas in the back, I've really got no major complaints about our society, so I don't think I'll vote today, thank you very much!"

Some will call this apathy,* but that casts an unfair connotation on the non-voter's expression of disinterest. Why is it apathy to be uninter-

* I just wish I were invited.

ested in current politics, while it is not apathy to be uninterested in current philosophy, poetry, or quantum mechanics? One never hears this reproach: "How dare you be so uninterested in the cosmological implications of string theory!"

It is a mark of immaturity and arrogance to consider our own passions to be of universal interest. Most of the people who spend a lot of time discussing politics are merely parroting propaganda and half-truths they have gullibly and unthinkingly adopted, anyway. The recent intensity of political discussion in America has not prevented the average politically-obsessed American from being staggeringly ignorant of political facts and realities.

When times are good, citizens can perhaps be forgiven for considering government to be like a big clock that runs fine on its own. When times are hard or government policies are controversial, though, as during the Great Depression, Vietnam era, Iraq invasion or the U.S. financial panic of 2008, neighbors scold each other for failing to stay informed politically. However, it is not at all clear that the greater intensity of interest caused by momentous times leads to any improvement in the political situation, not to any personal rewards for the political junkie. Recall that the Nazis were voted into power. When the U.S. reached its greatest intensity of political interest, during the Vietnam War, it elected Richard Nixon, and then it re-elected him. When the Iraq war was unarguably the most important political issue of the day (the 2004 election), the country re-elected George W. Bush and provided him with a Republican majority that allowed him to maintain and expand his disastrous occupation. We are therefore probably too self-righteous in our condemnation of apathy: voter apathy does not seem to hurt society in the good times, and a lack of apathy often does not help in the bad times.

Finally, we should observe that a lack of interest in voting does not automatically equate to a lack of civic responsibility. George Will notes that since 1980, while voting has been declining, the portion of Americans volunteering with charitable or social services groups has risen by about 20 percent and per-capita charitable giving has risen a remarkable 40 percent. Arguably, voting is one of the most trivial political acts that a person can perform, especially as compared with volunteering or giving charitable donations.

Conclusions: Finding Reasons to Vote

In summary, we think we vote to get our candidate elected, but that would be impossible. In reality we vote because evolution has wired our brains so that voting is simply fun and makes us feel good about ourselves (and also because we are afraid our friends will find out we didn't vote). It seems so obviously right to vote that it is practically an unassumed ethical imperative. Regrettably, however, we vote on the basis of the flimsiest political knowledge, or worse, on the basis of lies, errors and misunderstandings.

What's a country to do?

1. Leave the non-voters alone.

Given the Voter's Paradox, there really is no good reason for harassing non-voters. Abstention is just as rational as voting, if not more.

2. Leave the voters alone.

Voting is a fine and perfectly sensible way of expressing support for one's government. Most importantly — it feels good and puts you in tune with your fellow political junkies. If some people did not willingly sacrifice the time it takes to vote, our current system of government could become unworkable. So long as those voters refrain from self-righteous preaching, we have no reason to criticize them.

3. Make voting easier and more fun.

Voting today is too much of a pain in the neck. If I can vote for *American Idol* on my cell-phone, why can't I vote for McCain or Obama the same way? Since the value of voting to the individual is infinitesimal, the cost to the voter should logically also be as close as possible to infinitesimal, so that even a small sense of duty will tip the balance in favor of voting. It should be possible to vote on the Internet or by any digital device, even a cell-phone. I would even go further, with what I call "concierge voting" — you could program your local municipality to give you a wake-up voter call. Someone from the election bureau would call you on the phone to remind you that you wanted to vote that day, and they could take your vote right then, just like our helpful credit card companies do. My suggestion on the relevant security and fraud issues: fix them. If we can use our credit cards to pay money online or over the phone, there is no reason we cannot vote that way as well. Obviously, votes should generate a paper record which can be anonymously verified by the voter, just like our online credit-card transactions do.

However, I do not agree that voting should be extended over a week or month, as is practiced in some local elections. There is evidence that this diffuses the interest of the electorate, leading to even lower turnouts. You have to keep a sense of drama about the election if you want people to participate. Elections aren't logical processes, they are social events. No one wants to go to a party that lasts a month (after age 22, that is).

If we are not only concerned with voter turnout but with voter ignorance, then we should experiment with mechanisms that will force the electorate to educate itself. I am therefore in favor of "Deliberation Day," the national holiday proposed by political scientists Bruce Ackerman and James Fishkin.[67] Deliberation Day would take place a couple of weeks before a national election and allow citizen assemblies to debate the issues in a concentrated and in-depth fashion.

Finally, Election Day itself should also be a national holiday — this would thrill voters and non-voters alike.

4. Give people something real to vote about, so that they will actually learn something about the issues.

There is only so much improvement possible within the duopolistic mafia that is our current political system. It is virtually impossible to resist being suckered into partisan antagonism, because all of us naturally tend to prefer the images associated with one or the other parties. Unfortunately, this reduces our subsequent votes to nothing more than automatic expressions of our genetic and cultural biases.

There may be ultimate limits on the perfectibility of human society. In all conceivable large governments, a single human's vote will remain inevitably trivial. It is unlikely that any voting system could ever perfectly reconcile society's complex and conflicting interests. However, we can do better than we are doing today.

The first step would be to give voters interesting and meaningful things to vote about. This would be most the powerful possible incentive to overcome today's citizen ignorance and apathy. It must be fascinating to be a U.S. Senator. Ted Kennedy called it the greatest job on earth (though he had not much experience with any other jobs). U.S. Senators get to vote on the exciting and challenging issues facing the country, whereas our personal vote is little more than a matter of being asked to choose over and over again between "Scoundrel A" and "Scoundrel B" (under conditions in which it is completely unthinkable that we would ever choose "B").

Individuals should be given the same exciting and interesting elections as those facing Senators and Congressmen. The way to do this will be described in detail in Chapter 13.

CHAPTER EIGHT APPENDIX
Verbal Judo for Non-Voters

If America has anything like a national religion, it is the voting religion. For members of this religion, non-voters are like anti-Christs. Anyone brave enough to confess to not voting in a presidential election is either stout-hearted or foolhardy, depending on the situation. Since I know from experience how difficult it can be to explain the rational-choice analysis of voting behavior, I have provided the following Q & A session with helpful pointers for rational non-voters on how to deal with the most common objections and vituperation:

Q: What do you mean you don't vote? How dare you? *Oooh*, I'm getting so *angry*.

A: Why do *you* hate freedom? Are you working for Osama or something?

Q: (Baffled) What are you talking about?

A: America is known as the 'land of the free,' not the 'land of the voting.' Surely if there's one fundamental freedom we have, it's the freedom not to vote.

Q: But I just don't understand how you can be too lazy to vote, it only takes fifteen minutes.

A: I didn't say I was too lazy to vote, I said I *chose* not to vote.

Q: So then, if it's not laziness, why didn't you vote!?!

A: For several reasons. First of all, my vote couldn't possibly affect the outcome; second, I don't support either of the candidates, both of whom I think are wrong in many respects; third, I think a vote under these conditions makes a mockery of democracy, because it just props up a system that doesn't offer voters meaningful choices.

Q: So you don't believe in democracy, I take it? Are you a damn communist?

A: I believe in nothing but democracy, but as the Founding Fathers made quite clear, the U.S. was not established as a democracy but as a republic, which is another way of saying as an electoral oligarchy. In the *Federalist* papers, it's quite clear. If you don't believe me — just read the next chapter!

Now, if you're a big fan of real democracy and would like to do something to *finally* introduce it to the U.S., I'd be glad to work with you. You might want to read the last chapter of this book!

Q: But we have major problems facing the world right now! You're just copping out. Don't you realize how important it is for us to keep the Republicans out of office?

A: It seems that you're in favor of everyone voting, but only if it's *against* Republicans. Don't you see that if you encourage everyone to vote you will also be encouraging the Republicans? I see that you hate the Republicans, apparently, and I'm sorry if I don't hate them quite as much as you do,* but I really don't see how you think my vote could possibly make a difference, anyway. We live in New York, and it's well-known that the Re-

*Except for Orrin Hatch.

publicans will never carry New York in a presidential election. So in a very real sense, the next election in New York has already been held, and the next one after that as well. What need for us to vote, then?

Q: But how can you possibly argue that your vote wouldn't count? What about the contested Florida vote in the 2000 Presidential election, doesn't that prove that every vote counts?

A: No, for a lot of reasons. First, many voters were illegally and fraudulently scrubbed from the Florida rolls, so every vote did not count. Second, the winning margin was in the hundreds, so clearly one vote didn't matter. Finally, if there had been a margin of one vote it would have been contested, so once again, your vote would not have mattered. And all of that's assuming your vote wasn't "hanging a chad," as they say, which is truly *faux pas* in Palm Beach.

Q: But it's obviously a citizen's duty to vote. How can you deny that? Everybody knows that, don't they?

A: If it's so obvious, how come Dwight Eisenhower virtually never voted? How come Dick Cheney never voted in local elections? I would think Eisenhower would know something about duty (more than Cheney, certainly), since he directed the invasion on D-Day, when so many American boys did their duty by dying. Have you done military service?

Q: Uh, no. Actually, I'm just an imaginary straw person you put up here to look dumb, remember?

A: That's right, I forgot. Anyway, carry on, you're doing an excellent job! As I was saying, in some countries military service is obligatory and therefore a duty. Have you breached your duty to the U.S. by failing to volunteer for military service? Some people would argue that you have, but I wouldn't. The concept of duty is one that varies from country to country and time to time. So how did you decide that voting is a duty? No one appointed you the sole arbiter for the U.S. as to what is a citizen's duty and what isn't. There is absolutely no constitutional requirement to vote. Did you vote in the last local school board elections?

Q: Uh, actually, well... since I'm imaginary and all....

A: What a lame excuse. Of course you didn't, and most of your neighbors didn't either. Does that mean that none of you understands civic duty? I don't think so. In how many elections does a person have to vote? Like your neighbors, I do other things to help my community, like volunteering and contributing to charities, and I consider those a more important civic contribution than voting.

Q: But what if everyone did what you're doing, and refused to vote?

A: That's ridiculous. The very fact that you're standing here arguing with me about this proves how stubbornly and passionately most people want to vote in national elections. We are not ever going to get into a situation in a national election where suddenly everyone refuses to vote, because there are too many people like you.

Q: So you think it's stupid to vote. That's a fine lesson to be teaching our young people.

A: I never said it was stupid to vote. If you vote and you feel happy about voting, I have no complaints. You're the one that was criticizing me. I think voting is a fine symbolic expression of one's support for the government, and some people seem to think it's just plain fun, and those are perfectly acceptable motivations for voting from my point of view. Of course, I don't share those views, because I think we have a retarded and undemocratic system of government which we ought to change, but that's an argument for a later chapter.

Q: Hmm... (increasingly frustrated and confused).... Well, you do realize that if you don't vote, you have no right to complain.

A: Why not? That's like saying that if I don't check the weather report I can't complain if it rains. A single citizen can have about as much influence on national politics as on which way the wind blows. Anyone who enjoys kvetching about politics is entitled to do so, whether they have voted or not.

CHAPTER 9

Placebo Democracy

In reality, the word democracy signifies nothing more nor less than a nation of people without any government at all.... Remember, democracy never lasts long. It soon wastes, exhausts, and murders itself. — John Adams

DARK TRUTH #9
America is not a democracy
(at least not according to the terminology used by the Founding Fathers).

A Republic, Not a Democracy

Many beginning students of American history are surprised to learn that America was carefully and deliberately set up by its Founding Fathers *not* to be a democracy. Actually, most of the patrician Fathers harbored a deep mistrust for the rowdy system they called democracy — a government in which the people effected the popular will directly, as in ancient Athens. The master architect of the U.S. Constitution, James Madison, argued in the *Federalist Papers* that a democracy was impossible in any large country, because people could not deliberate and discuss from afar.

One has to wonder what Madison would say if he were alive today and we gave him a Blackberry and then asked him, "What was that you were saying about it being impossible to communicate from afar?" Would he reconsider his antipathy to democracy?

Probably not, because he had another very strong argument against democracy — human irrationality. Brilliantly anticipating the modern Culture War by more than two hundred years, Madison decried the tendency of humans to act irrationally in the political context:

> As long as the reason of man continues to be fallible, and he is at liberty to exercise it, different opinions will be formed. As long as the connection subsists between his reason and his self-love, his opinions and his passions will have a reciprocal influence on each other…. The latent causes of faction are thus sown in the nature of man; and we see them everywhere…. A zeal for different opinions concerning religion, concerning government, and many other points… an attachment to different leaders ambitiously contending for pre-eminence and power… have divided mankind into parties, inflamed them with mutual animosity, and rendered them much more disposed to vex and oppress each other than to cooperate for their common good. So strong is this propensity of mankind to fall into mutual animosities, that where no substantial occasion presents itself, the most frivolous and fanciful distinctions have been sufficient to kindle their unfriendly passions and excite their most violent conflicts.[68]

That is probably the finest brief analysis of political irrationality ever written. Although we cannot fault Madison for a lack of prescience, we may quibble with his prescription. Madison felt that the only way to avoid falling into the political trap set by human nature was to scrupulously eschew democracy:

> [D]emocracies have ever been spectacles of turbulence and contention; have ever been found incompatible with personal security or the rights of property; and have in general been as short in their lives as they have been violent in their deaths.[69]

Thus spoke the Architect of our Constitution, a man clearly uncomfortable with the very idea of democracy. In his fear of the irrational passions of the citizenry, Madison participated in a legacy stretching back to Thucydides and especially Plato, who hated democracy for having murdered his beloved Socrates. Sheldon Wolin, an expert on classical government, explains Plato's democratic reservations as follows:

> The usual claim was that the democrat had a passion for equality not merely because he was envious of distinctions of wealth, social status, birth, education, and virtue, but because he hated them. Plato went further and refined the idea by saying that the democrat loved freedom because he had no use for the forms of deference traditionally owed to various authorities. The *demos* was, in other words, disrespectful of social boundaries (*Republic,* 537b–d). Wherever the demos was incorporated as sovereign, the passions so to speak were collectivized. The result, so it was alleged, was "turbulence," "disorder," frequent changes in the laws, and erratic policies. In contrast, the counsels of reason, elaborated by the philosopher and attributed to the Few, produced prudent judgments and virtuous actions.[70]

Anticipating George W. Bush's characterization of terrorists as haters of freedom, the Platonists and Madisonians characterized supporters of democracy as haters of virtue and education.

M.I.T. political scientist Francis Dupuis-Deri has provided a historical analysis of the curious self-contradiction behind our use of the word "democracy." Dupuis-Deri traced the evolution of the popular usage of this term in both the U.S. and France, contrasting the term as employed by the founders with our present understanding:

> [A]lthough virtually all politicians today identify themselves with it, 'democracy' (and its derivatives 'democrat' and 'democratic') indiscriminately evoked chaos, irrationality, the tyranny of the poor, immorality and atheism at the time when the modern electoral systems of the United States and France were established. It was not until the nineteenth century that influential politicians began to identify themselves as 'democrats' and to place the political regimes of their countries under the heading of 'democracy'.[71]

It is hard for us to appreciate today how pejorative the term democracy was at the time of the U.S. Constitutional Convention in 1787. The word "democrat" was used as an aggressive epithet when one wanted to tarnish a political opponent as advocating mob rule, chaos or the abolition of private property:

> [T]he term 'democracy' and its derivatives unmistakably served to draw a visible negative distinction between the speaker and his adversaries, whom he sought to discredit by branding them as both irresponsible and dangerous.[72]

It was said that Alexander Hamilton lobbied for the Constitutional Convention largely out of his fear that the States were indulging the people's irrational "fondness for democracies." It should not be surprising that a good deal of discussion at the Constitutional Convention revolved around the "turbulence and follies of democracy" and the "vices of democracy."

Sheldon Wolin contrasted Athenian democracy with the system devised by the Founding Fathers by referring to the American system as "electoral democracy." Wolin pointed out that the American version was actually carefully designed to counteract the power of the people, which was supreme in Athens. Since the majority of the early American citizenry were poor, it was thought (in Philadelphia) that Athenian-style democracy would inevitably result in the rich losing their property. Virtually all of the delegates to the Convention were men of property and most were quite wealthy. They believed they had much to fear from Athenian democracy, so they built their system as a series of bulwarks against it:

> Among the main reasons Madison had recommended a republican constitution based on representative government was that it would control democracy by making it difficult for the majority to rule and that it would establish a political system in which there was a fair prospect that most of the major institutions of the national government — the senate, electoral college, the president, and the supreme court — would be staffed by republican *aristoi*.[73]

Not only were women and slaves not granted suffrage, in many states suffrage was further restricted to landed property owners and their first sons. The Founders must have felt fairly secure as they left Philadelphia that, whatever flaws their system contained, an excessive penchant for democracy was not one of them. And yet within fifty years the great Alexis de Tocqueville would author a famous book called *Democracy in America*, using a term that the entire world would come to associate with the American system of government. How was it that America came to be referred to as a "democracy," when its venerated Founders had striven to clearly mark the distinction between republic and democracy, and furthermore had strongly expressed their distaste for the latter?

Chocolate Becomes Vanilla, and Vice-Versa

When Benjamin Franklin left the Constitutional Convention at its conclusion, legend has it that he was approached by an old woman, who asked: "So, Dr. Franklin, what kind of government have you given us?"

To which the old sage responded, "A republic, madam — if you can keep it."

The purpose of this venerable chestnut is to further the hagiographic Founding Myth, that the Founders went to Philadelphia as did Moses to the Mount, returning with immutable wisdom inscribed upon sacred tablets. Franklin's oracular warning to the old woman was meant to convey that the Founders had done their part of the job, and that the rest — the future of the nation — would be up to the citizenry. However, upon closer scrutiny, the story seems curious. Did Franklin believe the old woman would understand the fine distinction between "republic" and "democracy" (with all of the attendant disparagement of democracy) as did the Founders? Unless the old woman was an intellectual ancestor of Susan Sontag, Franklin's *bon mot* probably would have gone right over her head. We can imagine her smiling beatifically at the Great Man as he walked away, then, a moment later, quizzically knotting her brows. A republic? What's that? And why are we going to have trouble keeping it?

Flush from their improbable victory over the British, and securely coddled in swathes of self-serving bias, the Founders had created a system in which all power and most privilege would rest securely in their own hands. They assumed that they could count on the support of those Americans who had essentially been forever excluded from direct participation in the political process.

In fact, the Founders' anti-democratic political philosophy did meet with support and understanding in most quarters, at least initially. Dupuis-Deri gives the example of a newspaper that appeared in the U.S. in 1801 under the unambiguous name of *The Republican, or the Anti-Democrat,* and which featured a supportive article entitled "The Government of the U.S. Not a Democracy." The article explained the distinction between republic and democracy and warned readers that a democracy is always "the curse of republics," a "volcano of licentiousness," and the "prolific mother of faction, cruelty, injustice, sedition, and tyranny."[74] By 1809 the Founders were already being venerated as great Solons for having *precluded* American democracy. In the words of Fisher Ames, the "sages in the Convention" had wisely chosen the governmental form of a republic, "which differs more greatly from democracy, than democracy from despotism."

But then the country changed. The addition of new states to the original thirteen brought new proponents of an egalitarian ideal into the picture. At the same time, American partisanship became a mass phenomenon. With the expansion of the nation, political parties grew into large, national organizations. Organizations, like organisms, follow their own evolutionary logic — they do whatever it takes to survive and reproduce. As the new parties and their candidates began to seek out voters for national campaigns, candidates discovered the attractiveness of pro-democratic rhetoric.

In 1824, five candidates ran for the Presidency, but none of them obtained a majority of the votes in the Electoral College, so the election was thrown to the House of Representatives. There, artful behind-the-scenes work by Henry Clay brought victory to John Adams. When President Adams appeared to reward Clay by making him Secretary of State, there was a national outcry at the appearance of a backstage agreement. Adams thus unwittingly provided one of the losing candidates, General Andrew Jackson, with the perfect ammunition for his 1828 campaign. In Jackson's view, a cabal of Eastern aristocrats had robbed the ordinary people of electoral victory. Although he had called himself a "republican" in his first campaign, in 1828 he sought to distinguish himself as a "democrat." Jackson waged America's first classic populist campaign, calling for support from the poor and working class to help throw out what was already perceived to be a privileged Washington elite.

Jackson's electoral victory confirmed the existence of decades of pent-up resentment against the Founders' anti-democratic spirit. The ordinary people did not hold themselves in as low esteem as had the Founders, and they wished for some of the political access that had been arrogated by Jefferson's "natural aristocracy." Soon newspapers began to jump on the Jacksonian bandwagon. While prior to 1800 not a single American newspaper had featured the word "democrat" or "democratic republican" in its name, after 1820 an explosion occurred and by 1850 there were 202 newspapers with some version of the word "democracy" in their names. By 1840 Jackson had chosen to rename his party the "Democratic" party. Conservatives began to flee the newly-unpopular word "republican,"even changing the name of the National Republican party to the Whig Party in 1834. When that was not enough, conservatives began claiming that they, too, were "democrats," much to the indignation of the renamed Democratic Party.

When the dust had settled, by 1850, it had become virtually impossible for a prudent politician not to classify himself as a supporter of "democracy." Chocolate had become vanilla, and vice-versa. America now considered itself a democracy, although its constitutional structure was unchanged: republican to the core.

Unpopular Populism

The tragedy of modern democracies is that they have not yet succeeded in effecting democracy.
— Jacques Maritain, *La Tragedie de la Democratie*

Given the undemocratic structures bequeathed to us by the Founders, and given further that those structures were not altered when the country began calling itself "democratic," it should not be surprising that many Americans have continued to clamor for "real" democracy. However, since the word "democracy" has already been appropriated by the major political parties, the malcontents are stuck with lexicographical leftovers: "populism" and "direct democracy." The first sounds suspiciously like socialism, and in fact has been associated with socialism in many specific campaigns. The latter sounds technical and kind of boring. Neither has made much progress in arousing support amongst the broader electorate. Populism hasn't been popular.

Which brings us to a crucial question — do the American people really want democracy (the old-fashioned, Athenian kind)? Or to use contemporary terminology, is there public support for direct democracy in America? Data from opinion surveys is contradictory. Americans report frustration that Washington politicians are not really responsive to the concerns of ordinary people, and majorities express support for democratic mechanisms like initiatives and referenda. At the same time, Americans exhibit a great lack of interest, and even antipathy, for the actual work of democracy: thinking, analyzing, debating and compromising. It seems that Americans would like the opportunity to participate in a real democracy, but they are secretly hoping that if the opportunity ever arises, their neighbors will rise to the chore.

If pressed, many Americans admit that they would just as soon have decision-making powers turned over to bureaucrats, "experts" or even business leaders. People want more democracy, so long as they don't have to get personally involved.

The above are some of the sobering conclusions reported in *Stealth Democracy* (2003) by political scientists John Hibbing and Elizabeth Theiss-Morse, who conducted a national survey on Americans' beliefs about how government should work. Most strikingly, the survey revealed an overwhelming lack of desire to get involved in politics:

> The last thing people want is to be more involved in political decision making: They do not want to make political decisions themselves; they do not want to provide much input to those who are assigned to make these decisions; and they would rather not know all the details of the decision making process. Most people have strong feelings on few if any of the issues the government needs to address and would much prefer to spend their time in nonpolitical pursuits. Rather than wanting a more active, participatory democracy, a remarkable number of people want what we call stealth democracy.[75]

This total absence of appetite for politics was nonetheless allied (paradoxically) with a feeling that citizens should be allowed greater access to politics because politicians weren't doing a good job of representing the citizenry.

In the national survey, more than 70% of respondents disagreed with the statement, "The current political system does a good job of representing all Americans."

Do Americans really want more democracy, or not? The answer appears to be: *we don't know*. It all depends on whether someone can come up with a kind of democracy that requires no work.

Those who are devoted to the dual ideals of democracy and laziness will be pleased to know that I have in fact come up with such a system, described in the concluding chapter.

Placebo Democracy as a Successful Meme

> Let the people think they govern and they
> will be governed. — William Penn,
> *Some Fruits of Solitude* (1693)

A meme is a unit of cultural behavior that can be passed from person to person by imitation.* Examples are songs, beliefs, fashions, customs, ideas, innovations and techniques. Specific instances of widespread memes today might include: the use of iPods, tooth-brushes, denim pants, the Happy Birthday song, Chinese food, text-messaging, etc.[76]

Like genes, memes must be transmitted to survive, and face strong competition. Memes are like software that we choose to install on the hard disks of our brains. Memes must serve some function, or possess some innate attractiveness or superiority, if they hope to win the battle over other memes. If a tune is not catchy, or if a new product is not effective, it will not be propagated. In our ordinary, everyday culture we find thousands of successful memes, each of which has temporarily won a "battle of the fittest" over other, rival memes.

Systems of government can be analyzed as memes. For most of recorded history, the most successful governmental meme was monarchy. However, memes, like genes, may go extinct. The democracy meme, for example, flared up briefly in ancient Athens before disappearing forever.

In the 18th and 19th centuries, the monarchical meme was replaced by the republican meme, led by the example of the American and French Revolutions. Within a few decades, the republican meme was itself replaced by a new hybrid meme – a government that functioned as a republic but simply called itself a democracy. I refer to such government as "placebo democracy." Placebo democracy has been an extremely successful meme, ruling much of the world for the past two hundred years. What explains its attractiveness?

Placebo democracy's success is in part due to the egotistical nature of our irrationality, which makes us susceptible to self-serving beliefs, whether true or not. The great advantage of placebo democracy is that it flatters the

---

*Richard Dawkins developed the concept of the "meme" in an attempt to apply Darwinian principles to human cultural evolution.

citizenry while expecting little of them. When the government of a placebo democracy invokes the term "democracy," it does so with a sacred solemnity it expects the public to share. The public is easily infected with that spirit of reverence — understandably. They are pleased to learn that they are members of a highly-privileged global elite — the lucky citizens of a democracy.

Placebo democracy's spread has been facilitated by a phenomenon unanticipated by the Founders (who, after all, were mostly republican). Electoral campaigns have proven irresistably entertaining. Aided by the modern media, elections have become the world's favorite competitive sport (we'll discuss why elections are so fascinating in Chapter 11).

Thus we see the enormous challenge faced by those who would like to see placebo democracy evolve into something more truly democratic. To win an evolutionary battle with placebo democracy, any new system must therefore be: 1) truly democratic; 2) incredibly easy; 3) flattering to the citizens; and 4) entertaining.

We'll try to rise to that challenge in Chapter 13.

Democracy: An Impossible Dream?

Most discussions of democracy today are based on the assumption that democracy is at least possible. We may not have very much democracy yet, but someday we could, right? The answer to this profound question is far from clear.

Amartya Sen is one of the world's leading economists, winner of the 1999 Nobel Prize for economics, with a dual academic appointment to both Harvard and Cambridge. In his Nobel biography, Sen recounts a life-changing incident that occurred when he was a struggling graduate student in economics at the University of Calcutta. He was sitting alone in his room when friend and fellow student, Sukhamoy Chakravarty, rushed in with news of the publication of an astounding economics paper. The monograph, *Social Choice and Individual Values*, was a Ph.D. thesis that had been published in New York in 1951 by Kenneth Arrow, a young economics professor at Stanford University.[77]

Sen and Chakravarty immediately repaired to a local student hangout, the College Street Coffee House, to pore over the mathematical proofs underlying Arrow's stunning "impossibility theorem." Sen never forgot that long afternoon, as the two friends sat by the window and the mild winter sun of Calcutta cast a fading glow over Chakravarty's features. The two friends spent hours pondering the amazing implications of what Sen would later later dryly refer to as "Arrow's demonstration that no non-dictatorial social choice mechanism may yield consistent social decisions."

The two young Indian economists were not the only ones left in stupefaction by the reach of Arrow's Theorem. It was instantly controversial and has remained so. A year after publication, the noted economist Paul Samuelson bewailed its impact:

> The search of the great minds of recorded history for the perfect democracy, it turns out, is the search for a chimera, for logical self-contradiction. New scholars all over the world — in mathematics, politics, philosophy, and economics — are trying to salvage what can be salvaged from Arrow's devastating discovery that is to mathematical politics what Kurt Gödel's 1931 impossibility-of-proving-consistency theorem is to mathematical logic.[78]

In the past fifty years, over 2,500 academic articles have cited Arrow's Theorem. No one has been able to disprove it technically, but many important thinkers, including Amartya Sen, have challenged its relevance, thereby participating in an age-old debate.

There are many ways of expressing Arrow's Theorem, but in essence it proves that any conceivable democratic voting system can yield undemocratic results. By implication, you can't vote your way to perfect democracy, because there is no single election procedure that can always fairly decide the outcome of an election. It seems the best you can do is accept the existence of some sort of non-democratic constraint, a dictatorial gatekeeper (like a parliament), which can intelligently limit the total number of options available.

In his essay, Arrow continued a distinguished lineage of voting theorists. The limitations of voting systems have long been known, ever since the Marquis de Condorcet established in the 18th century that if there were a choice between as few as three policies — X, Y and Z — it could easily occur that X was preferred to Y, Y was preferred to Z, but Z preferred to X. The outcome therefore depended on the order in which the alternatives were put. The poor Marquis ended up poisoned on the way to the guillotine — quite a dramatic demonstration of how trivial voting can be, as compared to other political methods. If Condorcet's theory seems too technical for you, just remember the child's game of "rock, paper, scissors," in which rock beats scissors, scissors beat paper, and paper beats rock. Condorcet established that voting can be a lot like playing this game over and over. The winner after any given play is not "better" than the other alternative, it is just lucky to have been matched that time against a weak opponent. Political scientists call this "cycling," and it is considered to be only one of the devastating critiques of democracy that issued from Arrow's work.

Although the debate over the reach of Arrow's theorem is far from over, it should leave us with a sense that democracy is a far more complicated concept than is popularly assumed. We can't vote our way to paradise.

To be fair, although it is generally conceded that Arrow's work is technically unassailable, the real-world significance of the theory has frequently been doubted. For example, political scientist Gerry Mackie has conducted an in-depth survey of dozens of real-world elections and come to the conclusion that Arrow's critique is irrelevant outside the ivory tower. In Mackie's analysis, most real-world elections actually are effective as a way of expressing the citizenry's political preferences. In particular, his analysis shows that cycling does not occur as frequently as Arrow's theory would predict.[79]

Regrettably, I cannot concur with Mackie's optimistic conclusions. Although his technical attack on Arrow is impressive, he failed to attack one of Arrow's assumptions which is actually favorable to democracy. Arrow began his analysis by assuming that voters actually have preferences. This is one of the fundamental tenets of "representative democracy" — namely, that the politicians must actually have something to represent. However, as we will see later in Chapter 11, most political science research bears out a contrary conclusion.

The average citizen really does not have many — or any — political preferences. At every election there are at most two or three issues that the average voter considers worthy of consideration (and some of these aren't even real issues, but merely contrived and ambiguous preferences for "change" or "moral values"). However, it is well known that any legislator will literally have to vote on hundreds of issues during his or her term. If the voters haven't expressed any preference on these less-salient issues (because they don't have any preferences), then who exactly are the politicians representing in our so-called representative democracy?

CHAPTER 10

Irrationality and the Politician

> I shall continue to believe that "great men" are a
> lie, and that there is very little difference in that
> superstition which leads us to believe in what the
> world calls "great men" and in that which leads
> us to believe in witches and conjurors. — Letter
> from Benjamin Rush to John Adams

DARK TRUTH #10
*We expect our politicians to act like gods,
but they're human, so they act like dogs.*

The Perils of Politocracy: Public Servants — or Public Masters?

> Nowadays, for the sake of the advantage
> which is to be gained from the public
> revenues and from office, men want to be
> always in office. — Aristotle, *Politics* 3.6

I sometimes refer to our current system of government as "elective oligarchy," but a more pungent equivalent might be "politocracy" — government by politicians. All so-called democracies in existence today are really politocracies. In fact, we are so ingrained to think that politocracy is the only possible form of democracy that it is very difficult for us to conceive of an alternative. Whenever the news media talk of "spreading democracy" they measure its progress in terms of "free and fair elections." For the press: elections = democracy. Given the evidence presented in preceding chapters, however, there is good reason to believe that this popular view is irrational. My task in this chapter is to explore the ramifications of a more accurate equation: elections = oligarchy.

Elections are fundamentally anti-democratic. I wish I could claim credit for this seemingly-radical viewpoint, but in fact it was already widely understood and accepted in ancient democratic Athens. The Athenians, far wiser than we, knew that government by election inevitably becomes government by the wealthy and powerful. Therefore, they chose most of their public officials through a system of lottery in which all free male citizens were eligible. Any Athenian citizen could wake up one day to find himself a magistrate or chair of an important public committee. I do not advocate a return to that Athenian system, but I recall it here merely to indicate that a full 2,500 years ago a highly-intelligent people had come to an important understanding about electoral politics which we appear to have entirely forgotten.[80]

The widespread acceptance today of electoral politocracy as the only available form of democracy is supported by a number of irrational beliefs. First comes our childish credulity in the rhetoric of "public service." All politicians refer to themselves as "public servants" and all express their ambition for public office as motivated by an intense desire to serve the public. Most politicians invest early on in some "back story," some community service or civil-rights-protest experience that they can trot out to prove their sincerity.

Such rhetoric is too self-serving. It's a rare CEO who claims to have obtained his MBA in order to render "public service." People get MBAs because they want to become rich. Likewise, no starlet ever hitched her way to Hollywood because she thought a career in films was the best way to serve the public. People go to Hollywood to become famous. Politicians are no different. They aim their careers toward Washington, D.C. or the state capitols because they desire power (in addition to fame and wealth; and let's not forget, sex).

If politicians were to admit that they were really motivated by a desire to achieve fame and power, it would be like the Wizard of Oz pulling away the screen on himself (without the assistance of Toto). The illusion would be dispelled. As in the case of Oz, that could prove to be a good thing.

The current political landscape confirms the notion that power is really the politician's ultimate motivator. Tycoons such as Michael Bloomberg and Jon Corzine were not satisfied by the mountains of cash they earned on Wall Street. It is an American cultural truism that money "makes the world go around," but for people with lots of money, money is not enough — there is a sweeter honey. After a successful career as a Teutonic robot, Arnold Schwarzenegger was not yet satisfied. Being the world's number one box office star was not enough. If you doubt the attractiveness of power, consider our former Secretary of State, Henry Kissinger, a dull, pompous, pudgy war criminal with a big nose, goofy glasses, funny accent and bad clothes, who was nonetheless able to seduce movie stars with that little something that even Brad Pitt himself still lacks: power.

Primatologist Frans De Waal, the world's leading observer of chimpanzee politics, compares our politicians to chimps and finds good reason to prefer the chimps:

> For males, power is the ultimate aphrodisiac, and an addictive one at that…. Given the obvious "will to power" (as Nietzsche called it) of the human race, the enormous energy put into its expression, the early emergence of hierarchies among children, and the childlike devastation of grown men who tumble from the top, I'm puzzled by the taboo with which our society surrounds this issue…. Everyone seems in denial…. Political candidates… sell themselves as public servants, only in it to fix the economy or improve education. Have you ever heard a candidate admit he wants power? Obviously, the word "servant" is doublespeak: does anyone believe that it's only for our sake that they join the mudslinging of modern democracy? Do the candidates themselves believe this? What an unusual sacrifice that would be. It's refreshing to work with chimpanzees: they are the honest politicians we all long for. When political philosopher Thomas Hobbes postulated an insuppressible power drive, he was right on target for both humans and apes. Observing how blatantly chimpanzees jockey for position, one will look in vain for ulterior motives and expedient promises.[81]

In every presidential campaign, each candidate must develop a sentimental narrative of how they came to "public service." Each election cycle, the public is asked to believe the same hypocrisy. As De Waal suggests, the main difference between the politicians and the chimps is that the chimps don't lie.

Bad Boys: When Politicians Go Wrong

> Offices are as acceptable here as elsewhere, and
> whenever a man has cast a longing eye on them, a
> rottenness begins in his conduct.
> — Thomas Jefferson, letter (May 21, 1799)

In early July, 2007, Senator David Vitter of Louisiana, a stalwart Republican opponent of same-sex marriage, should have been celebrating his greatest legislative victory. As the successful leader of a fight to stop an immigration bill supported by both President Bush and Senator Dianne Feinstein, Vitter had just helped guarantee the continued disenfranchisement of twelve million hard-working undocumented aliens. However, this Louisiana paragon of moral values, known particularly for his view that marriage is "the most important social institution in human history" (translation: it's not for gays), found himself unable to savor his moment of parliamentary glory. He had other catfish to fry. His name had been found in the call records of Deborah Jeane Palfrey, the "D.C. Madam." Following the script that had worked for so many other politicians, Vitter promptly admitted to a "very serious sin in my past."

A few days later, fresh reports indicated he probably should have used the plural for "sin." Jeannette Maier, the madam of *another* high-priced brothel, this one in New Orleans, paid Vitter the ultimate compliment that politicians don't want to hear when she called him "one of the nicest and most honorable men I've ever met" (by "honorable men," I suppose, meaning: "older men who reliably pay top dollar for exotic sex with young prostitutes"). In August, 2007, I participated in an online poll on America On Line (AOL) that asked whether the revelations concerning Senator Vitter were "surprising" or not. Approximately 89 percent of us were *not* surprised by the Senator's sexual hypocrisy, while a mere 7 percent of respondents were still capable of astonishment.

Senator Vitter first came to Congress in a 1999 special election to replace his predecessor, Robert L. Livingston. For those of you who have forgotten Mr. Livingston, he was one of the senior Republican Congressmen who led the fight to impeach President Clinton. Livingston, another paragon of Southern moral virtues, had to abandon the Clinton-hunting wolf-pack and resign from Congress when *Hustler* magazine exposed his own history of marital infidelity. Thus, in a sense, Vitter was merely carrying on a Louisiana tradition.

Despite the humiliation and scandal faced by Vitter in the summer of 2007, he still had to count himself a very lucky man. Why? He was lucky because his own sexual escapades were almost immediately wiped off the front pages thanks to the spectacular efforts of yet another Republican moral paragon, Senator Larry Craig of Idaho, caught soliciting sex under a bathroom stall in an airport. Senator Craig, of course, had also severely condemned President Clinton's Oval Office antics. Perhaps Craig felt that when it comes to illicit fellatio, it is better to give than it is to receive. Having excoriated Clinton for the inappropriateness of having sexual relations in the Oval Office, Craig showed us the right way for a politician to have sex — with complete strangers in a public toilet.

This is the story of but two months in the long sex life of Washington, D.C. I could go on; and on, and on…. A complete history of sexual scandal in Washington will probably never be written, because the public does not want to read a 20,000-page book that needs to be updated weekly (note to self: maybe they *do* — idea for next book). From the earliest days of the Republic, when our first Ambassador, Benjamin Franklin, fondled and groped the awestruck wives of his French hosts while on mission to Paris, shortly to be succeeded by the even-more-amorous Thomas Jefferson, who broke an ankle in the Louvre while leaping to an assignation with yet another married Frenchwoman, all the way down to our contemporary satyrs, the priapic Kennedys, Wilbur "Fanne Fox" Mills, "Slobbering" Bob Packwood, Bill "I did not have sexual relations with that woman" Clinton, etc., our political leaders have repeatedly proven to be incredibly horny old goats.

From amongst the innumerable peccadilloes known to history, my favorite is this gem from Ronald Kessler's book *Inside Congress:*

> Capitol Police Officer Gregory M. Lacoss will never forget turning the doorknob to one of Lyndon B. Johnson's seven Capitol hideaways when LBJ was majority leader of the Senate. It was 3 a.m. and Lacoss was making his rounds, checking to make sure all offices were locked. Lacoss opened the massive door and gasped. On the sofa, Johnson was having sex with Carole Tyler, a blond, curvaceous secretary.

"There was LBJ on top of Carole," Lacoss recalled. "I said, 'Excuse me.' He said, 'You son of a bitch.' He jumped up. I took off running because I knew that man's temper. I ran to the other end of the Senate building, down the marble stairway, past the Ohio clock. I ran through the Rotunda. He was running after me. I ran to the House wing, down to the terrace level, and to the chief's office.

"I just caught LBJ on top of Carole," Lacoss shouted at the desk officer on duty. "He's threatening to kill me."

The desk officer told Lacoss to hide in a locker. "Those lockers were little," Lacoss said. "I had a gun and flashlight, and I crammed myself in. I could hardly breathe. LBJ came flying in. I could hear him slam the door. I thought it would break. He said, "Where is that officer... that son of a bitch who came in here. I'll kill him."

Eventually Johnson tired of the hunt and the desk officer extricated Lacoss from the locker.[82]

So much for the role of politicians as "moral leaders" when it comes to extra-marital sex. History reminds us that in this respect, politicians are inveterate liars, Democrats and Republicans alike. This is one area where history is *guaranteed* to repeat itself. Mark my words, dear reader, before this year is out we will witness at least one more episode of the tawdry sort we should have become used to long ago: lovey-dovey text messages from congressmen to under-age pages, affairs with interns, madams with long memories, etc. ad nauseam.

[NEWSFLASH: It was extremely hard to keep this section of the book up to date. Inevitably, as this book was being revised for press, new political sex scandals continued to break out. For example, in March 2008 it was revealed that New York Governor Eliot Spitzer had engaged in trysts with a 21-year old prostitute. The world press gleefully shared the information that the Governor would pay as much as $4,500 for a single, sexual assignation. Regrettably for Spitzer, he paid a lot more in the end, as the scandal cost him his political career. Within a few days of announcing his situation, he resigned. In a heart-warming bipartisan display, his successor, former Lieutenant Governor David Paterson, was promptly sworn in before the State Assembly. Governor Paterson became only the third African-

American governor since reconstruction. Within *two days*, however, Paterson himself announced that he had been guilty of having several extra-marital affairs — as had his wife — but he considered such actions as *legal* (since not involving prostitutes) and therefore not relevant to his position. And so it goes. I can confidently promise new material for the next edition.]

In all fairness to our lusty male politicians, their behavior is no worse than that of privileged men and women in other walks of life. As the tabloid press never ceases to remind us, the glitterati are very romantically active. Evolutionary biology says: Duh! The primary motivation of any sexual organism is to reproduce with a mate who is likely to produce successful offspring. In our society, that means having sex with rich, beautiful or powerful people. As in chimp societies, those that can, do. Let us not be too quick to condemn those who are hotter (or hornier) than we are. We should recognize that our star male politicians appear to be besieged by extremely willing female victims. Sharon Stone herself got weak-kneed when President Bill showed up; Condoleezza Rice struggled to conceal the full extent of her worshipful admiration for her husband — I mean, her boss. Barack Obama must walk with care among his throngs of female supporters, lest he be dismembered with affection.

When a male chimp succeeds in knocking off his competition and finally becomes the alpha male himself, his main reward will be sexual. Evolutionary theory suggests that his body should adjust to this new-found status by producing hormones like testosterone that will enhance his sex drive. I know of no study measuring the testosterone levels of political victors, but I would conjecture that such levels rise after a successful election. Pump a man full of testosterone, then send in a nubile young woman carrying a pizza and flashing a thong, and the rest, regrettably, is CNN history.

How to Get Elected and Impress Chicks

> The pleasure of governing must certainly be exquisite, if we may judge from the vast numbers who are eager to be concerned with it. — Voltaire, "Government," *Philosophical Dictionary* (1764)

> **Nominee**, n. A modest gentleman shrinking from
> the distinction of private life and diligently
> seeking the honorable obscurity of public office.
> — Ambrose Bierce, *The Devil's Dictionary*

It is time for the electorate to develop a *politics of human nature*: an understanding of political action informed by evolutionary and cognitive psychology.

If we accept Frans De Waal's contention that humans have a genetically-acquired will to power, we stop expecting better behavior from our politicians. All humans possess a power drive — politicians are simply those people in whom the power drive is most extreme. If the behavior of chimps is any indication of early human evolution, it seems that societies have always been structured in power hierarchies in which dominant males had superior access to both sex and food resources. Thus, throughout human evolution it not only made sense for males to battle and jockey for power, but also, having achieved it, to exploit their privileges as unfairly as possible. LBJ's midnight charge through the Senate, still tumescent from his frolic with the curvaceous Miss Tyler, is reminiscent of nothing more than the angry bluster of an alpha chimp whose sexual monopoly has been challenged.

The anecdotes of sexual indiscretion recounted above concerned only male politicians, and there are perhaps good reasons for that. As has been argued earlier, sexism in the political sphere may well be a manifestation of evolutionary pressures. Some writers hold that any purportedly-scientific explanation of male dominance is actually a justification of that behavior. Others will point to the numerous examples of women who have achieved high political status (such as Margaret Thatcher, Golda Meir, Indira Gandhi, Mary Robinson, and Hillary Clinton) as evidence that gender is irrelevant in politics.

These critiques are misplaced. The objective here is a feminist one: obviously, women should have an equal role in the political sphere. However, so long as modern governments are based on the "electoral myth" which the Athenians debunked so long ago, politics will tend to be dominated by men, with resultant costs for society as a whole. By organizing our government on "free and fair elections," we are risking a polity marked by male dominance for a long time to come. It is as if we decided to choose our leaders through contests of who could drink the most beer, watch TV football the longest, or light their own farts on fire — i.e., contests more likely to be won by males than females.

No serious evolutionary theorist would argue that all men are essentially more political than women, nor that male political dominance is entirely explained by biology, nor that some women aren't extremely motivated by politics, nor that many women aren't extremely talented at politics. However, evolutionary theory is consistent with a slightly-higher political drive for men on average, and a slightly-higher tolerance for the ugly kind of adversary combat we find in electoral contests.

Over time, even very slight differences in interest are probably sufficient to generate huge political inequalities. So long as we choose leaders through election, we will tend to choose more males than females. Today, after four decades of women's liberation, women still represent only 18 percent of the U.S. Senate and 16 percent of the Congress. In Europe there have been attempts to mandate a minimum percentage of females in national parliaments, but such attempts will not easily overcome the latent sexist bias of an electoral system. Most top leadership positions in such countries still go to males. Astonishingly, Rwanda is the only country in the world where women represent a majority in the parliament. There are extremely few countries where women crack the 40 percent figure (outside of Scandinavia, there is no region in the world where women hold more than 22 percent of parliamentary seats).*

Electoral politics are sexist by their very nature, but that is not the only way in which they are undemocratic.

Political Leadership Today: Profiles in Boorish

> If the people can choose only from
> among rascals, they are sure to choose a
> rascal. — V.O. Key, *The Responsible Electorate*

> The public good requires us to betray,
> and to lie, and to massacre: let us resign
> this commission to those who are more
> pliable, and more obedient. — Montaigne

---

* I urge readers to visit the website of the Inter-Parliamentary Union to check the latest figures: www.ipu.org

What kind of person tends to be successful in politics? Is there any sort of uniform profile, or are there strong tendencies?

Our political leadership is both homogenous and peculiar. Politicians are similar to each other, but different from the rest of us. As I have established above, there is a strong likelihood that the majority of them will be male. It is also likely that they will be wealthy, white, tall, Christian, ambitious, workaholic, competitive, extroverted, intelligent, verbose, manipulative, deceptive (and secretly very horny).

This is not an ordinary person we are describing here. We are rather depicting an obnoxious type that many of us got to know in high school: the tireless self-promoter who takes himself too seriously and appears to believe his own hokum. Remember Tracy Flick? These are the people who want to join every club and committee and never shut up at any meeting. Not everyone wants to be one of these persons. Not everyone can even stand to be associated with them. Yet we allow ourselves to be ruled by them.

What if you want to enter politics but you are not stamped from the mold of the Stepford Senators? What is it like to try to join the political club if you don't look and act like everybody else? Consider the experience of several female British M.P.s who entered a male-dominated Parliament in the 1990s, as recounted in the BBC radio documentary, "A Monstrous Regiment."[83]

Says Labour's Barbara Follett, elected to Parliament in 1997: "Sometimes when women got up to speak, some of the men — not thankfully on our side of the House — would put their hands on their chests, wiggle them around and go 'melons'. It was like a schoolboy type of humor."

When former women's minister Joan Ruddock tried to address the issue of strip-searching women in Northern Ireland, she recounted: "I heard completely audibly in the chamber one of the men on the Tory side say, 'oh, I'd like to strip search you any day.'"

Former Labour MP Oona King concluded of parliamentary etiquette, "It's all willy-jousting."

Proving you don't need a willy to joust, Labour M.P. Fiona MacTaggart silenced a Tory critic, John Bercow, who had unmercifully teased her for her schooling at Cheltenham Ladies' College, by drawing attention to Bercow's short stature: "I said, 'I have no more influence over where I went to school than the honourable gentleman had over his lack of inches — I imagine we have both been affected by our experiences.' He's a completely short arse — and since I did that, he stopped it."

I wonder if Bercow was not in part silenced by the devastating *double entendre* lurking in MacTaggart's retort (a man lacking in "inches" vertically may also lack them *perpendicularly*; willy-jousting, indeed). Still, I'm sorry that MacTaggart had to stoop to Bercow's level (which apparently was quite low to the ground).

Having now considered the discomfiture of a group of privileged white women entering an enclave for privileged white men, let us imagine that you are a bit more exotic. Let's say you are black, or gay, lesbian, Muslim, fat, short, albino, vegan; or that you live in a trailer park, or were once arrested. How are you going to feel trying to fit into the rich white country club? Do you really want to join? Do you think you would be easily accepted? Would it be easy to communicate and get along with your peers?

It is no wonder that legislatures are always more homogeneous than the citizenry they supposedly represent. The in-group does not even have to discriminate to keep ordinary people out. When we see how obnoxious they appear at a distance, we don't even want to join.

The fundamental rule of partisanship is that we like people who are like us. We tend to join clubs out of a perception that the people in the club are like us in some important way. It takes an unusual kind of motivation to want to join a club where you are likely to be considered as a bizarre outsider. In 2007, the U.S. Senate was composed of 82 males and 18 females; two Senators were Hispanic, one Senator was African-American (and he was shortly to be lost to the Senate due to promotion). The figures for Congress speak of only marginally greater diversity. These statistics reveal the self-contradiction at the heart of "free and fair" elections. Elections by their very nature are neither free nor fair. Legislatures inevitably devolve into bastions of privilege, no matter how egalitarian the rhetoric.

We are led today by a homogenous elite. Let us describe the profile of this Stepford Senator, the statistically most probable politician:

White and male: Most politicians in the U.S. are white and male. If a political candidate were to join a country club as exclusive as the Senate, it would provoke popular discussion as to his commitment to equality.

Wealthy: Increasingly, candidates are wealthy. There are two main drivers for this trend. First, American politics has become more populist since the 1960s. Well-financed demagogic appeals to popular opinion have proved decisive in political campaigns and legislative battles. This was due in part to the rise of television as the chosen terrain for political warfare, and the corresponding decline in importance of old-boy partisan networks as the ultimate power brokers. The result is what one political scientist refers to as candidate-centered politics. In the era of candidate-centered campaigns, a personal financial fortune can more than substitute for a career rising gradually through the party ranks. As campaign consultants have developed the marketing science of political campaigning, it has become possible to create a credible presidential campaign out of nothing more than hot air and money. Consider the absurd candidacies of Ross Perot and Steve Forbes, arrogant crackpots who thought they could buy themselves a place in the national spotlight — and were proved correct.

Narcissistic: If one closely analyzes the rhetoric of political debates and speeches, one can eventually categorize all candidate statements as variations on the following:

"My ideas are much, much better than my opponent's stupid ideas."

"I love America way more than my opponent loves America."

"I really, really want this job. I have always wanted this job. That's why I'm the best person for this job. Therefore, please give me this job."

"Look how beautiful my wife and children are!"

We accept that people who run for office must be unbearably boastful. It is remarkable that we are then sometime surprised that these people exaggerate. As president, Ronald Reagan on more than one occasion boasted about his WWII experiences, without bothering to point out that his colorful memories were of heroic actions that he had performed in movies.

Unscrupulous: Legislatures are marketplaces of unbridled competition. Wherever competition becomes an obsession, there will be cheating.

The endless sporting scandals involving steroids are surprising only to the naïve. Our society lavishes its greatest hero worship on sports stars, but prohibits them from using substances that can help them win. The inevitable result is endemic cheating. In the political sphere, the key factor contributing to a candidate's election is money. Political campaign contributions are the steroids of politics. So long as they are helpful, candidates will figure out a way to get their hands on "the clear": cash.

Consider the above personal characteristics. Do they belong to the kind of people that we want in charge? So long as we maintain our currently flawed electoral democracy, these are the people who will run our lives, regardless of which party we support.

Equal Rights for Ugly People: Exploding the Meritocracy Myth

> Nothing appears more surprising to those who consider human affairs with a philosophical eye than the easiness with which the many are governed by the few, and the implicit submission with which men resign their own sentiments and passions to those of the rulers. When we inquire by what means this wonder is effected, we shall find out that, as Force is always on the side of the governed, the governors have nothing to support them but opinion. It is, therefore, on opinion only that government is founded....
> — David Hume, *On the First Principles of Government*

Why do we accept to be governed by an elite oligarchy? Sadly, one of the main reasons is that we think the powerful deserve to be powerful. Perhaps the most pervasive myth in our society is the unspoken one that high-status people are better than low-status people. Few people will own up to this belief, but it underlies so many of our social structures that it is impossible to deny. Indeed, social status is such a powerful factor in a person's life that there is medical evidence that it affects life-span. Higher-status men live longer and age in better health. In America as in so many other cultures, status is literally a matter of life and death.

However, though higher-status people may lead healthier and even more enjoyable lives, that is certainly no reason for concluding that they are morally superior to lower-status people. All citizens deserve equal respect from our society and our government. There is no valid reason to discriminate politically against low-status people.

Nonetheless, we do. Our government is composed almost entirely of high-status people who rule on the basis of the unspoken assumption that low-status people are somehow inferior, intellectually or morally. The growing economic inequality in American society, and the increasingly precarious position of our cognitive and social underclass, are in part due to the habitual tendency of politicians to make laws which reward the privileged while they neglect the unfortunate. The financial crisis and banking bailout of 2008 is just one more example. Politicians, like everyone else, "see" the world in a way that maximizes their self-esteem. Since politicians are viewed by society as "winners," they are inevitably predisposed to legislate in favor of other winners. In other words, rich bankers get bailed out while defaulting homeowners are evicted.

Of course, no politician would ever admit anything like that explicitly, but an anti-underclass bias is frequently implied. Thus, political campaigns are full of rhetoric praising work: "the working man," "a country where a person can get ahead with hard work," "a country where a person can achieve their dreams," etc. The implication is: "If you are poor, it is because you are slothful."

As a typical example of this kind of thinking, consider the following point of view from a 2008 conservative political column on the topic of the "IQ gap" in American society:

> Seek out the rich man in his castle: It is far more likely the case in the U.S.A. than anywhere else, and far more likely the case in the U.S.A. of today than at any past time, that he is from modest origins, and won his wealth fairly in the fields of business, finance, or the high professions. Seek out the poor man at his gate: It is likewise probable, if you track back through his life, that it will be one of lackluster ability and effort, compounded perhaps with some serious personality defect. I have two kids in school, eighth grade and tenth. I know several of their classmates. There are some fuzzy cases, but for the most part it is easy to see who is destined for the castle, who for the gate.
>
> Of the deciding factors, by far the largest is intelligence. There are of course smart people who squander their lives, and dumb people

who get lucky. If you pluck a hundred rich men from their castles and put them in a room together, though, you will notice a high level of general intelligence. Contrariwise, a hundred poor men taken from their gates will, if put all in one place, convey a general impression of slow dullness. That's the meritocracy. That's where we've come to.[84]

This author supports what might be called the Standard American Viewpoint on Success (SAVS): Anyone can become wealthy and successful if they work hard enough. Implicitly, people who fail to achieve wealth or social status in America are both lazy *and* dumb, hence unworthy. We would feel guilty of cruelty and lack of compassion if we condemned other people to a lifetime of poverty just because they were slightly less intelligent, so... cognitive dissonance sets in, and we find ourselves obliged to blame them for laziness as well. The poor and miserable usually deserve their unhappy fates, says SAVS (with relief). You probably believe this as well, dear reader, no matter how progressive you may pretend to be. We are all subjected to so many years of social brainwashing that indoctrinates us with the belief that wealth and status are always the result of greater *effort*, and are therefore deserved. Yet there are good reasons to doubt the basic validity of SAVS:

1) It is simply not true that everyone will advance equally with equal amounts of effort. Life is harder for some people than it is for others. You could say life is like a foootball game where some players have to wear heavy weights and handcuffs, while others get to ride around on motorcycles. It's not fair, under such circumstances, for the people on motorcycles to brag about how they scored touchdowns through hard work.

The marginal utility of effort will vary enormously depending upon differences in inherited social capital. For example, consider the case of two men, Bruce and Doug.

Bruce's dad is a wealthy doctor, his mom a former athlete and model; Bruce grows up in a wealthy suburb, attending private schools. His IQ is measured at 135; he reaches 6' 3", is good-looking (like his mom), extroverted, energetic, disciplined, and has a naturally happy, buoyant personality. Bruce has huge social capital. Every additional hour he invests in his career promises major payoffs down the road.

Doug is not nearly as lucky. Doug's dad is still in prison and his mom is dead, so he lives with his aunt, who is an alcoholic. Doug still limps from a car accident he had as a kid which was poorly treated at an inner-city hospital. He ate some paints chips off a peeling wall as a baby, but his IQ probably would-n't have been that high, anyway: about 80 (he is in the bottom 10 percent). He is slightly obese from adolescence on, and his height is 5' 6". He is described by teachers and counselors as "spaced out" and "lonely." Doug has no social capital. He can work really hard, but will the extra work do him as much good as it would Bruce?

Bruce has a chance to become a player in our global economy — if he works hard, he can become a corporate executive, plastic surgeon, trial lawyer, etc., making tens of millions of dollars in his career.

Doug has no choice but to work hard, just to stay alive, but what in-centive does he have to put in extra hours? What good will that do him in our economy? It's one thing to put in extra hours studying for the SAT so that you can get in to Princeton; it's another to work over-time as a cashier at your local supermarket.

If you know someone like Doug who has been promoted to manager of your local dry-cleaner's, give him your full respect, dear reader. He prob-ably worked as hard as any Bruce who ever made it to Senator.

2) Behavioral genetics (remember the twin Jims) suggests that inten-sity of motivation and concentration, and hence the capacity for hard work, are as likely to be genetically-determined as any other physical or behav-ioral characteristics.

If you were simply born with a particular trait, there is no reason for so-ciety to reward that trait as if it were a moral virtue. Venerating hard work is therefore about as logical as venerating red hair. With all due respect to our foxy fellow redheads, they have *done* nothing to earn our special esteem. The same is true of our fellow workaholics. Just as a St. Bernard dog can spend the afternoon sleeping while a Chihuahua drives one crazy with incessant yapping and skittering, different humans are born with different work drives. Worka-holics are people who were born with high-energy thermostats. They're not necessarily better than other people, they were just born with an inability to keep still — a characteristic that happens to be highly remunerative in today's capitalist marketplace, though frequently annoying to family and loved ones.

A low energy-level is not the only inheritable impediment a human being may face in the battle to acquire social status. There are fates arguably worse than laziness, such as fatness, shortness, ugliness, dumbness, a physical or psychological handicap or alcoholism. Try getting elected to public office if any of these adjectives apply to you.

Surveys have shown that tall men earn slightly more on average than shorter men. Other surveys have demonstrated that obesity can have a correspondingly negative effect. In other words, if you're a short fat guy, don't set your hopes on being referred to someday as the "the Senator." It appears that the negative impact of obesity is even more serious for women, and getting worse. In 1981 a slightly-obese American woman could expect wages 4.3 percent lower than her slimmer colleagues; by 2000 the wage penalty for female obesity had risen to 7.5 percent.[85]

Half of all Americans will always be below average in height, intelligence, looks, musical and athletic talent. It's not hard to end up in the bottom half of any of the above categories. It can happen to anybody. The problem is that in our capitalist society the below-average citizens make so much less money than the above-average. In our globally competitive economy, a few lucky breaks and a few IQ points may represent the difference between living in a mansion or in a trailer park. In the "old" societies of Europe, the accumulated wisdom of the ages has informed society that you never know when your kids are going to end up in the bottom half. Hence, the strong European safety net. The American middle class is different — like a gambler at the blackjack table who still hasn't lost hope. We hesitate to support "tax the rich" strategies because we still secretly hope to become rich ourselves.

The meritocracy myth prevents us from seeking a more just society because it provides us with a plausible justification for the inequity around us. Meritocracy is our excuse for inequality. If there are outrageously rich people who spend their money lavishly and wastefully, we tell ourselves that is because our markets must provide incentives for creativity and risk-taking. If there are miserably poor people, we tell ourselves it is because those people, to their discredit, lacked a sufficient respect for education, thrift and hard work.

However, behavioral genetics forces us to challenge the meritocracy myth. If the twin studies are correct, we must face up to the reality that achieving a match between one's genetic inheritance and one's environment is largely a matter of pure luck. To be lucky in the genetic lottery is its own reward. To wake up tall, beautiful, athletic, energetic and intelligent, is really to start the day off on the right foot.

Do we need political power and social privileges thrown in for extra measure?

CHAPTER 11

Irrational Elections

> You can fool too many of the people too
> much of the time. — James Thurber

DARK TRUTH #11
*American presidential campaigns are vicious, shallow,
mendacious and farcical, but at least they're entertaining.*

Presidential Elections: Adventures in Enjoyable Absurdity

The American presidential election is the world's most important political event, the Academy Awards and World Cup rolled into one. The winner of this election can plausibly claim the title, "Prince of the World." If ever an election demanded a full, balanced and informative discussion of the most important issues facing humanity, it would be this one. If ever we dreamed of seeing the glory of democracy on display, it would be here.

Given the height of our hopes, our disappointment is extreme. The Emperor is naked. Here is a brief list of what the world could hope for in the world's most important election, compared with what we actually get:

Issues: We hope for an informed, vigorous public discussion of the key policy concerns. *Disappointment*: We get a canned, strategic marketing contest, in which the candidates are paralyzed by fear of going "off message." Each candidate chooses his or her own preferred field of battle, even if that means endless discussion of false problems. In 2008 both parties jumped on the "offshore drilling" bandwagon, though energy economists decried as ridiculous the notion that such drilling could have any immediate impact.

Honest results: We hope that the outcome can be trusted as having been produced in a clean, transparent manner. *Disappointment:* The post-election mess in Florida in 2000, and the similar mess in Ohio in 2004, were not aberrations. Outright theft of elections has been surprisingly common in American history.

Democratic mechanism: We assume that the person with the most votes will win. *Disappointment*: We are saddled with a bizarre system called the Electoral College. In 2000, Gore earned a half-million votes more than Bush, but lost the general election. In 2004, Kerry was within a few hundred thousand votes of winning Ohio, and with it the presidency, even though he would have lost the popular vote by two million votes.

Responsible media coverage: We hope that the media will provide in-depth, balanced analysis of the candidates' policy positions. *Disappointment*: The media collude with the candidates to present us with a phony dog show. Instead of issues-analysis, we get celebrity profiles. In early 2008 the media followed Barack Obama like groupies on a rock tour. When Sarah Palin joined the contest they became like Britney-hunting paparazzi. In order to maximize revenues, the media frame the election as an exciting down-to-the-wire "horse race" — even in years (like 2008) when the outcome was a foregone conclusion.

Clean, substantive campaigns: We hope that the candidates will focus on the issues and not on vicious attacks of their opponents. *Disappointment*: Both sides commonly resort to smear tactics and outright lies. The Democrats scare us by presenting the Republicans as racist corporate war-mongers eager to cut funds off from the poor and elderly, while the Republicans present a frightening counter-portrait of the Democrats as America-hating, terrorist-loving, high-spending, atheist homosexuals.

Intelligent debates: We hope for lively exchanges that reveal the candidates' characters and explore the issues. *Disappointment*: We get carefully scripted recitations of market-tested pablum. Consequently, our estimate of who "won" turns on the tiniest of gaffes: who sweated or grimaced the most, or sighed least.

Why is the world's most important election decided so superficially and irrationally? As before, evolutionary psychology provides helpful clues. As a rational method of determining voter preferences and setting national policy, the election is worse than useless — it is preposterous. However, as an extremely entertaining combat for tribal supremacy, reminiscent of the millions of similar struggles that occurred throughout human evolution, it makes perfect sense.

We have been hard-wired by evolution to pay great attention to struggles for power that may impact our lives. We are also hard-wired to express our preferences in such contests — not on the basis of logic or reason, but rather as an expression of our underlying genetic and cultural affinities. We vote for the candidate we like best, and we tend to like best that candidate who is closest to us on the genetic, cultural and socio-demographic spectrum. Thus evolution has bequeathed us a wiring which a) makes political contests irresistibly interesting, b) makes us want to participate in them, and c) makes us prefer candidates who are culturally or genetically similar to ourselves. In many ways, our current political behavior is the continuation of the everyday activities of our ancestors over the past 1.5 million years.

How to Elect Tall, Deep-Voiced, Handsome, Happy People on Rainy Days

Most people assume that voters choose the president on the basis of some relevant criteria, such as a preference for the given candidate's policies, or the candidate's character and experience, or the candidate's party. What else could explain the preference for one candidate over another? This basic assumption is challenged by a welter of studies which show that voters are heavily influenced by a number of apparently irrelevant personal qualities. Often it seems that the voters are choosing the candidate they would most like to date or befriend, rather than the one best-qualified to lead the nation.

Height. In 2008, Barack Obama loomed in height over John McCain, and won the election. The taller of the two presidential candidates wins the election more often than not. Since 1888, the taller candidate has lost the popular vote in only five elections. Since the television era began in 1952, the taller candidate has only lost the popular vote four times out of thirteen elections.

George W. Bush's campaign team was so frightened of the height disparity in 2004 (Bush stood 5' 11" while opponent John Kerry loomed a formidable 6' 4") that they carefully kept Bush at least ten feet away from Kerry during the presidential debates. These results may be puzzling to rational-voter theorists, but are quite unremarkable to evolutionary psychologists.

As has been noted earlier, tall men benefit from a number of unfair privileges, political and otherwise. Studies have established that tall men are considered more attractive by women. On average, tall men cohabit with a greater number of sexual partners and have more children. A variety of evolutionary mechanisms have been proposed to explain this phenomenon. It could be that tall men were once better hunters or fighters, or it could be that height is simply an arbitrary form of sexual display, like the peacock's tail. Whatever the case, it should not be surprising if our unspoken but widespread preference for tall people, so important in other areas of social life, also has an effect at the polls.[86]

Voice. Another bizarre result is provided by voice-spectrum analysis. Deep-voiced candidates appear to have an advantage in campaigns. Close your eyes and listen to the vocal quality of Barack Obama, Mike Huckabee, John McCain, or Hillary Clinton. You will notice that all of these leading political figures have marquee voices — pleasant, engaging, steady, resonant, self-assured. Though most politicians have good voices, the winners tend to have the best ones. Social psychologists have discovered that during conversation low-status individuals tend to adopt the vocal patterns of high-status individuals. This process is known as "communication accommodation." Researchers Stanford Gregory and Timothy Gallagher studied the political impact of a specific low-frequency hum underlying human vocalization. Generally inaudible, the tenor of this hum nonetheless appears to communicate social status. The more confident and steadfast the tone, the higher the status of the speaker. Higher-status individuals also permit themselves a greater freedom in vocalization so their vocal patterns tend to be more expansive; lower-status individuals have a more timid, restricted vocal range. Lower-status individuals, it has been suggested, indicate an acceptance of their subordinate position by following the vocal lead set by high-status individuals.[87]

In a voice-spectrum analysis of presidential debates since the 1960s, Gregory and Gallagher demonstrated a correlation between vocal dominance and the popular vote. In each case, the candidate whose low-frequency vocal pattern was dominant ended up winning the popular vote. If a good voice can help you, it follows that a bad one hurts. Ross Perot's high-pitched nasal whine did not hinder him in the rough-and-tumble of the corporate marketplace, but it made his election to the Presidency a virtual impossibility.

Again, for evolutionary psychologists, this is no surprise. A strong, deep voice is a biological marker of high testosterone, which correlates with heavier musculature and aggressiveness. Anthropologists studying a hunter-gatherer tribe in Tanzania have established that deeper voice pitch predicts reproductive success. Men with lower voice pitch were found to have fathered more total children. Women who aspire to leadership may benefit from having a voice which is low enough to qualify as "masculine."

The impact of these two seemingly irrelevant characteristics — height and voice pitch — suggests that voters are actually acting like rational stone-age tribe-members assessing the conflict between two pretenders to the role of alpha male. Frans De Waal's observation of chimpanzee politics suggests that it can be dangerous for chimps to "abstain" from political participation. Alpha chimps keep track of who supports them in battles for power, and they punish defectors. Similarly, in proto-human tribes it may have been dangerous not to support the eventually-successful candidate for alpha status. It would have made sense for political spectators and supporters to learn to spot and support early favorites and front-runners — it was the safest bet. The taller, deeper-voiced, more testosterone-drenched candidate was often the right pick. Is it any wonder that Conan the Republican was elected Governor of California?

The problem, of course, is that a strategy that was rational for proto-human tribes struggling for survival on the African savannah (i.e., let the biggest, toughest person become alpha) is not at all rational for our complex societies today. We are not looking to elect a cave-man-in-chief. We are looking for someone who will represent the complex interests of a large society in an efficient manner. It is no longer rational to take height and voice quality into consideration. Yet we do.

Beauty. Physical attractiveness is another randomly distributed, innate characteristic which is irrelevant from a rational point of view but which we might expect to have a positive influence on voters. A number of studies have confirmed that voters — at least under laboratory conditions — exhibit a clear preference for candidates that look the part. When a handsome candidate is matched against an unattractive one in a simulated election presented to college students, the handsome one wins even when the accompanying campaign messages are identical. This finding corroborates a substantial body of research from social psychology which has established the presence of a powerful beauty effect.

When college students are shown pictures of attractive people and asked to speculate on their associated personal qualities, the students attribute qualities of intelligence, honesty and discipline to those people; conversely, unattractive people are associated with the opposite qualities. While it used to be said that "politics is show business for ugly people," that general principle no longer holds true. With the birth of the television era and the application of sophisticated Madison Avenue brand-marketing techniques to the political marketplace, personal attractiveness has become increasingly important.

From John F. Kennedy to Sarah Palin, the "hottie" candidate has been able to count on significant electoral support merely on the basis of looks. More importantly, it has become increasingly dangerous to be ugly. As the sophomoric saying goes, beauty is skin deep but ugly goes to the bone. Some portion of John Kerry's defeat in 2004 can surely be attributed to the odd, equine longitude of the candidate's cranium. If Dennis Kucinich looked more like George Clooney, at least half of the voting public (females) would begin to take him very seriously. But he looks like Dennis Kucinich, so he is treated the way people who look like Dennis Kucinich are treated (you know what I mean). Governor Bill Richardson of New Mexico probably had the most impressive resume of any of the Democratic contenders in 2008, but he was promptly dismissed by voters. He was simply 25 pounds too *gordo*. Americans might some day elect an ethnic candidate, but not a *panzón*. My advice to *compadre* Bill: cut back on the *chorizo* until you begin to look more like Barack.

Conservative political scientist Lee Sigelman conducted a tongue-in-cheek analysis of the respective attractiveness of Democratic and Republican office-holders. He had a single research subject go through the entire *Almanac of American Politics* for 1988, rating all 50 governors, 100 senators and 435 House members on an "ugliness scale" from –5 (yecch!) to +5 (hottie). Although the research subject was purportedly a liberal (she was identified only as "a middle-aged woman who has an inordinate fondness for looking at pictures of men"), the data indicated that the Republicans held a significant beauty edge (nearly 10 percent were hotties, compared to the Democrats' 1 percent; at the other end of the spectrum, 25 out of 26 politicians earning the lowest "yecch" rating were Democrats). It also appeared from the data that governors and senators were substantially better-looking than House members, suggesting that those with long-term political ambitions should consider plastic surgery sooner rather than later.[88]

Is it possible that a person's appearance could be in some way connected to true political competence? If so, is it possible that voters detect and accurately process these visual cues? The ability to intuitively "size up" a politician from his or her looks could be considered a variant of the "political heuristic" — emotional snap-judgments that work because they are based on the wisdom of our intuitive brain. For the most part I have been skeptical of the value of the political heuristic, given the presence of overwhelming partisan bias. However, under conditions where bias is not present, people have displayed a remarkable ability to judge strangers by their looks.

In an intriguing experiment devised by psychologists Nalini Ambady and Nicholas Rule, college students were shown pictures of the CEOs of the top-25 and bottom-25 companies in the *Fortune* 1000 list. They were asked to guess how competent a leader the CEO was, merely by looking at his picture (they were all men). To a remarkable degree, the students' evaluations of the leadership potential of the CEOs correlated with the level of profit earned by the company. In other words, students who knew absolutely nothing about the CEOs or their companies were nonetheless able, as a group, to predict which CEOs would perform better, merely by looking at their pictures. This suggests that there really is such a thing as "looking like a leader."

For voters in presidential primaries, who are not yet overly constrained by partisan bias (because all candidates are from the same party), and who know little of the candidates, a judgment made at face value may therefore contain a surprising wisdom. However, once our partisan bias kicks in, we become immune to the subtle charms of an opposing candidate's physique. Few Republicans fell in love with Bill Clinton's good looks, while Democrats proved equally resistant to George W. Bush's.

> A candidate for public office can have no greater advantage than muddled syntax; no greater liability than a command of language. — Marya Mannes, *More in Anger*

> Our great democracies still tend to think that a stupid man is more likely to be honest than a clever man, and our politicians take advantage of this prejudice by pretending to be even more stupid than nature made them. — Bertrand Russell, *New Hopes for a Changing World*

Intelligence. Intelligence is arguably the only one of the innate characteristics worthy of rational consideration by voters. Surely it would make sense for voters to prefer the more intelligent of the two candidates? Even here, however, we must be wary of a strong potential for irrationality, because most candidates do not write their own speeches or political platforms, so it is hard to tell who is sounding intelligent. When someone quotes a profound observation by President Reagan, they are almost invariably quoting his favorite speechwriter, Peggy Noonan. Humor is often associated with intelligence, but it's a rare president who writes his own material. Bill Clinton's best jokes were crafted by the presidential jokewriter, Mark Katz. When John McCain or Barack Obama makes a smart-sounding new policy proposal, chances are it was developed by a team of well-paid political consultants.

Moreover, American social attitudes toward intelligence are ambivalent. There appears to be no advantage to being considered the "egghead" candidate. The erudite Adlai Stevenson lost twice to Eisenhower, brainy Jimmy Carter was crushed by the vacuous Reagan, nerdy Dukakis was clubbed by the syntactically-challenged George H.W. Bush, and the encyclopedic Al Gore succumbed to good 'ole boy Dubya. Does it help to have a brain? I suspect that Karl Rove's answer would be: yes, but only if you hide it.

Don't ever mis-underestimate a savvy politician. In 2004 a conservative columnist, Steve Sailer, researched military and college records to extrapolate I.Q. scores for George W. Bush and his successive opponents, Gore and Kerry. The results showed they are all smart guys — Gore's I.Q. was 135, Bush's was 125, and Kerry's 120. As I have noted previously, voters tend to vote affectively — we vote for the candidate we like the most, and we tend to like those people who most resemble us. By definition the average human intelligence is set at 100. Politicians who are too intelligent are simply not like the rest of us — fully 80 percent of the population has an IQ beneath 110. As the 2008 presidential primaries developed, Hillary Clinton's evident intelligence was one of her greatest drawbacks.

There may even be good evolutionary reasons for being suspicious of extreme intelligence. The highest I.Q.s are estimated to be in the 200 range — literally twice the average. If we analogize I.Q. to height, coming across a person with an I.Q. of 200 is rather like meeting a person who is twelve feet tall. Wouldn't that frighten you? It should. Evolution may have bequeathed us a healthy fear of people who are too smart. Many of us have experienced that tingling "spider-sense" when we are receiving a sales pitch from a too-smooth salesman, the feeling that our pocketbooks are suddenly going to be made much lighter, whether we like it or not. Brainy politicians can make us feel the same way — at their peril.

Happiness. One of the most active fields in psychology today is known as "positive psychology," the study of human happiness. Dozens of popular books on the psychology of happiness have appeared in the past few years. As with so many other personal characteristics, it appears that genetics plays a determining role. Most psychologists now believe we are each born with a happiness "set point," a base level of happiness which does not vary much throughout our lives, no matter how hard we try. If you are naturally a happy person, this is good news. If you are naturally a sad person, well then....(you were probably already depressed).

The theory of "limbic resonance" posits that emotions are contagious, which suggests that a high happiness set point could be a great advantage to a politician. Neuroscientists have discovered that the human brain possesses "mirror neurons," brain cells which cause us to feel the same emotions being experienced by persons we observe. When we watch someone cry, it makes us feel sad; when we watch someone laugh, we feel happy.

It follows that watching happy politicians will make us happier. From my perspective, this is the only way of explaining the amazing success of Ronald Reagan, the ultimate "happy warrior." As a number of biographies have attested, Reagan was so uninterested in politics that he did not even recognize all the members of his own cabinet. But no one can deny the man's good-natured *bonhomie.* Even when he got shot, the assassin's bullet narrowly missing his vital organs, he was cheerful enough to josh with the surgical team before going under anesthesia! Limbic resonance explains why it was so often said about Reagan that he made "America feel good again." Of course he did — one only has to compare his bouncy demeanor to that of the preceding sour-pusses — Carter, Ford and Nixon. In the 2000 presidential campaign George W. Bush cultivated a happy-go-lucky quality, coming across almost as a bit of a frat-boy clown, which contrasted starkly with the gloomy Gore. It worked. Happiness is smart politics.

In early 2008 Barack Obama displayed an amazing ability to whip his supporters (and most of the nation's liberal pundits) into a fever of good feelings. Consider, for example, this article by George Packer in the *New Yorker* magazine, which describes an Obama speech:

> When [Obama] walked onto the stage, which was framed by giant vertical banners proclaiming "HOPE," his liquid stride and handshake-hugs suggested a man completely at ease....
>
> "We love you," a woman shouted.
>
> "I love you back," he said, feeding off the adoration he had summoned without breaking a sweat....
>
> Obama spoke for only twenty-five minutes and took no questions; he had figured out how to leave an audience at the peak of its emotion, craving more. As he was ending, I walked outside and found five hundred people standing on the sidewalk and the front steps of the opera house, listening to his last words in silence, as if news of victory in the Pacific were coming over the loudspeakers. Within minutes, I couldn't recall a single thing that he had said, and the speech dissolved into pure feeling, which stayed with me for days.[89]

Now *that's* limbic resonance.

Reagan continued to be a happy warrior all through the savings-and-loan debacle, as well as the Iran-Contra scandal. While those scandals are now fading into the mists of history, Reagan's happy smile grows ever more iconic, as increasing numbers of public buildings, airports and monuments are named after him. Happiness can even trump history.

Rain? Political scientist Brad Gomez led a team of researchers who analyzed the impact of rain and snow in 3000 counties across the U.S., in all presidential elections from 1948 to 2000. They discovered that one inch of rain reduces overall turnout by an average of 1% and cuts the Democratic vote by 2.5%. In America, it seems, rainy days can paint a state red, while sunny days will dry it blue. Gomez conjectured, for example, that two Northeastern thunderstorms would have been enough to throw the 1960 election from Kennedy to Nixon.[90]

In a presidential election year the citizenry hears endless discussion about the candidates' respective positions, character and past performance. But in the end, the outcome might just turn on a haircut, a smile, or a rainshower.

It's Not the Economy, Stupid

When James Carville posted the immortal slogan, "It's the economy, stupid," in the 1992 Clinton campaign war-room, he echoed the opinion of many political scientists. In particular, Carville's view found support amongst those brave political souls who have ventured into the world of presidential-election forecasting. Over the past fifty years, dozens of presidential-forecasting models have been developed. Many of these frameworks have been very successful in predicting presidential-election outcomes (though none has proved perfect). The factor most consistently taken into account by these models is the economic performance of the nation at a given date before the election.

According to the consensus view of the forecasters, voters really believe that a president's main job is to provide a healthy economy, no matter what they say. When interviewed, voters will claim that they are motivated by a candidate's "values" or "experience," but history tells us that a president or incumbent party that presides over a thriving economy will almost always be rewarded with re-election. Conversely, when the economy is weak or in recession, it is a near-certainty that the challenger will be elected. At first glance, this seems like a clear display of rationality on the part of the voters, contrary to my main thesis. Surely it makes sense to choose the president on the basis of the economy's performance? Actually, in my opinion — it does not, for the following reasons:

1) The president is only one of a large number of factors with an impact on the economy. Other important factors include the Federal Reserve chairman, the congress, the business cycle, international conflicts and competition, global financial crises, disruptive technological innovation, natural disasters and commodity shortages. It is much easier to attribute economic performance to the president than it is to trace the complex sequence of factors that would give a more accurate picture.

Thus, one president may raise taxes to eliminate a deficit, causing a temporary downturn during his or her own administration to the benefit of the succeeding administration. Another president may exhaust the public treasury to temporarily boost the economy in a fashion which will only be revealed as unsound in a subsequent administration. A president may implement a number of economically questionable policies and yet be rewarded with a good economy, while another might follow the most enlightened-economic policies and yet be punished by a recession. Voters' tendency toward rational ignorance will prevent them from ever being able to tell the difference. Incumbent presidents and parties will tend to be over-praised for a good economy and over-criticized for a bad one.

2) Only in theory can we compare the incumbent's economic performance to what the other party would have done. Even if the economy has done well, this is no proof that the other party would not have done better. If the economy has declined, it might have declined still more precipitously under the other party's leadership. We simply cannot know.

Of course, I agree that the economic performance of the nation is to some extent the president's responsibility. However, given the difficulty in ascertaining the scope of the president's responsibility, the state of the economy should not be enough to determine the preferences of rational voters. A truly rational voter would scrutinize the candidates' prospective economic platforms more than the economy's current performance. But that would be so hard!

To a large degree, therefore, the incumbent president or party is simply lucky to inherit a good economy the year before the election. Conversely, the challenger is lucky when the election cycle coincides with an economic downturn. Since it is not rational simply to reward the lucky, the evidence from the economic forecasting models supports the general theory of an irrational election process.

Rationally or not, though, the economy matters, and the forecasting models suggest that it is generally decisive. By mid-2008, an election year, it had become clear that the American economy was in such bad shape that a Republican victory in November was remote. The most well-respected forecasting models (such as Ray Fair's of Yale), predicted a clear Democratic victory.

The media, however, did not make such predictions widely known. Doing so might have spoiled interest in the election, which the media was counting on to fill the role of top-rated reality show of the year. Perhaps the most subversive implication of the success of the forecasting models is they suggest the existence of a "campaign fallacy" — an erroneous belief that campaigns matter. However, if the economic forecasts are accurate, political campaigns become meaningless. When forecasting models accurately predict the winner with data from the year before the election, we are hard-pressed to avoid the conclusion that campaigns are irrelevant in terms of persuading the voters.[91]

Consider the example of the 1988 election, for which the economic forecasts predicted an easy George H.W. Bush victory. At first, the forecasts appeared to be way off target, as the Democratic challenger (Michael Dukakis) garnered an early 17-point lead. Then, the polls began to see-saw back and forth, with Dukakis apparently losing a lot of steam when he looked silly riding in a tank, and later in a debate when he seemed strangely unperturbed by the thought of his wife's rape. The *coup de grace*, according to the conventional wisdom, was the devastating impact of Bush's infamous "Willie Horton" ads, which suggested that Dukakis was soft on crime. When Bush won the general election the pundits blamed Willie Horton, but the forecasters reminded everyone that their highly-accurate predictions had been made before *any* of those campaign maneuvers. In the forecasters' view, the 1988 campaign, for all its drama, just proved that campaigns really do not matter.

Fortunately for America's highly-paid political-campaign consultants, the forecasting models have not always proved correct. Most strikingly in

2000, the election forecasts by political scientists predicted an easy victory for Al Gore. Although the forecasters could claim some consolation in Gore's popular-vote victory, in truth their predictions were off the mark. A competing school of political scientists seized on the 2000 results to vindicate their claim for the existence of "campaign effects." Campaigns can matter, they proclaimed, especially when they are as maladroitly run as the Gore campaign in 2000. Perhaps campaigns do matter after all?

In 2008 the economic models correctly forecast an easy victory for the Democratic candidate. Once again, the victors attributed the results to the competence of their candidate, while the losers blamed the media.

Presidential Campaigns: The Negligible Role of Issues

> The people are that part of the state that does not know what it wants. — Hegel

Is there a place in the election process for the careful, rational analysis of policy positions and agendas by the voting public?

There are two competing schools of thought on this issue from political science. The first is represented by Philip Converse, especially as expressed in his classic 1964 paper, "On the Nature of Belief Systems in Mass Publics." Converse's research showed that most Americans don't really have political opinions or ideologies, though they can trot out a few seemingly-plausible factoids when prodded. In Converse's view, people vote primarily out of party identification. Most people carry around a grab-bag of half-digested political viewpoints to justify their votes, but they don't really understand any of those viewpoints in any depth. The campaign cannot be about issues because the people do not really understand any issues.

You can easily test this theory out on any of your politically-conscious friends. Next time they express an opinion on a political issue — such as U.S. withdrawal from Iraq, universal health coverage, or global warming — ask for a few details. *When* should the Americans withdraw, and *what* should they do if a civil war ensues? *Who* should pay for our universal coverage, and *how much* should they pay? *How* exactly are we to stop global warming, and *when* are we stop it, and *how* will we know when we have done enough? In most cases, the answers will be very fuzzy, and become fuzzier still the more you push for details. Most people think they have political opinions — but when pressed, can't say what they are.

Not everyone agrees with Converse. Some people think the voters know plenty enough to choose between politicians, and that voters can make a perfectly fine selection on the basis of minimal cues. This contrary view is best exemplified by Samuel Popkin's influential 1981 book, *The Reasoning Voter*. Popkin espouses a form of democratic minimalism generally referred to as "low-information rationality" or "gut rationality." In Popkin's view, voters do not need to know very much about the issues to form rational decisions on the candidate. Informal, superficial cues are enough.[92]

I refer to Popkin's view as the "hot tamale theory" of political science, due to his reliance on one memorable example. When President Ford was campaigning in the Texas Republican primary in 1980, he appeared for a photo-op in which he was called upon to enjoy that Mexican delicacy known as the *tamale*. Unfortunately for Ford, no one had informed him in advance that the corn shuck on the tamale is a *wrapper* — he took it as part of the dish, and bit lustily into it for the world's cameras. Ford thus made the front page of the *New York Times*, much to his own chagrin. Subsequently, after losing the Texas primary to Reagan, Ford said that the lesson he had learned about political campaigning was, "Always shuck your tamales."

The conventional wisdom held that Ford's culinary gaffe had soured the crucial Mexican-American vote. Popkin argued that it was quite rational for Mexican-Americans to take Ford's ignorance of their food as a lack of understanding for their culture and their needs. In Popkin's view, when the public makes up its mind on such seemingly-slight factors, there is actually a powerful underlying rationality at work.

Popkin confuses rationalization with rationality. Thus, he qualifies voters as rational if they can find any reason at all to justify their electoral decisions:

POPKIN: Why didn't you vote for Ford?

MEXICAN-AMERICAN: I don't like the way he eats *tamales*.

POPKIN: Okay, that makes sense.

Popkin is setting the bar for democracy too low. Voters should rely on good reasons, not just any reasons. With respect to Popkin, it is not sufficiently rational — and therefore not acceptable — for voters to choose their leaders based on the candidates' respective mastery of tamale-shucking protocol.

Multi-cultural ignorance of the sort demonstrated by Ford could rationally be considered at most a *minor* factor in assessing a candidate's competence. However, for it to be determinative is ridiculous. Ford was not running for President of Taco Bell. I say this as a Mexican-American, with some fondness for the controversial food in question.

Popkin's analysis is ultimately more insulting to Mexican-Americans than Ford's gaffe. Are Latinos assumed to be so intolerant that we reject Anglos who do not know our national cuisine by heart? We would also have to reject many of our own, under that stringent criterion. Many Mexican-Americans are unfamiliar with such traditional Mexican regional dishes as *cochinita pibil* or *huachinango a la veracruzana*. Yet greater numbers of Mexicans are unfamiliar with Caribbean and South American dishes. Extremely few Latinos are entirely familiar with the complete Ibero-American gastronomic gamut. It's a rare *gringo* who knows that tamales from Oaxaca are different from those made in Puebla. Most tamales are wrapped in corn shucks, but some are wrapped in plantain leaves. There are sweet, pink tamales made with raisins and cinnamon, and hot, spicy tamales with chicken mole or pork. Every Mexican presidential candidate knows all of this, but American candidates can surely be forgiven their tamale ignorance.

Both Wrong: The Howard Cosell Theory of Politics

> I never vote *for* anybody. I always vote *against*. — W. C. Fields

> Under democracy, one party always devotes its chief energies to trying to prove that the other party is unfit to rule — and both commonly succeed, and are right. — H. L. Mencken

> An attitude of permanent indignation signifies great mental poverty. Politics compels its votaries to take that line and

> you can see their minds growing more
> and more impoverished every day, from
> one burst of righteous anger to the next.
> — Paul Valery, *Tel Quel*

> Anger is the most seductive of the
> negative emotions; the self-righteous
> inner monologue that propels it along
> fills the mind with the most convincing
> arguments for venting rage. Unlike
> sadness, anger is energizing, even
> exhilarating.
> — Daniel Goleman, *Emotional Intelligence*

The electoral domain is characterized by the *ad hominem* attack. Both sides are always assailing each other, getting offended about it, retaliating, and getting offended again. Why is the political realm so suffused with anger? We can take a clue from the world of show business, where it has long been understood that if you want to sell tickets, you need a villain. When a candidate wants us to pay attention, he/she trashes the opponent. It always works.

Howard Cosell was a famous sportscaster whose career reached its peak in the 1960s and 1970s. He will live forever on ESPN Classics history as one of Muhammad Ali's principal interviewers, and baiters. I was always fascinated by the fact that virtually all Americans hated Howard, yet he was said to be a "popular sportscaster." One evening while watching Monday Night Football I realized that a key selling point of the show was that it permitted groups of men to assemble all over America to laugh at Howard's pomposity.

Cosell was known for his showy vocabulary, which was ridiculed by his fellow announcers, football legends Don Meredith and Frank Gifford. Whenever Howard would utter one of his classic inanities, such as, "It would appear that Staubach will have to expeditiously prestidigitate the Cowboys into the end-zone with a modicum of his customary legerdemain and savoir-faire," football fans throughout the nation would joyfully roar their contempt: "Howard, you a—hole!" Meredith and Gifford strove to keep their disdain for Cosell from showing, but were often unsuccessful.

This got good ratings, but everybody looked forward to the day when the annoying jerk would retire. When he did, he was replaced by another football legend, Joe Namath. Namath, Meredith and Gifford, all handsome, talkative, affable Hall-of-Famers, were a football-announcing dream team, expected to easily surpass the ratings achieved in the Cosell era. It never happened — ratings declined. People had loved hating Howard. Without him, the show lacked spice.

The same effect is common in politics. We love hating the other side. In most of our recent presidential elections, American voters have been more motivated by anger and disliking for the other side than by true admiration for their own candidate. In 1996, if you had been able to plumb the soul of the average Republican voter, you would have discovered that they were far more motivated by dislike for Clinton more than by love of Dole. Again, in 2004, Democratic voters were more motivated by their dislike for Bush than by their admiration for Kerry. Anger gets us to the polls. Love doesn't.

Anger is energizing — it releases catecholamines, neurotransmitters which act as energy stimulants, your brain's own version of Red Bull. We get a pleasurable little kick of out of political indignation, an anger buzz. It should not be surprising that anger and indignation are amongst the principal commodities of the political marketplace. In the political sphere, parties and politicians manufacture indignation and the media distribute it efficiently to eager consumers in the various markets. The next time you feel yourself getting angry during a televised documentary or news report on a political theme, ask yourself whether the broadcaster is peddling more than just a quick fix for indignation junkies.

An academic study of negative political advertising, *Going Negative,* by political scientists Stephen Ansolabehere and Shanto Iyengar, revealed that negative ads are effective in getting partisans to the polls, but moderates and independents are so turned-off that, in the end, overall voter participation actually declines.

Ansolabehere and Iyengar suggest that as a result negative advertising might be good strategy for at least one of the candidates in every election — the one who fears that a large turnout will benefit the opponent. Since today's professional pollsters can determine early in the campaign who is more likely to benefit from a high turnout, negative advertising is probably going to remain a staple of our elections for a long time to come:

Negative campaigning transforms elections into an entertaining spectator sport…. Those who do vote represent increasingly partisan groups within the electorate. Campaign advertising has contributed significantly to the disappearance of the non-partisan voter and the polarization of elections…. [A]dvertising removes the incentives for candidates, journalists and groups to foster public spiritedness. Candidates care only about their market shares, not about the total turnout. Reporters care only about their bylines, not about whether their stories foster faith in the political system…. [O]nce the gates of negative campaigning are opened, they are difficult to close. The best way to answer an attack is with another attack, and journalists, who thrive on political conflict, echo the negativity of the campaigns in their own critical and cynical reporting.[93]

The paradoxical role of political journalists in sustaining a vicious environment deserves greater scrutiny from voters. Journalists routinely claim to decry negative campaigning, but since no one benefits from it more than they do, we should anticipate a journalistic tendency to make political mountains out of campaign molehills.

How to Flout the Popular Will and Discourage Voting in the Name of Democracy: the Electoral College

The Electoral College system is the canary in the mine of American political irrationality. So long as the Electoral College exists, political irrationality thrives, and we must question whether Americans have any hunger for true democracy. The only possible explanation for the persistence of this antiquated mechanism is rational ignorance. If voters bothered to inform themselves, the Electoral College would collapse like a house of cards.

Our red vs. blue divide is a direct creation of the Electoral College. Without the Electoral College system, we would have no red-and-blue maps on election night. Instead, the maps would look like a crazy, fractal quilt, closer to our multicultural reality.

The Electoral College not only exacerbates our culture war, it fails to make sense from a democratic point of view:

1. We accept absurd results. Americans continue to accept that is possible to lose the popular vote and still win the election. George W. Bush was elected president in 2000 even though he had lost the popular vote by 500,000 votes. Liberal groups were furious with the 2000 election, but their fury failed to translate into a national debate on the Electoral College system. Our passivity is disconcerting. It is theoretically possible to achieve much greater disparities than the one observed in 2000. If a highly-polarizing candidate were to win all the red states by 51% but receive only a small fraction of the vote in the blue states (or vice versa), we could end up electing a president who would have lost the popular vote by twenty or thirty million votes. The Electoral College system leaves America open to truly ridiculous results.

2. The Electoral College strongly discourages voting. Every four years we are urged from all sides to do our civic duty of voting. Without delving into the larger irrationalities of voting already discussed earlier, let us simply observe here that the Founding Fathers understandably failed to foresee the overnight Gallup Polls. If one of the candidates has a 25-point lead in your state on the eve of the election, it can seem truly pointless to vote. All of those civic-minded appeals to vote, showered upon us by celebrities of every stripe, never address the simple question: why vote when you already know the outcome? Gallup and Roper are never going to be off by 25 points (the polls can be wildly inaccurate during the primary season, but as the general election nears they become increasingly reliable). It is a huge surprise when presidential election-eve polls are off by even three points. A five-point lead on election eve is close to insurmountable.

In some states, like Massachusetts, the result is a foregone conclusion years in advance. For the past thirty years it has been a safe bet that the next Democratic candidate would take Massachusetts. Why then, do the people in Massachusetts keep voting, since they know in advance which side is going to win? Many voters quite rationally choose to stay home, only to be castigated by the punditocracy for contributing to the "decline in voting."

In an era of increasing red vs. blue polarization, we can expect that more and more states will fall into the same category as Massachusetts, Texas and New York. In an unlikely but conceivable dystopia of total polarization, it would be possible to know the outcome in every state well in advance. No one would have to vote any more because everyone would know in advance how everyone else would vote — if anybody did. Our political system would validate Yogi Berra's classic restaurant review: "No one ever goes there anymore because it's too crowded."

3. The Electoral College is bizarre and peculiar. This strange contraption was cobbled together as a last-minute compromise when every other alternative had failed. It is now the conspicuous sore thumb of democracy. Every year America holds thousands and thousands of elections. In all those other elections, a margin of one vote provides victory. Only in our most important election is it possible to receive one million fewer votes than your opponent and still win. If there is any sense to the Electoral College mechanism, why don't we see it in place elsewhere? No other American state or municipality employs anything like it, nor does any other country.

4. The Electoral College was created out of fear of democracy. We all remember from our high school civics classes that the Electoral College was devised by the Founding Fathers to protect the interests of the small states. Since even the least-populous states are guaranteed two senators, no state can have fewer than three electoral votes. To this day, supporters of the Electoral College continue to parrot this single, solitary benefit. It forces the presidential candidates to focus attention on the smaller states; or at the very least, it keeps the candidates from focusing exclusively on the largest states.

This is a trivial, imaginary benefit. Does anyone really believe that the small-state focus in presidential campaigning measurably improves the lives of citizens in those states? There is an implicit understanding here that presidents will reach into the pork barrel to repay the small states that supported them — but is that a good thing? There is no proof that the republic as a whole is more efficiently governed because the candidates spend two or three extra days campaigning in a small state, or because they spend more of their TV advertising in a swing state. It is of no benefit to the nation as a whole that Florida or Ohio received a slightly-more-punishing regime of manipulative political advertising than the citizens of neighboring states. Nonetheless, it is largely for such illusory benefits that we accept a system in which the winner may have been rejected by the clear majority of voters — the *opposite* of democracy as commonly understood everywhere in the world.

The Presidential Survivor Show: Why We Love It So

The best that can be said about our presidential system is that it rotates power between two different kinds of elite. This is in accord with the minimalist conception of democracy put forward in the 1940s by the great Austrian economist Joseph Schumpeter. In Schumpeter's view, it was naïve to believe that democracy was a form of government controlled by the popular will. Rather, Schumpeter saw democracy as merely a system for periodically changing the leadership at random intervals. For Schumpeter, the potential for an orderly transfer of power was enough to mark significant progress over monarchy, in which ineffective leadership could persist for decades or centuries.[94]

However, Schumpeter's explanation does nothing to illuminate the vast popular interest generated by the American election. If our presidential campaigns are meaningless festivals of irrationality, why do we love them so much? Americans are completely besotted with presidents and presidential elections. Our national heartbeat is tuned to a four-year cycle. Every fourth year the entire media complex, from lowliest blog to the *New York Times*, growls noisily to life in anticipation of the election year, a long season of media obsession. If the campaign is as meaningless as the evidence appears to indicate, why are we (and all other nations) so fascinated by it? In previous sections I have focused on evolutionary reasons for a predisposition to be fascinated with contests for power. To this, let me add a cultural explanation.

To understand our obsession with presidential campaigns, we have to appreciate that our election is more than a political event. In a very real sense, it is a religious event. With the decline of traditional religions as national unifiers, the political process has stepped into the vacuum. The presidential election is our most important national ritual — it is a symbol of who we are as a people. To their credit, the Founders feared monarchy as much as they did democracy. They attempted to prevent the office of the presidency from acquiring monarchic importance and trappings by placing the Presidency on a status roughly equivalent to that of the Speaker of the House or the Chief Justice of the Supreme Court. Thus, the Constitution forces the President to get approval for all executive appointments from the Senate, and the right to originate legislation is left entirely to the Congress. The Founders hoped this fragmented structure would prevent the

President from becoming too pre-eminent. Their failure has been embarrassingly total. The Presidency and the election process have provided Americans with an unending source of popular entertainment in ways that the Founders failed to anticipate.

From the very first administration, the figure of the U.S. Presidency loomed over all other governmental branches in prestige. This should have been anticipated — whatever is rare is coveted. The Speaker of the House is one of 435; a Senator is one of a 100; a Chief Justice is one of nine. Only the President is unique. The imposing aura of the office was further dignified by its first holder, the most eminent American of all time. It is revealing that George Washington's portrait graces the dollar bill, unifying our two most potent national icons. Benjamin Franklin and Alexander Hamilton are the only non-Presidents ever to figure on U.S. paper currency, while all other bills feature former Commanders-in-Chief. No senator, governor, congressperson, military leader, artist, doctor or scientist has ever been successful enough in our eyes to merit this honor. The French, in contrast, were even known to put *poets* on their currency (in the days of the French franc).

The presidency is a mirror held up to the face of American society. We are defined by our presidents. Our schoolchildren learn a history paced in presidential administrations, as if history proceeded in four-year increments. Perpetually succumbing to the narrative fallacy, we use presidents to make sense of the inscrutable weave of history. Thus, to most Americans, the Civil War is as much a tale of Lincoln's leadership as it is of the nameless 600,000 dead and wounded. Did America survive the Great Depression? *Thanks to FDR's sweeping vision.* Were the 1950's calm and tranquil years? *Due to Eisenhower's serene but uninspiring leadership.* Were the 1960s exciting times of change? *Ushered in by JFK's bold new style.* Was America confident in the 1980s? *Reagan's inspiration.* Is American power resented around the world? *Bush's arrogance.*

The political world is infinitely, disturbingly complex, so we simplify it with an easy formula. When our party's president is in power, we are living the good times. When the opposite is true, we are in the bad times. Our large chaotic world is condensed into a single, affectively-weighted symbol.

Despite the best intentions of the Founders, the American president has become a secular monarch. Consider the regal trappings of the office. All monarchs have had splendid abodes and palaces, but our president lives in the most famous residence since Versailles. Monarchs have always traveled in style — but could any royal carriage rival the majesty of Air Force One escorted by a phalanx of F–16's? P. Diddy's posse of bodyguards makes him the king of New York, but they better step back when they see the Secret Service approaching in those trademark shades. The court of Louis XIV glittered with brilliance, but not more so than black-tie dinners at the White House in JFK's Camelot days.

Monarchs have always lived in fear of their lives, and our president is no exception. Whenever the American president ventures outside the imperial grounds of the White House to have a meal in any restaurant or hotel, a team of two Secret Service agents is assigned to watch the cooks prepare the Presidential repast, lest the great one be poisoned by a culinary assassin. Does anyone know how the Speaker of the House (or Chief Justice of the Supreme Court), travels? Or where they live? No one watches their food being prepared. Barely anyone knows their names. It is one thing to be grand vizier, another thing entirely to the monarch.

The president is thus a person of intense, almost overpowering interest. To this enormous celebrity we must now add the inherent drama of electoral conflict. Like sporting events, elections are sanitized forms of warfare. Any one-on-one election has an irresistibly fascinating story line. In the end, one side will be guzzling champagne and throwing party-streamers, while the other side will slink away, bloodied, beaten and unemployed.

When you combine the dramatic elements of conflict and defeat, inherent to elections, with the greatest prize offered by any contest in history — the American Presidency — you get a spectacle which is irresistibly riveting. Call it *Presidential Survivor,* the ultimate "must-watch" TV. No wonder that Hunter S. Thompson said that watching American elections was "better than sex." The battle may well be irrelevant and meaningless in terms of translating the policy preferences of citizens into governmental action, but that doesn't mean it's not incredibly fun to watch.

Joyce Carol Oates captured the gritty allure of prizefighting when she called it a "theater of reality." Politics, similarly, is a theater of reality, though it is more difficult than with boxing to tell where the theater ends and the reality begins. Still, victory and defeat can be equally glaring in both cases. The concrete reality underlying our highly-theatrical election process is that one of the candidates will end up a laughing stock, while the other will hold the levers of vast power. Even the most cynical of political observers must concede that it matters who wins. If not to the nation, it certainly matters to the candidates.

In the weeks leading up to a presidential election, Democrats and Republicans reveal their preferences in millions of discussions across the land. Some of the discussions are cordial, but many are not. "Trash talk" and banter are tossed back and forth, much of it by the candidates themselves. The day after the election, a lot of Americans are going to have to eat crow, and keep on eating it for four years. That is a true source of drama. There is a lot at stake on election night for all voting Americans. Many Americans watch the Super Bowl, but the number of spectators betting on the game is still a small minority. In politics, however, all voters are in a sense bettors, who have risked at least the time and effort it takes to vote, and usually more than that — their pride.

While it is moderately acceptable, at least in some parts of the country, not to watch the Super Bowl, it is practically morally reprehensible not to catch election fever. As the election approaches, the media collude to create an atmosphere of utmost urgency and suspense, practically screaming at us:

"It all matters so much!"

"The future of mankind depends on the outcome!"

"Keep watching TV!"

What will happen on America's next election night? One thing is a certainty: eyeballs will be glued to the TV screen, advertisers will pay top dollar for access to those viewers, and the coffers of the media giants will swell again with profit.

Conclusion: It's Time for a Change

Is any of this a bad thing? So what if we are obsessed with a trivial, negative and undemocratic mechanism? Even a meaningless election can provide us with a minimum, Schumpeterian form of democracy, and that is probably better than hereditary monarchy. Although policy issues may not have decisive importance in the election, the campaign process does allow Americans to vent their political spleen. Studies show the citizenry is not greatly educated by the process, but they do pick up a few things. The great interest generated by the dramatic subtext of the election forces the people to think about politics a little more than they do in other years, and that also may be a good thing.

Nonetheless, there is much to be condemned in our national campaign obsession. Americans are encouraged to believe that by participating in this quadrennial spectacle they have done their political duty. Americans who vote walk away from each election feeling they have accomplished something that they can be proud of. They may not have researched any of the issues; they may not have changed parties in thirty years; their vote may be a purely automatic response to environmental stimuli or manipulative advertising; they may be completely unaware of local politics and community issues; their exposure to campaign rhetoric may have made them more polarized and angry; but, they've voted, and feel they can go home and rest for four more years.

Here, the citizenry sets the bar for democracy too low. What good are you doing your country if you vote like an automaton without any deep understanding of the issues? Conversely, what real choice is your country giving you if your only option is to periodically confirm your partisan prejudices?

The harsh truth, as the Athenians discovered two millennia ago, is that elections are good for demagogues but bad for democracy. If we want democracy, we will have to find a better way. In the meantime, though, elections are extremely fun to watch.

CHAPTER 12

Obama Zen: The Color of Hope

DARK TRUTH #12
*Our hopes reveal not only our dreams but also our fears
and frustrations; no one hopes for something they already have.*

A leader is a dealer in hope. — Napoleon, *Maxims* (1804–1815)

Every political rationalist must accept that rationality is often about as welcome as a cold shower. When the opposition political party is in power, our fellow partisans laugh heartily when we satirize the irrationalities of government. However, when our own president is in power, those governmental irrationalities become less interesting, and our friends would rather not hear about them.

As a rationalist with liberal inclinations, therefore, it was with mixed feelings that I watched President Barack Obama succeed President George W. Bush. President Bush, for all his defects, had been one of history's greatest promoters of the concept of political irrationality. While he was in office, it was not difficult to make the case that there was something fundamentally irrational about our political system.

President Obama, on the other hand, presented a new challenge. His victory appeared to symbolize the opposite of political irrationality, a triumph of tolerance over the irrationality of racism. When President Obama announced that he wanted to make government "cool again," the multitudes (the liberal multitudes, at least) responded with a throbbing adoration that showed that, whatever they thought of government, they considered their new president to be the coolest man on the planet. As Reagan had twenty years before him (and JFK twenty years before that), Obama made the country feel good again. Americans fell back in love with America. Ethnic minorities around the world looked on with wonder and a sense of inspiration. School-children of color dared dream bigger dreams than they had ever dreamed before.

Of course, it is always nice to see Americans (or anyone else) feeling so good about themselves. Nothing is more human than the urge to celebrate an accomplishment. However, as we saw in Chapter 2, human vanity is a powerful driver of erroneous perceptions. Although it was a basic tenet of New Age parenting that a child's self-esteem should always be boosted, recent research has come to a contrary conclusion. A balance is needed. Too much self-esteem and you fail to see your own flaws. Studies have shown, for example, that bullies and violent criminals tend to have very high self-esteem. National self-esteem, like personal self-esteem, is an unreliable indicator of rationality and psychological health. When we see someone celebrating immoderately, we are not impressed but rather suspect that they have some psychic wound or sense of inferiority to conceal. America's orgy of self-congratulation over the victory of Barack Obama was in this way suspiciously extravagant.

The overpowering hunger for celebration was certainly understandable. With two costly wars underway and an economic recession looming, Americans were starved for good news, which explains in part why Obama's election became such a national obsession. As a liberal, I am inclined to agree with other liberals that President Obama is a brilliant and dedicated statesman. However, as a committed rationalist I also feel obliged to cast a few drops of cold rain on this happy parade.

Despite the new president's undeniable qualities, the American political system remains today exactly what it was before his election. Our government is an oligarchy masquerading as a democracy. The election of a single inspiring leader cannot possibly change that. The election of one enlightened politician is insufficient to redeem a flawed system. This was amply demonstrated by the corruption scandal which broke out immediately after the election (in which Governor Rod Blagojevich of Illinois was charged with attempting to sell Obama's newly-vacant Senate seat). As I have argued in the preceding chapters, our current system will always tend to produce more politicians like Blagojevich than like Obama.

It was on the issue of race that Obama's election was taken to be most symbolically inspiring, and it is here that we will find the greatest popular self-deception.

In the 2008 election Barack Obama dominated almost every American demographic, yet gained only 53% of the final vote. Obama received over 95% of the black vote, 78% of the Jewish vote, 68% of the Latino vote and 62% of the Asian vote. Why, then, was the winning margin so narrow? The answer lies in the fact that Obama soundly lost the nation's largest demographic: whites. Obama received only 43% of the white vote and only 41% of votes from white men. Although Obama actually did better among whites than John Kerry had in 2004, the results in 2008 are regrettably quite consistent with a substantial residue of anti-black prejudice from whites (no Democratic candidate has carried the white vote since 1964).

Between 2000 and 2008 the U.S. Hispanic population grew by 32%, the Asian population by 30%, the black population by 9% and the white population by 2%. The proportion of whites who harbor racist prejudice has therefore probably diminished as a percentage of the total, but there is little evidence that the historical effects of racism are fading.

As President Obama began his administration, African-Americans represented 13% of the American population but 55% of federal prisoners. In early 2009, as the economic recession began to take its toll in jobs, unemployment was 6.6% among whites and 11.9% among blacks. From the point of view of statistical equality, the U.S. Senate in 2009 should have included thirteen African-Americans; instead, there was only one.

It would be naïve and unrealistic to believe that the election of Barack Obama could have any major positive impact, in the short term, on the above-cited statistics. Indeed, the incoming president announced specific time-tables on ending the Iraq War and on achieving energy independence, but made no specific promises as to when Americans would begin to achieve racial equality. As the above statistics show, that time is not likely to come soon. America's racial problems are far from over.

With Obama's election Americans must confront the growing chasm between symbolic racial victories and racial realities. The success of individual African-Americans can no longer be taken as a symbolic proxy for true equality. Symbols of equality can be enormously attractive and inspiring, but they can never satisfy our desire for true equality.

One of the reasons that America's racial divide is so intractable is that there are aspects of racism which Americans stubbornly refuse to acknowledge. In this chapter, I will focus primarily on one aspect of this refusal, our national oversimplification of race.

Obama and the Diversity of African-American Experience

> Other than color, Obama did not — does not — share a heritage with the majority of black Americans, who are descendants of plantation slaves.... So when black Americans refer to Obama as "one of us," I do not know what they are talking about.... — Stanley Crouch, *NY Daily News* (2006)

> "I go by the one-drop rule. One drop [of black blood], and you're black. The truth is, every African-American is biracial. Go back far enough, and you'll find the massah was in the slave quarters." — Spike Lee, quoted at Democratic Convention (2008)

Barack Obama's 2008 victory in the U.S. presidential election was historic because it represented the first time a predominantly white nation had elected a non-white head of state. The global press trumpeted Obama's victory as a triumph over racism which was particularly redemptive in light of America's legacy of slavery.

Given the public attention to the candidate's racial background, it made news when a few African-American pundits expressed the opinion that Obama was not really "black." These contrarian journalists pointed out that Obama had been raised by a white mother and grandparents and had had little contact with African-American culture prior to adulthood. Was Obama "black enough?" Given that over 95% of African-Americans voted for him, the resounding answer seemed to be: yes.

The critiques of Obama's blackness never attracted popular support. When Obama gained victory in the Iowa primary, the issue virtually disappeared. After the 2008 election, discussion of Obama's blackness was increasingly interpreted as churlish or even racist (though the issue had in fact arisen first in the black community). A new taboo had formed.

Given President Obama's early popularity, America's disinterest was perhaps understandable. Nonetheless, a reluctance to fully engage the issue of the president's ethnicity masked several important contradictions. American racism is a complex phenomenon, replete with contradiction and self-deception. The writers who raised the issue of President Obama's blackness were prematurely silenced. By avoiding a potentially awkward discussion of the president's bi-raciality, we missed an important opportunity to come to a deeper understanding of racism.

A profitable discussion of the president's ethnicity does not necessarily imply a criticism or rejection of the president. Even the first writers who raised the issue of Obama's blackness (Stanley Crouch and Debra Dickerson, for example) ended up supporting Obama and celebrating his victory.

The issue of "black enough" for politics did not arise with Obama nor will it disappear with his election. It is a recurrent American political theme which we should now try to decode. Prior to Obama's 2008 candidacy, for example, it had recently been observed in the 2002 electoral duel between two African-American candidates, old-school Sharpe James, the former Mayor of Newark, and his challenger and eventual successor, Cory Booker. Booker, a Stanford grad and Rhodes scholar with suburban roots, was notoriously ridiculed by James as a "faggot white boy" and a "white Republican." Booker's authenticity as a representative of under-privileged blacks was challenged in light of his economically-privileged background and ties to wealthy and glamorous financiers.

In 2002, Jesse Jackson and Al Sharpton endorsed Sharpe James, who was running for his fifth consecutive term as mayor. James squeaked out a contested victory. Booker, however, did not slink away. When Booker returned for another scrap in 2006, James abandoned his mayoral campaign and Booker cruised to a 70% landslide, establishing himself as a rising star of American politics (while James was left to face indictments for corruption). By 2006, Booker was no longer criticized for not being black enough.

Obama himself failed to overcome the not-black-enough rhetoric in his first attempt at national office. In his 2000 Congressional race against the highly-respected former Black Panther leader Bobby Rush, Barack Obama was defeated by thirty points. Although Rush did not specifically tag Obama with the not-black label, he did point out Obama's lack of experience with the civil rights struggle: "[Obama] went to Harvard and became an educated fool.... Barack is a person who read about the civil-rights protests and thinks he knows all about it."

On the street, the action was rougher. One of Obama's political operatives, Al Kindle, recalled the harshness of these early encounters:

> "The accusations were that Obama was sent here and owned by the Jews. That he was here to steal the black vote and steal black land and that he was represented by the—as they were called—'the white man.' And that Obama wasn't black enough and didn't know the black experience, the black community. It was quite deafening...People would say, 'Oh, Kindle, man, we trust you, you being fooled. Obama's got you fooled.' And some people called me a traitor."[95]

Obama overcame the bruising defeat to Rush, returning in 2004 to win a special election for the U.S. Senate with the overwhelming margin of 70%. Obama's opponent in the 2004 Senate race, Alan Keyes, also attempted to make a not-black-enough attack on Obama (Keyes is African-American). This time the approach drew more ridicule than support.

The experiences of Obama and Booker suggest that young black politicians with elite backgrounds will commonly face this challenge in their first electoral appeals to black working-class voters. The Ivy-league interlopers must first establish their "street creds" if they hope to be viable candidates. When Cory Booker challenged him in 2002, Sharpe James taunted Booker by insinuating that Booker had to "learn to be black." Booker responded by demonstrating the sincerity of his commitment to the black community. Astonishing the press (and his neighbors) he chose to live in the downtown projects in Newark.

Booker and Obama invested heavily in acquiring the necessary credibility with the local community, and they both achieved that credibility. Obama spent years as a community organizer on Chicago's South Side, later marrying into a prominent South Side family and becoming a pillar of the local community. However, the fact that both men had to work so hard suggests the existence of an underlying dynamic of rational scrutiny. There is nothing wrong with black working-class voters wanting to make sure that their representatives have shared their experiences. Later, though, when those same African-American candidates seek state-wide or nation-wide office, the not-black rhetoric becomes increasingly strained, because it is harder to understand why white voters should care whether a candidate is black enough.

On at least one occasion, a politician was rejected by the electorate as not black enough. In the 1984 elections for the Stockton City Council, a black incumbent by the name of Ralph White was unseated by a "black" challenger named Mark Stebbins. The problem, in Mr. White's view, was that Mr. Stebbins was not really black. Although Stebbins possessed frizzy hair, the overall physical impression he gave was of an ordinary white American.[96]

After losing the election, Mr. White conducted some research on Mr. Stebbins. He then called a news conference at which he angrily brandished a copy of Stebbins' birth certificate, which listed Stebbins' race as white, as well as that of both of Stebbins' parents.

"If the momma is an elephant and the daddy is an elephant, they durn sure can't have no lion," explained White, "They got to have a baby elephant."

When pressed on how he could be sure that Stebbins was not black, White responded: "I know white when I see it." He further explained: "His hair is the big thing. I know he's had a permanent."

Stebbins protested that he was, in fact, black. He claimed to be "socially, culturally and genetically black," tracing his ancestry to an unspecified black grandparent. He sniffed that the question could even be raised: "It's terribly significant that you can still ask a man's race twenty years after the Civil Rights Act."

Stebbins pointed out that he was married to a black woman, lived in the black community, and had been an active civil rights protester and activist for twenty years. Indeed, many prominent members of the local black community were of the opinion that Stebbins was black enough, or at the very least, felt that it was unfair for White to raise the issue. Thus, the Rev. Bob Hailey, chairman of the Stockton chapter of the Black American Political Association of California, said that Stebbins was, "one of the bright spots here. In my estimation, he thinks black and is black."

In terms of credibility as a representative of the ordinary black voter, Stebbins seemed to have a slight edge. Stebbins was known as a tireless activist and the organizer of community gardens, while White was primarily known for his opulent 27-room mansion and numerous rental properties. After two recall elections, the Stockton voters were perhaps confused. A man named White who was actually black was claiming that his opponent was a white claiming to be black. Mr. White was indubitably black, but was the other white black as well? For reasons that were hard to decipher, Stebbins was booted out on the second recall. The baby lion was snubbed by the somewhat puzzled elephant herd.

What does it mean to be black in America? The experiences of Stebbins and White, like those of Booker and Obama, suggest that the answer is not always as simple as one might think. In fact, both white and black Americans habitually oversimplify the issue of race.

Oversimplification #1: All blacks in America share a common cultural bond.

This common misperception is unfortunately magnified by the popular use of the term "African-American." Although the term's popularity is understandable (it promotes a sense of historic pride), it is nonetheless confusing. Most black Americans have only a distant and remote African ancestry, while many newer African immigrants (including whites and North-African Arabs, for example) have a more direct tie to Africa. This illogic was exposed when a white teen-ager who had grown up in South Africa applied for an "African-American" scholarship at his new high school in Colorado. Quite correctly, the school decided that he was not eligible, though no one could deny the boy's technical claim to status as an "African-American." The scholarship was intended to benefit under-privileged black people who had grown up in the U.S., not over-privileged white people who had emigrated from Cape Town. However, the mix-up revealed the potential for confusion.

The term "African-American" became increasingly popular after 1988, when the Rev. Jesse Jackson held a news conference to urge its widespread adoption. At first, the change caught on slowly. In a survey of blacks conducted by the *Washington Post* in 1989, 66% of respondents still preferred the term "black," while only 22% preferred "African-American" and 10% liked both terms. However, by 2003 those preferences had largely reversed. The same survey now showed that 48% preferred "African-American," 35% preferred "black" and 17% liked both terms.

Meanwhile, over the time period in which the term "African-American" became ascendant, the U.S. received a very large number of immigrant blacks with roots in the Caribbean or Sub-Saharan Africa. In the 1990s, the number of American blacks with roots in Africa tripled, while the number of blacks of Caribbean origin grew by 60%. By 2000, foreign born blacks constituted nearly a third of all blacks in New York City and Boston.

The potential ambiguity within the term "African-American" became not just a matter of semantics, but an issue with true political significance. In 2004, for example, the *New York Times* reported on a conference of public health experts in Silver Springs, Maryland, on the topic of how to educate African-Americans about the dangers of prostate cancer. An Ethiopian-born activist, Abdulaziz Kamus, had attempted to argue that there should be more of a focus on African immigrants. He was surprised to find himself rebuked by black Americans, who insisted that the purpose of the campaign was to focus on native-born blacks.[97]

According to Kamus: "I said, 'But I am African and I am an American citizen; am I not African-American?' They said, 'No, no, no, not you.' The census is claiming me as an African-American. If I walk down the streets, white people see me as an African-American. Yet African-Americans are saying, 'You are not one of us.' So I ask myself, in this country, how do I define myself?"

In fact, black America is every bit as multi-cultural as the rest of America. Americans with a high percentage of African ancestry fall into many culturally-distinct groups: black Americans descended from West African slaves (the largest group); African-Native American descendents; Spanish/French/English/Creole-speaking West Indian immigrants; Central American immigrants; Brazilians; African first- and second-generation immigrants; blacks born in Europe; and, bi-racial and multi-racial mixtures between these groups and other groups (e.g., Tiger Woods).

Both white and black Americans tend only to "see" the first group, and to lump everyone else of color into that group, which leads to misunderstanding and resentment. West Indian, African and Brazilian immigrants often complain that the distinctions between their cultures and black American culture are insufficiently appreciated.

Increasingly, black Americans have also maintained that ambiguities of race and class can be detrimental to American-born blacks with a slave ancestry. Thus, at a 2004 reunion of Harvard University's black alumni, Professors Lani Guinier and Henry Louis Gates issued a statement of concern that more than half of Harvard's "black" students were West Indian and African immigrants or their children. Their statement generated a sharp debate within the black educational community about whether or not the ancestry of black students was relevant. Thus, Orlando Patterson, a Harvard sociology professor and West Indian native, said he wished others would just "let sleeping dogs lie."

But Prof. Mary C. Waters, another Harvard sociologist and an expert on West Indian immigrants in the U.S., demurred: "You need a philosophical discussion about what are the aims of affirmative action. If it's about getting black faces at Harvard, then you're doing fine. If it's about making up for 200 to 500 years of slavery in this country and its aftermath, then you're not doing well. And if it's about having diversity that includes African-Americans from the South or from inner-city high schools, then you're not doing well, either."

These cultural fault-lines are quite apparent to those who experience them in their daily lives.* Sheila Adams was a Harvard senior in 2004. She had met many blacks at Harvard, but few with backgrounds like her own: born in the Bronx to a school security officer and a subway token seller. Adams said that there were so few black students like her at Harvard that they had taken to referring to themselves as "the descendants." Aisha Haynie, another Harvard student at the time, said she had been spurred to research the ancestry of black students by the reaction of her black classmates when she told them that she was not from the West Indies or Africa, but from the Carolinas: "They would say, 'No, where are you really from?'"

A similar type of cultural oversimplification is found in the American custom of grouping a number of highly-diverse cultures under the general rubric of "Latino" or "Hispanic." If a candidate of Cuban or Argentine descent were to reach the White House, it would probably be celebrated by the press as a victory for Latinos in general. However, we might find some reticence from the most-populous Hispanic minority, Mexican-Americans. Cuban-, Argentinean- and Mexican-Americans have highly distinct cultures and each of these groups would like the rest of Americans to know it.

Another over-simplification is represented in the term "Asian-American," which also melts down dozens of rich, distinct cultures into a single stereotype.

Oversimplification # 2: Exposure to racism in America is similar for all blacks.

---

*See, e.g., "Definition of 'African-American' Becoming a Debate of Heritage," *New York Times,* April 29, 2004.

African-American culture has greatly stratified according to skin-tone and class. The life experience of wealthy, highly-educated blacks is fundamentally different than that of poor, working-class blacks. We could almost speak of two separate cultures linked by a common color, except that even the color is different. African-Americans are subject to "colorism" from both whites and blacks (colorism is the tendency to treat light-skinned people better than the dark-skinned). As we will see further below, pervasive colorism is the secret shame of African-American culture (as it is, indeed, of global culture). Our squeamishness in dealing with the president's racial mixture allows related issues, such as that of colorism, to remain un-explored, hence un-solved.

The black population has not only stratified according to skin tone, but also economically and educationally. For a young black person with only a high school diploma, it is much harder to land a job than a comparably qualified white person. The same is not necessarily true for black graduates of Harvard Law School. America's top law firms and government agencies — all committed to the ideals of diversity — must compete against each other to recruit from the limited pool of black and Hispanic candidates at the leading law schools. For African-Americans from privileged backgrounds or with elite educations, race is not a disadvantage in the same way it is for African-Americans from working-class backbrounds. From a socio-economic perspective, African-American society (like white society) is a gold-capped pyramid, a small wealthy triangle perched atop a vast base of the middle-class and poor. For African-Americans in the top section of the pyramid, the traditional American narratives of racial oppression can be inappropriate and even patronizing.

Oversimplification #3: When a black person marries a white person, their children are black.

Americans today have agreed by consensus to classify race according to a simple formula, which is literally black and white. A person is either entirely black, or entirely white. It seems impolite, and even a trifle racist, to talk of "in-between." When President Obama referred to himself as a "mutt" in an early press conference, the national response was an awkward silence. In America we are nonplused by the concept of the half-breed. Despite this, the category of "in-between" has a long and rich history which is increasingly relevant today.

Many Latin American and Caribbean nations, with much higher proportions of black and brown peoples than the U.S., are composed almost entirely of "in-between" populations. Most of these societies were once structured on caste systems which corresponded to gradations in skin color.

The American custom, in contrast, is known as the "one drop rule." It was notoriously exemplified in the *Plessy v. Ferguson* ruling of the U.S. Supreme Court in 1896. In that case, the Supreme Court upheld the State of Louisiana's right to prevent Homer Plessy from boarding a "whites only" train compartment, though Plessy was only one-eighth black. The Supreme Court's ruling implicitly supported the "one-drop" theory, which held that one drop of black blood was enough to taint a person as non-white. Ironically, though, that "racist" one-drop principle still underlies our current black/white simplification of the American racial divide. In particular, it is responsible for our classification of President Obama as black. Since the president is precisely half-black and half-white, from a logical perspective it makes just as much sense to classify him as "white" as it does to classify him "black." When we call the president a black man we are guilty of a culturally-approved form of racism.

Compare the American approach, which might be called "one-drop of black," with Brazilian custom, which we could call "one-drop of white." The Brazilian census allows Brazilians to classify themselves as white, brown ("pardo"), black, yellow or indigenous. As a practical result, Brazilians make great use of the in-between concept of brown. In everyday usage, the terms "moreno" (brown) and "moreno claro" (light brown) are used more often than "pardo." Roughly forty percent of Brazilians identify themselves as "moreno" or "moreno claro."

If a Brazilian "moreno claro" comes to the U.S., he may be disconcerted to find himself classified by Americans as "black." If the Brazilian protests, he may be criticized for trying to "pass" and deny his blackness (the same experience is common for Caribbean and Central American immigrants).

The opposed one-drop principles represent differing approaches to the social fact of racism. The American one-drop principle set a high barrier to entry (i.e., genetic purity) to the privileges of white society. In America's slave-holding days, "brown" was placed on the black side of the white/black fence. The Brazilian approach, in contrast, derived from the response of non-whites to racism. Aware of the social stigma that attached to blackness, but allowed by Brazilian custom to self-classify, Brazilians of color adopted the broad "moreno" category, which encompasses a large number of ethnicities and cultural mixtures. The concepts of "whiteness" and "blackness" in Brazil are consequently ones of gradation. Many Brazilians who self-identify as white would be considered people "of color" in America. It is noted with self-deprecating humor by Brazilians that in Brazil color is enhanced by wealth and status. Wealth has a detectably "whitening" effect on the self-perceptions of upper-class Brazilians.

If we looked at President Obama's election from a Brazilian or Caribbean perspective, we could arrive at an interpretation that might seem shocking or cynical to Americans. When voters elect a candidate like Barack Obama it is not, strictly speaking, a victory for "blacks." More accurately, it is a victory for the "moreno." As the independent historian J.B. Bird observed with regard to former Secretary of State Colin Powell:

> Many other countries of the Americas do not follow the one-drop approach. As an example of the U.S. distinction, consider the case of U.S. Secretary of State Colin Powell. Though he clearly appears to be of mixed African-European ancestry, in the U.S. Powell is described simply as "black," and in fact it would be considered offensive if *The Wall Street Journal* described him as a "light-skinned black"... Such is not the case in all countries of the world. In most countries of the Caribbean, Colin Powell would be described as a Creole, reflecting his mixed heritage. In Belize, he might further be described as a "High Creole," because of his extremely light complexion. So which is he, black or Creole? It depends on the culture making the distinction. Ethnicity purports to be based on human biology — on the dubiously scientific notion of "race" — but in reality, it reflects cultural norms as much or more than the alleged composition of someone's "blood."[98]

Why It Matters: The Skin Color Paradox

> "What makes blue-veiners [light-skinned blacks] so aristocratic, is that we blacks like them, the white folks like them, and they like themselves." — Sutton E. Griggs, *The OverShadowed*, (1901)

> "I guess I've benefited from the colorism, because I'm light-skinned…. I've always had the long, straight hair. I thought I was just pretty….
> — Markita, African-American college student quoted by ABC News (2005)

> The worst insult a dark-skinned boy as a child ever got is to be called African…. You can call me anything in the book when I was younger. Just don't call me African. — Jason, African-American college student quoted by ABC News (2005)

The racial over-simplifications described above contribute to the persistence of prejudice. One of the themes of this book is that is impossible to address problems that aren't perceived. Thus, for example, one of the most harmful forms of skin-based discrimination is rarely discussed: the self-inflicted form of discrimination known as "colorism." Many African-American and Latino families will admit that subtle (and sometimes not-so-subtle) preferences are expressed within them for the lighter-skinned members. In fact, both whites and blacks in America discriminate against darker-skinned black people. For many dark-skinned blacks and Latinos, the most painful prejudice they ever face in their lives comes from their own peers.

The impact of colorism is not at all trivial. Studies show that dark-skinned black Americans have lower economic status, diminished social prestige, receive harsher treatment from law enforcement and have a lower likelihood of holding elective office than light-skinned blacks. In one study of male felons incarcerated for their first offense in the State of Georgia, it was found that light-skinned blacks received sentences three months longer than those of whites, medium-skinned blacks received sentences six months longer than light-skinned blacks, and dark-skinned blacks received sentences six months longer than that. The difference in average sentence between the whites and dark-skinned blacks was 571 days (and in the Georgia penal system, those are undoubtedly some very long days) — about a year and a half.

Another study found that black defendants in capital cases with a white victim are twice as likely to receive the death penalty if they have dark skin and Afrocentric racial features. People with darker skin color are more likely to have grown up in poor families, less likely to finish their education, less likely to marry, and if married, have spouses of lower socioeconomic status.

Colorism is rampant in Hollywood and on Madison Avenue, as has been attested to by generations of black actors who have had to learn the type-casting that goes with their skin-tone and "look." Actor Mel Jackson was quoted as saying that light-skinned men like him tend to get the role of the "business executive:" "If the character's supposed to be more successful or more articulate or have a better background, they'll easily cast me in that character." Actress Wendy Raquel Robinson made a similar observation: "I've never been offered... the distressed mother. I play the very upscale, educated young lady. I do have some peers that are a lot darker than myself. They don't get the opportunities."

American black politicians are predominantly light-skinned. A study of all African Americans elected to the House of Representatives, Senate or a governor's office since 1865 revealed that "light-skinned blacks have always been considerably over-represented and dark-skinned blacks dramatically under-represented as public officials." When the American press touts a "promising" young African-American politician, the odds are they are speaking of a light-skinned candidate. In a survey experiment that varied the skin tone of black candidates in a hypothetical election for Senate, the light-skinned hypothetical candidates beat their dark-skinned rivals by eighteen points. Respondents rated the light-skinned candidates as being more intelligent, more experienced and more trustworthy than their dark-skinned opponents.

Although it is a painful reality for American society to face, we must come to admit that some African-Americans benefit from what political scientist Jennifer Hochschild refers to as the "Skin Color Paradox." The paradox is that blacks are aware of colorism but do not resent light-skinned blacks because of it:

> Engagement with colorism would war with a strong sense of racial identity. Black racial identity is premised on recognition of primary marginalization, whereas skin color differentiation is a form of secondary marginalization. In an environment in which members of a group feel deeply threatened by institutional or individual racism, it is very difficult for members of that group to protest in-

ternal differences…. [I]ntense concern for disfavored group members seems like a luxury that cannot at present be afforded… or even like a betrayal of the comradeship and collective spirit needed to fight the external threat.[99]

In other words, colorism has been allowed to persist because racism has always been a more pressing problem. To confront colorism risks being taken as disloyalty in the battle against racism.

While the election of Barack Obama suggests that, at least in some small measure, American racism has finally begun to diminish, it does not say the say same thing about colorism. On the contrary, it appears that colorism and the skin color paradox are alive and well, lurking in the long shadows cast by racism. Although Barack Obama's campaign for the presidency in 2008 was welcomed by many as an opportunity to address racial issues in greater depth, no one raised the issue of colorism.

Colorism is not only an American problem, it is a global phenomenon. There is a huge market in developing countries in Africa and Asia for skin-whitening creams. While an awareness of racism has allowed Americans in the past to combat discrimination on a national scale, an awareness of colorism would enable us to attack discrimination globally, helping literally billions of people. That is one change worth hoping for.

Obama as Hero

"Calmness is always Godlike."
— Emerson, *Journals* (1840)

"Mr. Obama is handsome, fit, smart, and a great speaker… and Americans tend to get giddy over winners, especially underdogs who take the measure of a foe thought to be impregnable…. But I've seen charismatic politicians and pretty families come and go…. There was something more that was making people go gaga over Obama…. We've been watching that something this week, and it's called leadership. Mr. Obama has been feeding the almost desperate hunger in this country for mature leadership, for someone who is not reckless and clownish, short-sighted and self-absorbed." — Bob Herbert, *New York Times* (January 28, 2009)

Was the tsunami of love and good feeling that followed Obama's inauguration an indicator of rationality? Or to use Bob Herbert's phrasing, quoted above, did Americans "go ga-ga" over Obama because they could instinctively tell he was going to be a great leader? As this book went to press it was not yet possible to comment substantively upon President Obama's performance in office. However, his initial popularity was a matter of established fact. After his first week in office, Obama's approval rating was 68% (Gallup) — one of the highest initial scores ever recorded. John F. Kennedy had begun office with an initial approval rating of 72%, Dwight Eisenhower had begun at 68% and Jimmy Carter at 66%.

Is presidential popularity a good indicator, for a rational person, of that president's past or future performance? If so, it is an extremely imperfect predictor. The highest presidential approval rating ever recorded (92%) was achieved by George W. Bush shortly after 9/11. George W. Bush also holds the highest disapproval rating (76%) ever recorded (in 2008). More often than not, presidential popularity faces a steep downward slope. From its highest to its lowest point, George W. Bush's popularity declined by 73 percentage points, Harry Truman's by 65 points, George H.W. Bush's by 60 points and Jimmy Carter's by 47 points.

Historians have not always ratified the citizenry's popularity ratings. Thus, Harry Truman finished his administration with abysmal ratings (22% in 1952), but his reputation has been refurbished since then. Ronald Reagan is now considered the pinnacle of conservative achievement, but he began office with modest ratings (51%), which dropped to a low of 35% by 1983, before recovering in his second administration.

Commentators who sought to explain the dynamics of Obama's early popularity frequently commented upon the president's "Zen" equanimity. Throughout the campaign marathon of 2007–2008, Obama had displayed an increasingly impressive serenity, looking like Tiger Woods calmly striding toward certain victory on the 18th hole (while feverish competitors blew themselves up trying to keep pace). Was the positive reaction of the American electorate to Obama's self-assurance a demonstration that voters can intuitively sense the type of leader they really need?

Once again, our viewpoint is likely to be colored by self-serving partisan bias. Liberals will answer one way, conservatives another. While Obama's campaign serenity was undeniably impressive, it did remind one of another display of cool composure by a politician — George W. Bush's in the days leading up the Iraq invasion. In March, 2003 American newspapers and magazines vied with each other to present steely, heroic images of President Bush and his Cabinet as they prepared for war. On the eve of the invasion, much was made of George W. Bush's "almost eerie" calm. Sometimes, history reminds us, calm precedes a storm.

Obama's early popularity (like Bush's) reveals our innate human preference for calm leaders. This preference has been demonstrated by a number of studies. Calm interpersonal behavior has been associated with high serotonin levels. Blood samples of leaders (college fraternity presidents in one study, alpha chimpanzees in another) show high serotonin levels. In one experiment, a single monkey in a group of monkeys was given Prozac (which raises serotonin levels). The Prozac-enhanced monkey would then become the dominant male.

In our long evolutionary past, calmness was a valuable characteristic for leaders. One of a leader's primary tasks was to anticipate and resolve disputes, a vital activity which required calmness. By emulating a leader's calmness in difficult times, followers were more likely to survive themselves. Our evolutionary programming causes us to gravitate toward calm leaders.

Obama's exceptional serenity is one element of his rock-star appeal. However, neither his early popularity nor his calmness provide any rational basis for evaluating him nor for predicting his future success.

The Rationality of Hope: Reasons to Like Obama

Obama possesses all of the qualities that were conducive to alpha-male status in our evolutionary past. He is tall, good-looking, and intelligent, with a deep voice and a calm, reassuring demeanor. For the most part, however, I think the rational voter should ignore these types of personal characteristics. They have been possessed by both Democrats and Republicans in the past, and by unsuccessful presidents as well as successful ones. Great leaders like Gandhi and King have possessed charismatic qualities, but so have demagogues like Mussolini and Peron.

Likewise, Obama's soaring campaign rhetoric of change and hope left the rationalist in me unmoved. The political challenger always promises change, but this is not helpful unless we are told what kind of changes are intended.

It is human nature to hope. As Dr. Johnson observed, "The natural flight of the human mind is not from pleasure to pleasure, but from hope to hope." However, as studies of the over-confidence bias have revealed, humans tend to hope too much and are consequently prone to disappointment. Thus one of the principle tenets of Buddhism, the most psychologically-astute of all the major religions, is that we must learn to tame our longings and hopes. Hope usually feels good, but it is not always rational.

Why, then, do I count myself amongst President Obama's supporters, rather than as a rational agnostic? It is because I approve of two of Obama's central policy themes:

1) his opposition to excessive partisanship, and

2) his insistence on government transparency.

This book has argued that our partisanship is not only irrational but that it allows politicians to exploit us. The great appeal of Obama's political philosophy is that it attacks political irrationality on both of these crucial fronts. Americans who imitate Obama's example will become less partisan. Policies of transparency will make it that much harder for self-serving politicians to exploit us.

Evolutionary psychologists Patrick McNamara and David Trumbull have emphasized the role of emulation in the lives of great leaders. Many great historical leaders modeled themselves closely after an influential mentor. In turn, the great leaders themselves tended to become the source of widespread imitation. Human beings, like other apes and monkeys, are extraordinarily imitative ("monkey see, monkey do"). Obama's noble, post-partisan example has the potential to be enormously influential in the long run, which is a good thing.

However, while I approve of Obama's post-partisan goals, I think it is important to remain realistic as to his chances of overcoming partisanship in the short term, which are modest at best. Our irrational partisanship has deep biological roots which have been strongly reinforced by lifetimes of cultural programming. Political irrationality will not be easily vanquished.

CHAPTER 13

Overcoming Political Irrationality

> The public can best speak for itself when it can gather together in some way to hear the arguments on the various sides of an issue and then, after face-to-face discussion, come to a collective decision.
> — James Fishkin, *The Voice of the People*

DARK TRUTH #13
If you want real democracy, you'll have to learn to trust your neighbors (at least, more than you trust the politicians).

Is Rational Democracy Possible?

Political irrationality is the source of some of our most fundamental social problems:

Partisan polarization and the Culture War — Our two-party political system encourages social conflict. Innate ideological predispositions are reinforced and exacerbated by partisan bias, which makes our conflicts bitter and hard to resolve. Parties, politicians and the media each have good (self-interested) reasons to stir up our latent biases. The result is an angry society, divided against itself.

Self-serving social mythology — The failures of our political system are camouflaged by myths that are difficult to debunk because they make us feel good. At the party level, partisans refuse to accept that their party's policies or leaders have flopped. Consequently, our political landscape is cluttered with moribund failures, propped up by "true believers" (e.g., sugar subsidies, the drug war, the Electoral College, the Cuban embargo, Iraq, etc.).

Un-democratic political structures — Though we pride ourselves on our democracy, we are in fact the subjects of an oligarchy. In the U.S., the ordinary people are only rarely allowed a direct vote on any important issue, and then only at the state or municipal level (never at the federal level).

The citizenry therefore does not vote directly on federal tax levels, government expenditures, compensation for elected officials, decisions to engage in war, revisions to the law or Constitution, or any other important public matters.

Instead, every few years the citizens are allowed to choose between two groups of rich people, one of which goes on to make all important decisions. These politicians hold absolute power, so they are besieged by wealthy lobbyists.

The Way Out — Instead of entrusting all our political decisions to politicians, which leads always to partisan conflict and corruption, we need to return power to the citizens. However, we need to do so under conditions that minimize political irrationality. In practice, this means giving power to small groups of citizens who are required to really learn about a given issue, and who are expected to debate and discuss the issue before voting.

The Next Big Thing in Democracy: Citizens

In a speech given on July 3, 2007 the United Kingdom's incoming Prime Minister, Gordon Brown, announced to some consternation that his government would make extended use of a device known as the "citizen jury." Brown said that the purpose of this democratic innovation was to "[B]ring government closer to the people... by devolving more power directly to the people."[100]

A citizen jury — as the U.K. soon learned — is a small group of randomly-selected citizens who are asked to deliberate upon a policy question, such as gun crime or public healthcare. After hearing evidence and discussing possible solutions for a day or more, the jury reports its findings and recommendations. It functions rather like a focus group, except that it is meant to influence governmental action rather than corporate or political strategy.

Prime Minister Brown's announcement of official governmental support for the citizen jury was big news in the world of democratic theory. Growing public frustration with the failures of electoral democracy has created support for direct democracy, and Brown's experiment was one of the boldest steps taken in that direction. Although I support Prime Minister Brown's overall objectives, I am not surprised the program left voters underwhelmed. In fact, Brown's juries were met with scorn in many quarters.

An editorial in *The Observer* (England) reported "growing concerns that they [citizen juries] are a 'sham' listening exercise used for political purposes, rather than a genuine way of canvassing opinion." One academic said, "There is a lot of worry about whether these are genuine consultations and deliberations. If used in the wrong way, they can actually close down debate rather than open it up." Soon, news reports began to crop up highlighting the high cost of the juries. In October 2007 *The Guardian* (London) reported that juries had cost 500,000 pounds in the first four months of implementation. Other reports pegged first-year expenditures at over three million pounds. Conservative critics attacked the juries as being unaccountable, undemocratic, unqualified and overly powerful, not to mention — phony: "fake listening."[101]

By 2008, all talk of citizen juries had evaporated as Gordon Brown fought for his political life. Ironically, he was attacked above all for a failure to provide leadership. By leading the British people toward democracy, he had apparently been taking them in a direction they were not especially inclined to go. Perhaps this is because the British electorate found the citizen jury to be a phony, political ploy by the Prime Minister. However I think a more important reason is that the average voter, British or otherwise, is not overly desirous of more democracy. Most people are still comfortable with placebo democracy, a system in which voters are assured that they have democracy but that someone else will do the hard work of making all the decisions. Thus, the so-called democratic public often expresses anger when its leaders fail to act monarchically.

The U.K. experience is also instructive as regards the perverse difficulties that will always obstruct democratic reforms that originate with either party. If a democratic innovation is introduced by one of the established political parties, it will be attacked by the other party because it was "not invented here." No political party wants to admit that the rival party has just made a great step forward in democracy. Sadly, the psychology of partisan bias suggests that any democratic reform's opposition will become entrenched over time. If one party introduces democracy, the other party will fight it, and confirmation bias will ensure that the opponents become increasingly dogmatic. Democratic reforms therefore have a better chance of widespread acceptance if they are developed through non-partisan mechanisms.

Citizen Panels, Citizen Juries and Deliberative Polls

Despite the birthing pains of citizen juries in the U.K., the device should make a large impact on democracies worldwide. Similar approaches have also been referred to as citizen panels, citizen councils, deliberative polls, consensus panels, and by a variety of other terms. Two of the most influential methodologies are the *Deliberative Poll,* developed by James Fishkin, and the *Citizen Jury,* developed by Ned Crosby.

The common element is that citizen-participants are expected to "deliberate" — that is, to receive information and then discuss and debate amongst themselves — before coming to a final decision. Note the contrast with ordinary surveys and elections, in which participants are allowed to respond instinctively and without information (i.e., irrationally). The deliberative poll and citizen jury provide a context in which people are encouraged to activate System 2, the reasoning module of the brain. With deliberative polls and citizen juries we are looking to create an ideal micro-polity — a group of informed and concerned citizens — to help guide the rest of us.

The idea has been catching on around the world. In 2007 the Prime Minister of Bulgaria, Sergei Stanishev, pledged that his government would make use of the results of a Deliberative Poll on the plight of the impoverished ethnic minority known as the Roma (more commonly known as Gypsies). The inability of Bulgarian society to integrate the Roma has been one of the country's most intractable problems. Following Fishkin's procedure, the Bulgarian government first surveyed 1,344 people on a variety of issues related to the Roma, including housing, crime and education. From the initial survey group, 255 were selected to participate in a two-day conference. All participants received briefing materials, including proposals from political parties and non-governmental organizations. During the conference, participants broke into small groups to discuss issues and raise questions, which they later posed to experts in a full session. Six hours of the proceedings were broadcast on national television.

Some of the initial discussions were brutal, revealing widespread antagonism against the Roma. "They should be given just bread and water," said one woman. However, by the end of the process, it had become clear to most participants that the further integration of the Roma was not only possible but necessary. Participants were surveyed again at the close of deliberation. The percentage who thought that the Roma should live in separate neighborhoods had declined from 43% to 21%. Those supporting an increase in the number of Roma police officers increased from 32% to 52%. Most Bulgarians appeared willing to support the integration of Roma into society, despite the divisive rhetoric of nationalist politicians. The Deliberative Poll results were evidence of the underlying tolerance of the Bulgarian people.[102]

Also in 2007, a group of 400 Australians came together in Sydney to use the Deliberative Polling method to explore ways for Muslims and non-Muslims to live together without prejudice. In 2006 Taiwan held what it called a "deliberative democracy debate" in the election for Mayor of Taipei. Citizens and citizen representatives participated directly in the televised debate. In 2005 in Zhejiang Province in China, a Deliberative Poll was used to determine public attitudes toward spending priorities. In Greece in 2004, former Foreign Minister George Papandreou helped organize a Deliberative Poll which actually decided an issue (albeit a relatively minor one) — the selection of a Socialist candidate for the mayor of Marousi, an Athens suburb.

Deliberative Polls, Citizen Juries and other forms of citizen panels have also been widely used throughout the United States. The Public Utility Commission of the State of Texas, for example, has used Deliberative Polls to determine service satisfaction with eight of the state's publicly-regulated utilities companies. Recently, federal wildlife officials announced a controversial plan to use a citizen panel for the management of grizzly bears reintroduced into the

Bitterroot Mountain range of Idaho and Montana. If citizen panels can effectively govern grizzly bears, management of humans may not be far away.

Which Way Forward: Panels or Direct Democracy?

Panels. Citizen panels offer a promising solution to problems caused by our ingrained political irrationality, but they do not bring us all the way to political paradise. Let us examine why.

The strongest benefit of the citizen panel is that it provides an opportunity for citizen rationality. No other currently existing democratic mechanism allows ordinary citizens to participate in politics in a truly rational manner. While studies show that ordinary voters do not acquire much information prior to voting, members of a citizen panel are *forced* to learn about an issue in depth. Moreover, citizen panelists are required to confront divergent views through discussion and debate. Every participant must learn to accept that well-intentioned fellow citizens may hold radically different views. The citizen panel is like a mini-legislature, providing its members with a deliberative experience similar to that of a working Senator's or Congressperson's.

The other principal benefit of citizen panels is that they are fundamentally democratic mechanisms. Citizens express their views directly, without the need for representatives. Citizen panels provide a democratic alternative to our traditional political oligarchy. The citizenry, at long last, is allowed to comment directly on political issues.

When the panel makes its report, the general public is provided with a trusted source of political information. As we have seen earlier, one of the endemic problems of electoral democracy is that the citizenry does not fully trust its elected leaders. Despite their oft-repeated assurances of love for public service, we suspect that they are self-interested humans (just like everybody else) who will make policy decisions to reward supporters even when it might not benefit the general public. Ordinary citizens also suspect that elected leaders are "out of touch," that their cushy lives of power and privilege prevent them from understanding the travails of ordinary people.

As opposed to an elected legislature, the citizen panel is much more likely to contain a mix of backgrounds, including those who have been less fortunate economically and otherwise. Citizen panels help diversify the political sphere by introducing opinions that do not emanate from the social and political elite. We may not agree with the recommendations of a citizen panel, but we are likely to accord them a certain respect that we might not accord a politician. The politician can claim to represent the polity, but he or she may be lying. The citizen panel, on the other hand, *is* the polity. Citizen panelists may prove to be wrong, but we cannot doubt their sincerity.

Another advantage of citizen panels — as currently constituted — is that they do not have much capacity to do harm. They represent a form of incremental utopianism, low-risk democratic experimentation. Radically-utopian political designs, from Plato's to Lenin's, have failed to take into account that governments and societies are intertwined systems. Even minor utopian tinkering is apt to produce surprising systemic feedback. Government emerges from national culture the way a tree grows from its roots. Radical utopians have often been like people trying to plant trees with no roots.

Political innovation is more like gardening or farming than it is like architecture. One must accept the constraints of climate and soil, and wait to see whether the new seed will bear fruit. A plant that flourishes in one climate may fail in another. Thus it makes sense to set aside a test patch, where you can experiment with a few different strains before planting the whole field.

To date, citizen panels represent a very modest test patch. As currently practiced, citizen panels provide a source of persuasive information to the political elite — but they do nothing to change the basic structure of our government. This is simultaneously a virtue and a vice. Panels won't do much harm, but they can't do much good.

Direct democracy. Contrast the citizen panel with those other democratic mechanisms, sometimes lumped together under the rubric of "direct democracy": initiatives, recall and referenda. These latter tools allow citizens to originate and pass legislation. The referendum and initiative can do some good, theoretically, because they can allow a frustrated citizenry to circumvent obstructionist leaders.

However, as most prominently seen in California, experience with these measures has been mixed. Although the objective of initiatives and referenda is to allow the citizenry to speak directly without the intermediation of the legislature, initiatives and referenda have at times become vehicles for special interests. In order to place an initiative on the ballot, all that is needed in most states is a certain number of signatures. Corporations and lobbyists have learned that you can simply pay people to get those signatures, which is not that different from buying votes. Initiatives and referenda expose politics to the risk of becoming purely a money game.

These criticisms are persuasively advanced by journalist David Broder in *Democracy Derailed: Initiatives and the Power of Money*. However, Broder's arguments are themselves systematically critiqued by political scientist John Matsusaka.[103] Matsusaka's historical analysis of American direct democracy suggests that Broder's fears are over-stated, and that direct democracy has already provided powerful benefits. For example, Matsusaka compares overall tax levels and government expenditures in states that have initiatives and referenda with states that don't. States with direct democracy had consistently lower tax rates than states without it. Direct democracy may be a powerful force for government efficiency.

Small, incremental improvements and innovations will probably make the initiative and referendum more powerful in years to come. For example, it might be helpful to use citizen panels to oversee the initiative process, in order to focus citizen attention on important issues rather than only on those that are pushed by special interests.

Problems with Panels. Experience from the past few decades of democratic tinkering suggests we should expand the role of citizen panels but remain cautious on the rapid expansion of initiatives and referenda. However, the legislative power of initiatives and referenda does suggest a possible avenue for the future role of citizen panels: they can be given real power.

Recall that the main criticism leveled at citizen panels in the U.K. (especially by Tory voters) was that they were sham exercises, mere public relations charades for the Labour Party. There was a strong answer available to this criticism, but one had to be willing to go through with it. Prime Minister Brown could have followed the lead of his Bulgarian colleague, Prime Minister Stanishev, by promising to take citizen panel results into account. Of course, even when politicians have the temerity to promise something, they can still change their mind. The future of citizen panels therefore lies in finding ways to make their results binding and compulsory.

One important difference between the legislator and the citizen panelist — and an implied criticism of the citizen panel — is that the legislator has a chance to learn the job and become a professional or expert, while the panelist must remain a beginner. Thus citizen panels are said to entrust important decisions to amateurs. Fishkin's Deliberative Polls require direct citizen participation for at most two days, while Crosby's Citizen Juries convene from one to five days. Can we expect ordinary citizens to be converted into Solons over a long weekend?

Participants in citizen panels commonly receive information on the issue they are asked to consider, but they are not briefed or trained on the power of cognitive bias, nor on methods of negotiating and resolving policy disputes. Without such training, much of the potential value of the panel is lost. Supporters of panels will reply that the inexperience of panelists is a small price to pay for their impartiality. Although our elected representatives can plausibly pretend to the status of experts, surveys show that we still do not trust them. It makes sense to prefer sincere amateurs to dishonest professionals. In the future, however, this criticism should be taken into account. Methods should be devised to introduce a training regimen into the panel process. Even an hour or two of training on the concept of cognitive bias could enable participants to come to better decisions.

Another criticism of citizen panels is that they provide a democratic voice for only a tiny fraction of the public. Initially, only a very small proportion of the citizenry will get to sit on panels. However, as time goes on, a greater proportion of citizens will have had the chance to participate. Gradually, the benefits of panel membership will spread throughout the population. Eventually the point may be reached when citizens strive just as creatively and energetically to escape citizen panel duty as they do now to escape regular jury duty.

We should not be naïve in assuming that people will be instantly ennobled or enlightened by their participation on citizen panels. Just as with regular juries, citizens may come away disgusted and disillusioned. Studies show that most people do not like argument or conflict, so it would not be surprising if a significant proportion of panelists ended up with a negative view of the process. Would that be a good reason to stop using panels? Not in my view — the main purpose of panels is not to increase the personal happiness of those participating on the panels, but rather to produce rational political decisions that are untainted by elite bias.

A final inherent weakness of panels is that they have the capacity to generate extremely unpopular opinions. This seems counter-intuitive at first. Since the panels are composed of ordinary citizens, shouldn't the broader citizenry accept the panel's recommendations? Not necessarily. Remember that the panelists start out as ordinary citizens, but by the end of the process they have undergone a profound transformation: they have become knowledgeable. This actually makes them extremely un-typical. In a sense, they have become a mini-elite. As with decisions emanating from any elite, their recommendations may be met with incomprehension. Thus, in Australia in 1999, a Deliberative Poll was organized to consider Australia's relationship to the British monarchy. The results of the Deliberative Poll suggested that it was time to sever the relationship between Australia and the monarchy, but a subsequent citizen vote went the other way. The public did not agree with its own Deliberative Poll.

Fishkin blamed the apparently anomalous result by blaming it on a sophisticated pro-monarchy advertising campaign. The same thing happened in Canada in 2006 when a large citizen panel was entrusted with considering electoral reform, and proposed several radical new changes which were in turn rejected by the general public when put to a vote. Again, one could blame campaign effects. However, it makes more sense to simply accept the vote as revelatory of an expected rationality gap between the panelists and the broader public. It is normal that people who have received a great deal of information on a social topic will come to somewhat different views on that topic as compared with people who have no information at all. It will therefore be a common experience for citizen panels to produce results that are slightly, or substantially, mystifying to the general public.

How should we react to puzzling decisions emanating from citizen panels? First, consider the alternative: puzzling decisions made by politicians. Do these not provoke complaints as well? Our elected politicians make a great number of unpopular decisions, but for the most part these do not lead to civil unrest because our societies accord a degree of traditional legitimacy to the work-product of our elected leaders. Citizen panels, likewise, will eventually be trusted by the citizenry. We have seen in the U.K. that this trust will not always be attained easily or quickly. As with any social innovation, trust takes time to earn. Citizen panels are a new device and it will take time for citizens to learn to appreciate their benefits. Like that other venerable device based on citizen participation, the legal jury, citizen panels will eventually become accepted as one of the essential mechanisms of a truly democratic society.

The Let's Try Democracy (LTD) Party: Government by Citizen Panel

> BOSWELL: So, Sir, you laugh at
> schemes of political improvement.
> JOHNSON: Why, Sir, most schemes
> of political improvement are laughable
> things. — James Boswell, *Life of Johnson*

The principal improvement that could be made to citizen panels is to give them real legislative power. Here, however, an oligarchic Catch-22 blocks the way. Citizen panels can only acquire true power if politicians are willing to give it to them, but that is unlikely — because politicians won't vote themselves out of a job.

I propose, therefore, to put the citizen panel to a general vote by creating a political party based *entirely* on the citizen panel. This theoretical party will be dubbed the "Let's Try Democracy Party," ("LTD Party") in recognition of the fundamental challenge facing our political system, namely, that of achieving true democracy.

The LTD Party Concept. The LTD Party would be based on an agreement to submit all legislative votes to a panel of constituents. The LTD Party legislator agrees to be remote-controlled by the constituency.

Let us consider the hypothetical case of the first LTD Party candidate elected to the U.S. Congress. After being elected, the LTD Party legislator immediately creates a citizen panel of 100 citizens, each of whom will be invited to serve a term of one year. When the time arises for a vote on a particular issue, the citizen panel deliberates and decides (most deliberations will be accomplished on-line, through a secure web-site). The LTD Party legislator will follow the orders of the panel regardless of his or her own preferences.

How it Will Work. The LTD Party legislator will help prepare, structure and coordinate the deliberations of the participants, but in the end the panel will decide. The LTD Party thus voluntarily transfers power from the political class to the citizenry. While most politicians claim to speak for the people, but in fact are heavily influenced by their financial stakeholders, the LTD Party politician is immunized from undue influence by being rendered powerless. No one bribes the powerless. Unlike other politicians, the LTD Party legislator actually does have some claim to the term "public servant." Even though LTD Party candidates may still be motivated by the usual combination of personal self-love and lust for glory (assuming they are human and not saints or robots), when it comes to legislative votes — their most important activity — they would be forced to act as public servants.

Benefits: neutrality and rationality. The LTD Party not only provides us with a more rational way to make political decisions, it provides us with an avenue of escape from the red state / blue state culture war. As political scientists like Morris Fiorina have established, most Americans fall in the middle of the political spectrum, but our two-party system creates an artificial barrier in the center. For years, surveys have shown that Americans are unhappy with harshly negative, polarizing political campaigns, and are therefore disgusted with the two main political parties. However, there is no place for these disgusted moderate voters to go. If they retreat into apathy, they are harassed and chided by self-righteous college kids. If they choose one of the two main parties, they perpetuate the polarizing culture war. If they choose an alternative party, such as the Greens or Libertarians, they are roundly derided for "wasting their vote." The LTD Party finally provides a home for these disgruntled rationalists.

Legislative Focus. The LTD Party deals with the vote-wasting argument by focusing exclusively on legislative elections, which are of much lower interest to the general public than presidential, gubernatorial or mayoral elections. Most Americans cannot name their congressional representative, much less their state representative or city council-person.

The LTD Party candidate says to the voter: "Vote for whomever you want for president, governor or mayor. But since you don't know who your legislator is anyway, go ahead and vote for the LTD Party for Congress, the state legislature and the city council. By doing so, you vote for direct democracy and reduced power for politicians."

Alternative parties have failed to gain traction in the U.S. mainly because they always seek to establish a foothold in the impossibly competitive presidential election. The only kind of third party could that could seriously compete in the presidential election would be one led by a telegenic billionaire. This will not be the LTD Party's approach. Consequently, the LTD Party willingly foregoes the presidential campaign. It would be harder to structure a remote-controlled executive than a remote-controlled legislator, anyway. The LTD Party concept is better suited to legislative than to executive elections.

A Non-partisan Party. Unlike other alternative political parties, the LTD Party does not compete on the ideological spectrum. There is only one issue on the LTD Party platform: direct democracy through citizen panels. This is neither a left-wing nor a right-wing point of view. Citizen panels will produce conservative recommendations as well as liberal ones. Moreover, surveys show that conservatives support greater democracy as much as liberals. Consequently, the LTD Party has a true claim to the vacant position of Middle Party. The LTD Party will provide a refuge for those citizens who don't want to be polarized. In fact, for such people, the LTD Party will be the only rational option. All other parties place you somewhere on the ideological spectrum, open to red vs. blue sniping.

In an LTD Party campaign the main strategy would be to sell the virtues of the citizen panel concept, not the virtues of the candidate or of a particular platform. The candidate's personal beliefs and preferences would be quite unimportant, since they would not necessarily be carried out. If one wanted to know what the candidate would do in office, one would have to consult the citizens — they would be the "deciders."

Since the LTD Party will preach no particular platform, there will be no need to attack the other side's platform. Negative campaigns will become a thing of the past. The LTD Party campaign will be completely open and welcome support from Democrats and Republicans, even those actively campaigning for their party's presidential candidate. Instead of phony campaign events, the LTD Party campaign will be organized around a series of Deliberative Polls. Instead of a campaign in which the politician announces his or her policies, here the politician listens as the policies are dictated by the citizens.

Impact. Let us imagine that a small percentage of legislative seats around the country, perhaps 5%, were captured by the LTD Party. What impact could we expect? Thousands of ordinary citizens would be drafted into an intensive civics-training program. After service on a legislative panel, citizens would return to their communities with deep, practical knowledge of how our government works, and of the key challenges facing our society. As opposed to regular citizen panelists, who deliberate on a single issue, members of an LTD Party panel would become true policy experts after their year of service. During their deliberations, the citizen panelists could be expected to discuss issues with family and co-workers, bringing knowledge of legislative issues to a broader public.

The LTD Party would create a vital swing bloc in the middle. The politicians of both sides would begin to appeal to this party for support; but they would learn that in such appeals their former demagogic strategies would be of no use. For the first time, they would have to rely on logic, evidence and reason.

Criticisms. The LTD Party concept is open to most of the criticisms which have been leveled at the citizen panel, and to a few more as well. The most obvious objection is a pragmatic one — could it work in practice? Modern legislators spend much of their time in negotiations, conferences and committees. Many votes take place at the last minute, sometimes late at night, and many votes are on re-drafts or minor amendments to prior legislation. How could a citizen panel follow this labyrinthine process, much less provide effective and timely decisions when needed? How could a citizen panel participate in a drafting committee? How could it originate legislation?

My answer to these general objections is that these difficulties can be overcome. Attorneys represent complex corporate interests in negotiations without having to check with the Board of Directors on every edit to every clause. Citizen panels could set clear parameters on what would be acceptable legislation. It would even be possible, using modern digital technology, for large numbers of panelists to participate in last-minute decisions on revisions to legislation. As for the drafting and development of legislation, citizen panels could appoint sub-committees to carry out these tasks. It is true that the LTD Party legislator would have much less freedom of action than his/her Republican and Democratic colleagues. But then, that is the whole point.

"Field of Dreams" Democracy: Build It and They Will Come

The LTD Party concept is only one of many proposed innovations that have been put forward to deal with the deficiencies of our current system. A number of proposals have been based on replacing some our American "winner-take-all" style elections with proportional systems like those of European parliamentary democracies. While this might represent an improvement over our current duopoly, proportional systems still leave politicians in charge. I favor systems that allow citizens to express their preferences directly.

Political scientist Kevin O'Leary proposes an interesting democratic innovation he calls the *Virtual National Assembly* (VNA). Under his system, each of America's 435 Congressional districts would draft 100 ordinary citizens into a group that would function much like a citizen panel or deliberative poll. The citizens would be provided with information and a digital forum in which to air and express their views. They would then vote on the same legislation that was proposed to Congress.

Who would listen to their votes? At first, the deliberations and votes of the VNA would carry no formal weight, and politicians would certainly be free to ignore them. That's why I refer to the VNA as "Field of Dreams Democracy": as in the baseball film, we first build the ballpark, on faith to some extent, then hope that players will come.

I believe O'Leary is right that the politicians would come to play. They would be forced to. Opinions emanating from 43,000 well-informed ordinary citizens would have thunderous clout. The VNA would become an extremely powerful organ of public opinion.

Eventually, O'Leary believes the VNA could be formally entrusted with some important decision-making powers, which would represent an epochal change in American democracy. This would require major amendments to the Constitution, no small matter.

Although I support O'Leary's proposal for a national citizen assembly, I think there is still a lot of work to be done in refining the VNA's assumptions and proposed procedures. For example, O'Leary prefers face-to-face meetings for citizen assemblies, rather than web-based or electronic meetings. His reasoning is that much of human communication is "non-verbal" and would be lost or garbled by electronic transmission. However, I would argue that some of the "non-verbal communication" which would be lost is non-verbal communication of social status. Losing it might be a good thing. The perception of social class could tend to replicate — within the citizen panel — the same uneven playing field that exists outside in society.

In many cultures, gradations of social status are clearly marked by dress, accent, tone, posture and even physiognomy. Our perception of a speaker's social status directly affects our evaluation of the speaker's persuasiveness. Face-to-face meetings are always subject to the risk that high-status individuals will intimidate their colleagues. Web-based discussions are an alternative, but in that case we might just be transferring political primacy to our most nimble-fingered typists. We should probably explore mixed or hybrid systems, with part of the process conducted online and part in face-to-face meetings.

I would further recommend that each citizen representative be allowed to delegate his or her position to a friend or family member. There are many people whose self-perceived lack of social status might make them bashful in political debates; but most of these shy persons probably know at least one friend or family member brave enough to go down to the citizen assembly and tell the folks a thing or two.

Another aspect of the VNA which should be further explored is the possibility for an international counter-part, a Virtual Global Assembly. Arguably, there is even more need for a global assembly than a national one, because the democratic deficit is greatest at the international level (there is very little democracy at the domestic level, but virtually none at the global level). As the lone superpower, the United States can unilaterally undertake actions which will affect the lives of citizens everywhere (which is why our presidential election is avidly watched by the entire world), but only 5% of the world's citizens are allowed to actually vote for the American president. The U.S. invasion of Iraq, for example, arguably taxed the economies of every country in the world by disrupting global oil supplies and driving up the price of crude petroleum. This is a form of global taxation without representation.

In every American election, whether presidential, gubernatorial, mayoral or legislative there are at most two or three salient political issues upon which the election may turn (e.g., the economy, a foreign war, a particular scandal, etc.). One issue that never makes it into the top three is our United Nations policy. The citizenry is woefully ignorant of geopolitical affairs. An American citizen might have a positive or negative view of the United Nations, but in either case is almost certain to lack specific opinions on any particular U.N. action. It's the same in all other countries. The citizens of the world may love or hate the U.N., but they cannot tell you what it does or how it works.

How then, do the world's "democratically-elected" political leaders know what instructions to give to the U.N.? The politicians have no choice but to devise such instructions on their own, without consulting the citizenry. International policy of all kinds is therefore developed in a kind of bureaucratic black-box, permanently shielded from all democratic influence and scrutiny. The citizens of the world are obviously affected by globalization and international relations, but they have no way of reacting to events or of expressing themselves, because there are always more-salient domestic issues that will determine national and local elections.

Admittedly, there are very great technical challenges facing the creation of a Virtual Global Assembly (language, for example). However, given the current democratic vacuum at the international level, the need is even greater.

However, is the VNA realistic? Isn't it — like the LTD Party — just another example of ivory-tower utopian dreaming?

Marketing Democracy: Open Letter to the Rich and Famous

If we are to transform our current system of government into something more democratic and more rational, we must overcome one final paradox. Our arguments so far against political irrationality have been entirely logical. Unfortunately, this entails a certain self-contradiction. If people really are irrational when it comes to politics, what makes us think that we could use rationality to convince them to change? Indeed, one of the central arguments of this book is that most of our political orientation is impervious to logical argument.

What are we to do? One answer is to wait for citizen discontent with politicians – already substantial – to grow to a point that the need for democratic evolution becomes painfully obvious. One might call this the "silver-lining theory," in that it suggests that any serious social crisis represents an opportunity for political growth. Although the global financial turmoil generated in 2008-2009 by the failure of the sub-prime mortgage market may eventually lead to better governance, it is rather a large price to pay. There has to be a more systematic approach that we can follow while we are patiently waiting for the next financil crisis or political scandal.

So let us consider another tack, following the path blazed by Madison Avenue. If you want to create demand for new products, it's not enough to create devices with wonderful, innovative features. You also need good marketing. "Social marketing" is the use of modern market-research and advertising techniques to effect social change. Advertisers have taught us that if you want to make something cool, use an admired celebrity to peddle it. In our celebrity-obsessed culture, there is a great, un-used social power waiting to be tapped. As our TV, film and recording stars age, their earnings plummet while the bonfires of their vanity continue to blaze brightly. Rather than letting these paragons of entertainment wash up on the shores of some reality show, let us offer them a more dignified alternative. Give us your help, let us say, and we will make you even more famous than you were before — and what's more, we'll make you honored and respected (which you never were before), as one of the founders of true democracy.

In recent decades, political parties have increasingly recruited future candidates from the ranks of recycled celebrities — e.g., Ronald Reagan, Arnold Schwarzenegger, Sonny Bono, Jesse Ventura, Al Franken, Fred Thompson, etc. Let us follow their example, but with considerably less risk for the general public. When a celebrity runs for office as an LTD Party legislator, we don't have to fear that he or she will make empty-headed decisions, because the LTD Party legislator doesn't make any decisions. The citizen panel makes the decisions, the legislator just carries out their orders. Consequently, the LTD Party is not afraid of the damage that celebrities can cause through their inexperience. An LTD Party politician is harmless. We can just sit back and enjoy their antics without worrying that they will start an unnecessary war or destroy Wall Street.

Our recent political history has taught us that a candidate's likeability can be his or her most powerful asset — and celebrities are experts at being likeable. Any sufficiently well-liked figure would be sufficient to launch the first LTD Party campaign, or serve as the VNA's first spokesperson. For a politically-oriented comedian like Jon Stewart or Stephen Colbert, the transition would be a smooth one, from political entertainer... to entertaining politician. Revered sports legends like Tiger Woods, Michael Jordan or Larry Bird could easily be elected as LTD Party candidates.

While the LTD Party will require only an engaging first candidate to get off the ground, the Virtual National Assembly (or Virtual Global Assembly) could be started even more easily. Here, only one ingredient is required: money. There is no legal impediment to creation of such bodies, and all the managerial impediments can be overcome with enough capital. If the politicians sell out to wealthy lobbyists and corporate interests, then let us return the favor, by using crusading billionaires to battle plutocracy. Bill Gates and Warren Buffett could create democracy with pocket change. Let's encourage them to do so.

When I observe philanthropists like George Soros, celebrity activists like Sean Penn or Arianna Huffington, or activist organizations like moveon.org — all supporting traditional left-wing causes and structures like the Democratic Party, I lament the missed opportunity to support the more fundamental and progressive reforms of citizen panels and citizen assemblies. These activists are currently just promoting one branch of electoral oligarchy over another.   There is a better way.

Education for Rational Democracy: Starting with the Mirror

> Self-reflection is the school of wisdom.
> — Baltasar Gracian, *The Art of Worldly Wisdom*

> Go to your bosom,
> Knock there, and ask your heart what it doth know.
> — Shakespeare, *Measure for Measure*, 2.2.136

The increased use of citizen panels, as through the LTD Party concept, is a promising avenue for the development of true, rational democracy. An ultimately more powerful avenue is through public awareness and education. If citizens become aware of the pervasive extent of human political irrationality, they can begin to combat it in the most powerful way — by looking in the mirror.

The key concept in this book is that our political orientations emanate from deep biological and cultural sources. It therefore makes no sense for us to feel great pride in our own politics, nor to despise other people for their politics.

Strong partisan bias comes very close to racism — it is at heart a failure to accept human diversity. If you are one of the many Americans who feel an intense antagonism or even hatred for the other party's leaders, ask yourself why you need that feeling. Do you not accept to live in a society where people hold political beliefs that are different from your own?

Likewise, try to understand why you support candidates. Have you made a rational analysis of your candidate's policy proposals and compared them with your own preferences? Or are you falling prey to a normal human fascination with images of celebrity, beauty, and power? It is all right to love and support a particular politician, but we should not confuse that kind of support with participation in democracy.

If you want to participate in democracy, *learn about something*. Learn a lot, not just a little; learn about both sides. I hope that this book has challenged you to face up to your own ingrained tendencies toward political ir-rationality, but that is only the beginning. I urge you to find out more about global warming, stem-cell research, the WTO, conflict in the Middle East, immigration policy, social security, etc., but please: try to counter your own confirmation bias.

This will be hard work, but I can promise you that it is very reward-ing. In the long term, knowledge can be more powerful than voting, but only if tempered by an awareness of our human penchant for bias and irrationality. If we really want democracy, the best way to prepare for it will be by becoming an informed, rational citizenry.

EPILOGUE

The "Ten Suggestions"
For Greater Political Rationality

> Order a purge for your brain, it will be
> much better employed there than upon
> your stomach. — Montaigne, "Of the
> resemblance of children to their fathers"

1. Be humble with respect to your political knowledge.

You should be humble about your political knowledge because studies show that if you are an average citizen, you don't have much. Even if you are a fanatical news junkie and fervent C-Span watcher, your knowledge of issues is probably no deeper than a sound-bite. If you are highly-partisan, your confirmation bias has probably effectively shielded you from a great deal of data. The odds are that you haven't listened to contrary evidence for years.

There is a lot out there, politically speaking, that you don't know. As Socrates said, the beginning of wisdom comes in a person's realization that "I only know that I don't know."

2. Accept that your community will always contain people very different from you.

If you are a Democrat, you must learn to accept that Republicans are not going away. America's future has Republican presidents in it, and your fellow conservative citizens are going to abide as well. If you are a Republican, similarly, you must come to grips with the likely future health of the Democratic Party.

In a large society, people will always have views based on radically different cultural premises. Sometimes, the views of our fellow citizens will shock us, but we should be cautious about reacting with contempt. Instead, we should look at their behavior as a puzzle, asking ourselves, what is so different about their value systems that it drives them to come to such a strange viewpoint? How can we negotiate a compromise?

3. Weaken your partisan attachments.

There is a good chance that you are genetically predisposed to be either liberal or conservative. Strangely, however, that predisposition does not necessarily correlate with your choice of party. Many people are in the "wrong" party — natural conservatives in the Democratic Party, natural liberals in the Republican Party. That this is possible suggests that most people are strongly susceptible to childhood partisan indoctrination, the primary method of acquiring a partisan perspective.

What would happen if you were to change political party tomorrow? I wager that you would be embarrassed and uncomfortable in front of many of your friends and co-workers. But is that a good reason for remaining in your political party? Why do you need to feel allegiance to any political party? This book has argued that it is simply irrational to have strong loyalties to the Democratic or Republican parties — neither of which has an internally consistent ideology. The Democrats do not always support liberal politics, and the Republicans do not always support conservative viewpoints. Since you cannot rely on these parties to provide consistent ideological positions, you shouldn't blindly follow them. Think for yourself.

4. Don't despise those people who hold political views contrary to your own.

There is disturbing evidence that humans are innately susceptible to racial and xenophobic hatred and intolerance. In modern, secular society, partisanship unfortunately becomes one of the principal means for the expression of these atavistic, destructive impulses. If you find yourself despising other people because of their political opinions, ask yourself what has become of you. What is the point of becoming involved in politics if it makes you a hateful human being? The costs to you and to society of your animosity far outweigh any imaginary benefits from the potential victory of your political party.

5. Don't pay too much attention to presidential elections.

The irresistible spectacle of the presidential election offers a fascination which is out of proportion to the slender opportunity it provides for a rational discussion of the issues. Becoming greatly interested in presidential elections is no substitute for acquiring informed political opinions. For many citizens, coming to a vote in a presidential election is a good excuse for not doing any political thinking otherwise. Don't be one of those lazy citizens. By all means, have fun following the electoral spectacle, but don't delude yourself: watching the televised *Presidential Survivor* show is no substitute for becoming an informed, rational citizen.

6. Leave the non-voters alone.

The choice between Democratic and Republican parties is a sterile one. In either case, a detached political elite will continue to run the country. In such a context, non-voting is perfectly rational. A rational understanding of voting allows us to appreciate that in any event, voting is primarily a symbolic act. Non-voting is therefore an acceptable way of symbolically expressing one's refusal to accept the choices presented. A true democracy should accept such symbolic expressions of disagreement.

7. Learn about something.

Studies show that most people don't learn about political issues in depth. When someone does get riled up enough to want to research a political issue, it is pretty likely that partisan bias and confirmation bias will lead that person to highly-biased sources. Thus we have a polity that is principally composed of citizens who are either ignorant or irrevocably biased.

Don't fall into this trap. Learn about political issues in depth, making sure to give equal time to opposing viewpoints.

8. If we want more representation of women and minorities, we will have to be willing to experiment with new democratic mechanisms.

I have argued that there is an inherent sexist bias in electoral politics. An analogous bias exists against racial minorities. If we want more representation of women and minorities, we will not soon achieve it through traditional electoral means. When qualified women and minority candidates appear, they will tend to face rationalized objections, a cover-up for subterranean sexism and racism. Citizen panels and direct democracy provide a necessary alternative to government by a biased elite.

9. Don't try to export democracy.

In the Founders' terminology, we are not a democracy, we are a republic. Since we do not have democracy, we cannot really export it. Indeed, our attempts to "export democracy" have been hampered by our own linguistic self-hypnosis. So-called modern democracies are really enlightened oligarchies. Those countries that we call most "advanced" are the ones where the oligarchies play by the rules. However, for republican government to work, the law-abiding oligarchies themselves must already be in place, and if they are not ready for the importation of republican power-sharing, the results will be disappointing. Thus in the late 20th century we have seen the growth of sham democracy and even democratically-induced civil war. It is not that the citizens are not ready for democracy, but that their oligarchs are too immature to share power.

10. Build utopia slowly and cautiously.

Public disgust with the failures of our current system often leads to broad, utopian proposals to "turn government over to the citizens." However, all our research indicates that the citizens as a whole are genetically-predisposed to partisan conflict, and are therefore susceptible to demagoguery.

Reformers should therefore learn to accept the constraints of biology and human nature. Moreover, the protean capacity of powerful elites to manipulate government reforms to their advantage suggests that we should proceed carefully, lest we make things worse than they already are. The best way forward is to experiment cautiously with different ways of increasing the participation of ordinary citizens in real democratic decision-making. From amongst the alternatives available, the increased use of citizen panels seems like the most promising experiment.

NOTES

Chapter 1

1 The modern theory of political irrationality has rich historical roots. It has, for example, classical antecedents in the work of many early philosophers, such as Plato (e.g., *The Republic,* with its enduring metaphor of the irrational cave-theater that so eerily presages our own flat-screened cocoons, and *The Apology,* with its implicit condemnation of the criminal irrationality of the citizenry in condemning to death its greatest citizen, Socrates) and Aristotle (whose rational classification of governments into monarchies, oligarchies and democracies was history's first systematic debunking of political nonsense). Thomas Hobbes's *Leviathan* contributed the viewpoint that society requires mechanisms for negotiating the perpetual clash of self-interests, but he viewed the basis of this struggle as an individual one, and failed to capture the extent to which civil conflict is caused by tribal, partisan or ethnic allegiances. The great French aphorist, La Rochefoucauld, was a keen observer of the ability of personal self-interest to skew perception, anticipating the work of cognitive psychologists by several centuries. At the founding of the United States, James Madison argued strongly for a dispersed, diffuse system of government, in which committees of elites were delicately counter-balanced against each other, because he felt that any other course would lead either to monarchy or to true democracy (which he feared would give the irrational masses control of the government, leading in turn to chaos and ruin); see particularly *Federalist Paper* No. 10 (Hamilton, 1787). Ralph Waldo Emerson, Henry David Thoreau and Friedrich Nietzsche are re-

membered for their intense dedication to intellectual autonomy; each believed that intellectual independence requires freedom from irrational partisanship and cant. The great Austrian-American economist, Joseph Schumpeter brought his profession's capacity for sober observation to bear on the issue of citizen irrationality, observing simply that since most citizens did not show any understanding of political affairs, it was evidently fallacious to attribute the operation of modern, so-called "democracies" to the people's will. For Schumpeter, what we call democracy is not characterized by the expression of the popular will (which is either irrational or non-existent) but by an orderly and lawful alternation between different kinds of elites (see Schumpeter, 1942). Kenneth Arrow's Impossibility Theorem, and Anthony Downs' economic analysis of democracy, provided us with a new rational framework for the analysis of politics, and new paradoxes of irrationality to decipher. The tools of cognitive psychology, particularly the "heuristics and biases" approach developed by Daniel Kahneman and Amos Tversky (see Kahneman, 2002), have enabled contemporary social scientists and political philosophers to analyze political irrationality in great depth and with increasing precision. See, especially, Tyler Cowen's paper, "Self-Deception as the Root of Political Failure," (2003), and Michael Huemer's "Why People are Irrational about Politics" (2008). The psychological and biological roots of political irrationality have been brought to popular attention through the work of journalists such as *New York Times* columnists Nicholas Kristof and David Brooks and *Newsweek* science writer Sharon Begley. See, for example, Begley's article, "When It's Head Versus Heart, The Heart Wins," (Begley, 2008), and Bryan Caplan's "The Myth of the Rational Voter."

2 The study which used twin data to determine whether politics are inherited is John R. Alford, Carolyn L. Funk and John R. Hibbing's "Are Political Orientations Genetically Transmitted?" Alford, 2005). A variety of press articles reported on the study and interviewed the authors, including Benedict Carey's "Some Politics May Be Etched in the Genes," *New York Times*, June 21, 2005, and Mathew Hansen's "University of Nebraska Political Scientist says Genetics, Politics Linked," *Lincoln Journal Star*, June 23, 2005.

3 For an analysis of the evolutionary psychology of politics, see Paul H. Rubin, *Darwinian Politics: The Evolutionary Origin of Freedom* (2002).

4 For an interesting discussion of how beliefs are like clothing, see Robin Hanson, "Enhancing Our Truth Orientation," (2004).

5 See, for example, James Q. Wilson, Political Organizations (1973).

6 See Ellen Langer, *Mindfulness: Choice and Control in Everyday Life* (1989). Langer's work is a thoughtful exploration of the human potential to counteract innate irrationality. A number of experimental psychologists are now seeking to establish to what extent it is possible to learn to override our own prejudices and biases.

7 Nolan McCarty, Keith Poole and Howard Rosenthal reported that Congressional polarization varies directly with internal economic stress; their research involved a historical analysis of Congressional votes, as set forth in "Polarized America: The Dance of Ideology and Unequal Riches" (2006).

8 Karen Kaufman, "The Gender Gap," *Political Science and Politics* (2006).

9 Anthony Downs, *An Economic Theory of Democracy* (1947).

10 Reported by James Q. Wilson in "How Divided Are We?" *Commentary* (2006).

Chapter 2

11 Soon, Brass, Heinze and Haynes, "Unconscious Determinants of Free Decisions in the Human Brain," *Nature Neuroscience* 11, p. 543–545 (2008).

12 See generally, Joseph Ledoux, *The Emotional Brain: The Mysterious Underpinnings of Human Life* (1996).

13 Gerd Gigerenzer, *Gut Feelings: The Intelligence of the Unconscious* (2007).

14 See, for example, Paul Ekman, *Emotions Revealed: Recognizing Faces and Feelings to Improve Communication and Emotional Life* (2003).

15 Martha Stout, *The Paranoia Switch* (2007).

16 See "Are We Happy Yet?" Pew Research Center Study, February 13, 2006, http://pewresearch.org/pubs/301/are-we-happy-yet, last accessed March 29, 2009.

17 Paul Slovic, Melissa L. Finucane, Ellen Peters and Donald McGregor, "Risk as Analysis and Risk as Feelings: Some Thoughts About Affect, Reason, Risk and Rationality" (2002), p. 3–4.

18 See generally Kahneman, *Id.* (2002).

19 For a number of examples of research on cognitive bias see Cordelia Fine, *A Mind of Its Own: How Your Brain Distorts and Deceives* (2006), p. 3–29.

20 Philip Tetlock, *Expert Political Judgment* (2007).

21 Brad Pinter and Anthony Greenwald, "Exploring Implicit Partisanship: Enigmatic But Genuine Group Attraction and Identification" (2002).

22 Anthony Greenwald and Linda Hamilton Krieger, "Implicit Bias: Scientific Foundations," *California Law Review* (2006).

23 See Stanley Milgram, *Obedience to Authority* (1974).

24 C.G. Lord, L. Ross and M.R. Lepper, "Biased Assimilation and Attitude Polarization: The Effects of Prior Theories on Subsequently Considered Evidence," *Journal of Personality and Social Psychology*, 37: 2098–2109 (1979).

Chapter 3

25 Daniel Kahneman and Jonathan Renshon, "Why Hawks Win," *Foreign Policy* (January/February 2007).

26 *Id.*, p. 1.

27 Dominic Johnson, *Overconfidence and War* (2004).

28 Bryan Caplan, *The Myth of The Rational Voter: Why Democracies Choose Bad Policies*, p. 23–49.

Chapter 4

29 Alford, Hibbing and Funk (2005).

30 *Id.*

31 Hulda Thorisdottir, John T. Jost, Ido Liviatan and Patrick E. Shrout, *Psychological Needs and Values Underlying Left-Right Orientation: Cross-National Evidence from Eastern and Western Europe* (2007), p. 177.

32 For a clear introduction to Maynard Smith's work, see David Sloan Wilson, *Evolution for Everyone: How Darwin's Theory Can Change the Way We Think About Our Lives* (2007).

33 Bouchard's research is nicely summarized by William Wright in *Born That Way: Genes, Behavior, Personality*, pp. 34–45, 62–76.

34 James H. Fowler and Cindy Kam, "Beyond the Self: Social Identity, Altruism and Political Participation" (2008).

35 Vedantam, Shankar "Study Ties Political Leanings to Hidden Biases," *Washington Post*, January 30, 2006. See generally Westen (2007). The experiment in which partisans were subjected to MRI-scans was first described in an official Emory University press release entitled "Emory Study Lights Up the Political Brain," issued on January 24, 2006. The

results of Dr. Drew Westen's research were presented at the 2006 Annual Conference of the Society for Personality and Social Psychology.

36 The Implicit Association Test (IAT) was developed by a team of psychologists including Anthony Greenwald and Mahzarin Banaji. One of Banaji's academic papers on implicit association is "The development of implicit attitudes: Evidence of race evaluations from ages 6, 10 & adulthood," *Psychological Science* (2005). Readers who are brave enough to explore their own implicit prejudices and biases are encouraged to take the quick tests available on the IAT website at: https://implicit.harvard.edu/implicit/demo/.

37 Vedantam, p. 2.

Chapter 5

38 Frans De Waal recounts this story from different perspectives in various books, including *Chimpanzee Politics* (1982), *The Human Ape* (2005) and *Primates and Philosophers* (2007).

39 Rubin (2002), p. 5–8.

40 James H. Fowler, Christopher Dawes and Laura Baker, "Genetic Variation in Political Participation," *The Journal of Politics*, 69: 813–827 (2008).

41 *Id.* (2008).

42 Richard Dawkins, *The Selfish Gene* (1974).

43 For a thorough exposition of the evolutionary psychology of hostility toward out-groups, see Richard Wrangham and Dale Peterson, *Demonic Males: Apes and the Origins of Human Violence* (1996) and David Buss, *The Murderer Next Door: Why the Mind is Designed to Kill* (2005).

44 Frans De Waal, *Our Inner Ape* (2005).

45 For a discussion of the evolutionary origins of deception and self-deception, see Robert L. Trivers, "The Evolution of Reciprocal Altruism," *Quarterly Review of Biology*, 46: 35–37 (1971).

46 For a discussion of the asymmetrical nature of male and female reproductive strategies, see Robert L. Trivers, "Parental Investment and Sexual Selection," in B. Campbell, *Sexual Selection and the Descent of Man* (1972).

47 This research was summarized and interpreted by Roy R. Baumeister in "Is There Anything Good About Men?" denisdutton.com, (2007).

48 Aristotle, *Rhetoric*, Book II.

49 Ruth Mace, "Evolutionary Psychology of Human Life History," *Animal Behaviour* (2000).

50 For a thorough account of Margaret Mead's fall from academic grace, as well as a history of the battle between cultural and biological determinism, see Derek Freeman, *Margaret Mead and Samoa: The Making and Unmaking of an Anthropological Myth* (1983).

51 Louann Brizendine, *The Female Brain* (2006), p. 11–56.

Chapter 6

52 Robert Sapolsky, "Are the Desert People Winning?" *Discover Magazine* (2005).

53 *Id.*

54 All of the data on international comparison of cultural dimensions is drawn from Geert Hofstede, *Cultures and Organizations: Software of the Mind* (2005).

55 Robert Levine, *A Geography of Time*, pp. 131–163 (1997).

66 George Lakoff, *Moral Politics*, p. 366 (1996).

Chapter 7

67 Thomas Frank, *What's the Matter with Kansas? How Conservatives Won the Heart of America*, pp. 1–67 (2004).

58 Morris P. Fiorina, Samuel J. Abrams and Jeremy C. Pope, *Culture War? The Myth of a Polarized America* (2004).

69 McCarty, Poole and Rosenthal (2006), pp. 1–14.

Chapter 8

60 Anthony Downs, *An Economic Theory of Democracy* (1957). For an overview of rational choice methods in the analysis of voting behavior, see Kenneth A. Shepsle and Mark S. Bonchek, *Analyzing Politics: Rationality, Behavior and Institutions*, pp. 5–136 (1997).

61 The influential political scientist William Riker's thinking on democracy and voter behavior is developed in works such as *The Theory of Political Coalitions* (1962), *Liberalism Against Populism* (1982) and *The Art of Political Manipulation* (1986). Riker essentially argues that it is irrational to believe that a legislature can somehow represent an unformulated popular will; consequently, democracy is merely an arena for contending elites who produce positive externalities only insofar as this is nec-

essary for their own advancement. For a relentless attack on Riker's thinking, and on the theory of democratic irrationalism in general, see Gerry Mackie, *Democracy Defended* (2003). I believe that Mackie is on the whole correct to argue that rational choice critiques *à la* Riker fail to capture aspects of the electoral process which permit citizen preferences to be communicated to policy-makers. In other words, Mackie is right that democracy is theoretically possible despite the Arrow theorem, and he is further right that there are some elections that can be pointed to as having communicated something important about the citizenry's desires. However, that is only half the story, the rational half. Mackie does not deal with the overwhelming evidence for the presence of endemic irrationality in the political system, nor he does he deal with the critique which has been contributed by cognitive psychology and behavioral economics.

62 Samuel Abrams, Torben Iversen and David Soskice, "Interests, Parties and Social Embeddedness: Why Rational People Vote," American Political Science Association Annual Conference (2005).

63 *Id.*

64 Frans De Waal, *Chimpanzee Politics*, p. 89 (1982, 1989, 1998).

65 Jennifer Hochschild, "Where You Stand Depends on What You See: Connections Among Values, Perceptions of Fact, and Political Prescriptions," in *Citizens and Politics: Perspectives from Political Psychology*, ed. James H. Kuklinski (2001).

66 Steven Hill, *Fixing Elections: The Failure of America's Winner Take All Politics* (2002).

67 James Fishkin, *The Voice of the People: Public Opinion and Democracy* (1997).

Chapter 9

68 Alexander Hamilton, John Jay and James Madison, *The Federalist Papers* (1787), p. 55–56.

69 *Id.* at 58–59.

70 Sheldon Wolin, "Democracy: Electoral and Athenian," *Political Science and Politics* (1993)

71 Francis Dupuis-Deri, "The Political Power of Words: The Birth of Pro-Democratic Discourse in the United States and France in the Nineteenth Century," *Political Studies* (2004).

72 *Id.*

73 Wolin (1993).

74 Dupuis-Deri (2004).

75 Hibbing and Theiss-Morse (2002).

76 Dawkins (1976); for an engaging and somewhat trippy introduction to the concept of the meme see Susan Blackmore's *The Meme Machine* (1999).

77 This story, recounting the initial reaction of Amartya Sen to Kenneth Arrow's 1951 *Social Choice and Invididual Values*, is found in Sen's *Nobel Prize Autobiography*. Stockholm: 1998.

78 Paul Samuelson's lament on the reach of Arrow's Theorem is quoted in *Archimedes' Revenge*, by Paul Hoffman (Fawcett Crest, New York, 1993), pp. 215.

79 Gerry Mackie, *Democracy Defended* (2003).

Chapter 10

80 Wolin (1993).

81 Frans De Waal, *Our Inner Ape*, p. 84 (2005).

82 Ronald Kessler, *Inside Congress: The Shocking Scandals, Corruption and Abuse of Power on Capital Hill* (1998), p.4

83 "A Monstrous Regiment," Television Documentary, British Broadcasting Corporation (2005).

84 John Derbyshire, "Smartocracy," National Review Online (2008).

85 David Lempert, "Women's Increasing Wage-Penalties From Being Overweight and Obese," *U.S. Bureau of Labor Statistics* (2008).

Chapter 11

86 For a review of a number of studies dealing with perceived social preferences for tall men, see Robert B. Cialdini, *Influence: Science and Practice* (2001).

87 Stanford W. Gregory and Timothy Gallagher, "Spectral Analysis of Candidates' Vocal Communication: Predicting U.S. Presidential Election Outcomes," *Social Psychology Quarterly* (2002).

88 Lee Sigelman (1990).

89 George Packer, *New Yorker*, (January 28, 2008).

90 Brad T. Gomez, Thomas G. Hansford and George A. Krause, "The Republicans Should Pray for Rain: Weather, Turnout and Voting in the

U.S. Presidential Elections," *Journal of Politics* 69: 649–663 (2007).

[91] Ray Fair, "Econometrics and Presidential Elections," *Journal of Economic Perspectives*, 10: 89–102 (1996).

[92] Samuel L. Popkin, *The Reasoning Voter: Communication and Persuasion in Presidential Campaigns* (1991).

[93] Ansolabehere and Iyengar (2005).

[94] Joseph A. Schumpeter, *Capitalism, Socialism and Democracy* (1942).

[95] Lizza, Ryan, "Making It: How Chicago Shaped Obama," *The New Yorker*, July 21, 2008.

[96] Sweet, Frank M. "Features of Today's One-Drop Rule" (2005). http://backintyme.com/essays/?p=14 Last accessed Jan. 12, 2009.

[97] Swarns, Rachel L., *New York Times*, Aug. 29, 2004, "Definition of 'African-American' Becomes Issue of Heritage."

[98] Bird, J.B. "Rebellion" – a web-based documentary. http://www.john-horse.com/black-seminoles/faq-black-seminoles.htm Last accessed Jan. 12, 2009.

[99] The cited studies on colorism and the quotation are from Hochschild, Jennifer and Weaver, Vesla, "The Skin Color Paradox and the American Racial Order," *Social Forces*, Volume 86, No. 2, December 2007, p. 14.

Chapter 13

[100] Alex Barker, "Brown Sets Up Citizen Juries," *Financial Times* (September 4, 2007).

[101] Jo Revill, "Sham Juries Face Controls," *The Observer* (September 30, 2007).

[102] Nicholas Wood, "To Invigorate Public Interest, Bulgaria Invites 255 for a Day of Intense Democracy," *New York Times* (May 7, 2007).

[103] John G. Matsusaka, "Direct Democracy Works," *The Journal of Economic Perspectives*, 19: 185–206 (2005).

For comments on, and updates or corrections to the Notes
and Bibliography, please consult this book's companion website:
www.redgenesbluegenes.com

BIBLIOGRAPHY

Abrams, Samuel, Torben Iversen and David Soskice. 2005. "Interests, Parties and Social Embeddedness: Why Rational People Vote." American Political Science Association Conference.

Ackerman, Bruce and James Fishkin. 2003. "Deliberation Day." Internet: http://www.ssc.wisc.edu/~wright/deliberation%20day.pdf Last accessed: July 20, 2008.

Alford, John R., Carolyn L. Funk and John R. Hibbing. 2005. "Are Political Orientations Genetically Transmitted?" *American Political Science Review:* Vol. 99, No. 2.

Ariely, Dan. 2008. *Predictably Irrational: The Hidden Forces That Shape Our Decisions.* New York: HarperCollins.

Aristotle. *Rhetoric.* Translation by W. Rhys Roberts. Web edition made available by Lee Honeycutt at: http://www.public.iastate.edu/~honeyl/Rhetoric/index.html. Last accessed July 28, 2008.

Barker, Alex. 2007. "Brown sets up citizen juries to shape policy." *Financial Times,* National News: September 4, 2007.

Baumeister, Roy R. 2007 "Is There Anything Good About Men?" Denis Dutton: www.denisdutton.com. Last accessed July 30, 2008.

Beard, Charles A. 1913. *An Economic Interpretation of the State.* New York: MacMillan.

Begley, Sharon. 2008. "When It's Head Versus Heart, The Heart Wins." *Newsweek:* February 2, 2008.

Berman, Morris. 2006. *Dark Ages America: The Final Phrase of Empire.* New York: W. W. Norton & Company, Inc.

Bird, J.B. "Rebellion," a web-based documentary," http://www.johnhorse.

com/black-seminoles/faq-black-seminoles.htm" Last accessed Jan. 12, 2009. The cited studies on colorism and the quotation are from Hochschild, Jennifer and Weaver, Vesla. The Skin Color Paradox and the American Racial Order. Social Forces, Volume 86, No. 2, December 2007, p. 14.

Blackmore, Susan. 1999. *The Meme Machine.* New York: Oxford University Press.

Brafman, Ori and Rom Brafman. 2008. *Sway: The Irresistible Pull of Irrational Behavior.* New York: Doubleday.

British Broadcasting Corporation. 2005. "A Monstrous Regiment." Radio Broadcast.

Brizendine, Louann. 2006. *The Female Brain.* New York: Broadway Books.

Broder, David S. 2000. *Democracy Derailed: Initiative Campaigns and the Power of Money.* New York: Harcourt, Inc.

Burton, Robert A. 2008. *On Being Certain: Believing You Are Right Even When You Are Not.* New York: St. Martin's Press.

Buss, David M. 2005. *The Murderer Next Door: Why The Mind Is Designed To Kill.* New York: The Penguin Press.

Caplan, Bryan. 2007. *The Myth of the Rational Voter: Why Democracies Choose Bad Policies.* Princeton: Princeton University Press.

Carpenter, Siri. 2008. "Buried Prejudice." *Scientific American Mind.* Vol. 19: p. 33–39.

Chua, Amy. 2003. *World on Fire: How Exporting Democracy Breeds Ethnic Hatred and Global Instability.* New York: Doubleday.

Cialdini, Robert B. 2001. *Influence: Science and Practice.* Needham Heights: Allyn & Bacon.

Cosmides, Leda and John Tooby. 1994. "Better than Rational: Evolutionary Psychology and the Invisible Hand." *American Economic Review.* Vol. 84, No. 2, p. 327–332.

Cowen, Tyler. 2003. "Self-Deception as the Root of Political Failure." Website last accessed July 28, 2008: http://www.gmu.edu/jbc/Tyler/PrideandSelf.pdf

Cutler, Fred. 2002. "The Simplest Shortcut of All: Sociodemographic Characteristics and Electoral Choice." *The Journal of Politics,* vol. 62, No. 2, May 2002, pp. 466-490.

Dawkins, Richard. 1974. *The Selfish Gene.* New York: Oxford University Press.

Dean, John W. 2007. *Broken Government: How Republican Rule Destroyed the Legislative, Executive and Judicial Branches.* New York: Viking.

Delli Carpini, Michael X. and Scott Keefer. 1996. *What Americans Know About Politics and Why It Matters.* New Haven: Yale University Press.

Derbyshire, John. 2008. "Smartocracy." *National Review Online.* Internet:

http://article.nationalreview.com/?q=NjEzOTM1YmM4ZmYxO-
TExMTg1MTZmODlhZGM0N2RkY2I=.

De Sutter, Pascal. 2007. *Ces Fous Qui Nous Gouvernent: Comment La Psychologie Per-
met de Comprendre Les Hommes Politiques.*

De Waal, Frans. 1982, 1989, 1998. *Chimpanzee Politics: Power and Sex Among Apes.*
New York: Harper & Row.

— 2005. *Our Inner Ape.* New York: Berkley Publishing.

— 2006. *Primates and Philosophers: How Morality Evolved.* New Jersey: Princeton
University Press.

Didion, Joan. 2001. *Political Fictions.* New York: Alfred A. Knopf.

Dowbiggin, Ian Robert. 2003. *Keeping America Sane: Psychiatry and Eugenics in the
United States and Canada 1880–1940.* Ithaca: Cornell University Press.

Dowd, Maureen. 2008. *New York Times,* Op-Ed, January.

Downs, Anthony. 1947. *An Economic Theory of Democracy.* Boston, Mass: Addison-
Wesley.

Dunbar, Robin, Louis Barrett and John Lycett. *Evolutionary Psychology: A Beginner's Guide.* Oxford, UK: Oneworld.

Dupuis-Deri, Francis. 2004. "The Political Power of Words: The Birth of Pro-
Democratic Discourse in the United States and France in the Nineteenth
Century." *Politcal Studies:* 2004, Vol. 52, 118–34.

Dutton, Denis. 2003. "Darwin and Political Theory." *Philosophy and Literature:*
Vol. 27: 241–254.

Dworkin, Ronald. 2006. *Is Democracy Possible Here? Principles for a New Political
Debate.* Princeton, NJ: Princeton University Press.

Ekman, Paul. 2001. *Emotions Revealed: Recognizing Faces and Feelings to Improve
Communication and Emotional Life.* New York: Times Books.

Ellis, Joseph J. 2007. *American Creation: Triumphs and Tragedies of the Republic.*
New York: Knopf.

Fair, Ray. 1996. "Econometrics and Presidential Elections." *Journal of Economic
Perspectives,* Vol.10, No. 3, pp. 89–102.

Faux, Jeff. 2006. *The Global Class War: How America's Bipartisan Elite Lost Our Future — and What it Will Take to Win It Back.* Hoboken, NJ: John Wiley &
Sons.

Fine, Cordelia. 2006. *A Mind of its Own: How Your Brain Distorts and Deceives.* New
York: W.W. Norton.

Fiorina, Morris P., Samuel J. Abrams and Jeremy C. Pope. 2005. *Culture War?
The Myth of a Polarized America.* New York: Pearson Longman.

Fishkin, James. 1997. *The Voice of the People: Public Opinion and Democracy.* New
Haven: Yale University Press.

Fowler, James H. and Christopher Dawes. 2008. "Two Genes Predict Voter Turnout." *The Journal of Politics*, Vol. 70, No. 3, pp. 579–594.

Fowler, James H., Christopher Dawes and Laura Baker. 2008. "Genetic Variation in Political Participation." *American Political Science Review*, Vol. 102, No. 2, p. 233–248.

Fowler, James H. and Cindy Kam. 2007. "Beyond the Self: Social Identity, Altruism and Political Participation." *The Journal of Politics*, Vol. 69, No. 3, pp. 813–827.

Frank, Thomas. 2004. *What's The Matter With Kansas? How Conservatives Won the Heart of America.* New York: Henry Holt and Company.

Franken, Al. 2005. *The Truth (With Jokes).* New York: Dutton.

Freeman, Derek. 1983. *Margaret Mead and Samoa: The Making and Unmaking of an Anthropological Myth.* Cambridge: Harvard University Press.

Galton, Francis. 1869. *Hereditary Genius.*

Gigerenzer, Gerd. 2007. *Gut Feelings: The Intelligence of the Unconscious.* New York: Penguin.

Gilovich, Thomas. 1991. *How We Know What Isn't So: The Fallibility of Human Reason in Everyday Life.* New York: The Free Press.

Ginsberg, Benjamin, and Alan Stone, Eds. 1991. *Do Elections Matter?* Armonk, NY: M.E. Sharpe

Gladwell, Malcolm. 2005. *Blink: The Power of Thinking Without Thinking.* New York: Little, Brown and Company.

Gomez, Brad T., Thomas G. Hansford and George A. Krause. 2007. "The Republicans Should Pray for Rain: Weather, Turnout and Voting the U.S. Presidential Elections." *Journal of Politics*, Vol. 69, Issue 3, pp. 649–663.

Gore, Al. 2007. *The Assault on Reason.* New York: Penguin Press.

Goleman, Daniel. 1995. *Emotional Intelligence.* New York: Bantam Publishing.

Green, Donald with Bradley Palmquist and Eric Schickler. 2002. *Partisan Hearts and Minds: Political Parties and the Social Identities of Voters.* New Haven: Yale University Press.

Green, Mark with James Fallows and David R. Zwick. 1972. *Who Runs Congress? The President, Big Business, or You?* New York: Bantam Books.

Greenwald, Anthony and Linda Hamilton Krieger. 2006. "Implicit Bias: Scientific Foundations." *California Law Review*, July 2006.

Gregory, Stanford W. and Timothy Gallagher. 2002. "Spectral Analysis of Candidates' Vocal Communication: Predicting U.S. Presidential Election Outcomes." *Social Psychology Quarterly*, Vol. 65, No. 3, pp. 298–308.

Gumbel, Andrew. 2005. *Steal This Vote: Dirty Elections and the Rotten History of Democracy in America.* New York: Nation Books.

Haidt, Jonathan. 2006. *The Happiness Hypothesis.* New York: Basic Books.

Hamilton, Alexander, John Jay and James Madison. 1787. *The Federalist.* New York: Modern Library Edition.

Hanson, Robin. 2004. "Enhancing Our Truth Orientation." Website: http://hanson.gmu.edu/moretrue.pdf Last accessed: July 27, 2008.

Hauser, Marc D. 2006. *Moral Minds: How Nature Designed Our Universal Sense of Right and Wrong.* New York: HarperCollins.

Hibbing, John R. and Elizabeth Theiss-Morse. 2002. *Stealth Democracy: Americans' Beliefs about How Government Should Work.* New York: Cambridge University Press.

Hibbing, John R. and Kevin B. Smith. 2007. "The Biology of Political Behavior: An Introduction." *Annals, AAPSS.* Vol. 614, November 2007.

Hill, Steven. 2002. *Fixing Elections: The Failure of America' Winner Take All Politics.* New York: Routledge.

Hirschman, Albert O. 1977. *The Passions and the Interests: Political Arguments for Capitalism Before Its Triumph.* Princeton, NJ: Princeton University Press.

Hochschild, Jennifer. 2001. "Where You Stand Depends on What You See: Connections among Values, Perceptions of Fact, and Political Prescriptions." *Citizens and Politics: Perspectives from Political Psychology,* ed. James H. Kuklinski. Cambridge: Cambridge University Press.

Hofstede, Geert. 2005. *Cultures and Organizations: Software of the Mind.* New York: McGraw Hill.

Hudson, William E. 2001. *American Democracy in Peril: Seven Challenges To America's Future.* New York: Seven Bridges Press.

Huemer, Michael. 2008. Why People are Irrational About Politics. http://home.sprynet.com/~owl1/irrationality.htm. Last accessed July 28, 2008.

Johnson, Dominic. 2004. *Overconfidence and War.* Cambridge: Harvard University Press.

Johnson, Steven. 2004. *Mind Wide Open: Your Brain and the Neuroscience of Everyday Life.* New York: Scribner.

Joseph, R. 1993. *The Naked Neuron: Evolution and the Languages of the Brain and Body.* New York: Plenum Publishing.

Kahneman, Daniel. 2002. "Maps of Bounded Rationality: A Perspective on Intuitive Judgment and Choice." Nobel Prize Lecture.

Kahneman, Daniel and Jonathan Renshon. 2007. "Why Hawks Win." *Foreign Policy,* January/February 2007. http://www.foreignpolicy.com/story/cms.php?story_id=3660

Kaminer, Wendy. 1999. *Sleeping with Extra-Terrestrials: The Rise of Irrationalism and Perils of Piety.* New York: Random House.

Kaufman, Karen. 2006. "The Gender Gap." *Political Science and Politics,* July, 2006.

Key, V.O. 1966. *The Responsible Electorate*. Cambridge, Mass: Harvard University Press.

Kessler, Ronald. 1997. *Inside Congress: The Shocking Scandals, Corruption and Abuse of Power on Capital Hill*. New York: Simon & Schuster.

Klein, Joe. 2006. *Politics Lost: How American Democracy Was Trivialized by People Who Think You're Stupid*. New York: Doubleday.

Langer, Ellen. 1989. *Mindfulness: Choice and Control in Everyday Life*. New Jersey: Addison-Wesley.

Lakoff, George. 2008. *The Political Mind: Why You Can't Understand 21st-Century American Politics with an 18th-Century Brain*. New York: Viking Penguin.

Lakoff, George. 2006. *Whose Freedom: The Battle over America's Most Important Idea*. New York: Farrar, Straus and Giroux.

Lau, Richard. 2006. *How Voters Decide*.

Lau, Richard and David P. Redlawsk. 2001. "Advantages and Disadvantages of Cognitive Heuristics in Political Decision-Making." *American Journal of Political Science*, Vol. 45, No. 4, pp. 951–971.

Ledoux, Joseph. 1996. *The Emotional Brain. The Mysterious Underpinnings of Emotional Life*. Simon & Schuster.

Lempert, David. 2008. "Women's Increasing Wage-Penalties From Being Overweight and Obese." U.S. Bureau of Labor Statistics. Reported in *Atlantic Monthly*, March 2008, p. 32.

Lewis, Justin. 2001. *Constructing Public Opinion: How Political Elites Do What They Like and Why We Seem to Go Along With It*. New York: Columbia University Press.

Levine, Robert. 1997. *A Geography of Time*. New York: HarperCollins.

Lipset, Seymour and Stein Rokkan, eds. 1967. *Party Systems and Voter Alignments: Cross-National Perspectives*. New York: The Free Press.

Lizza, Ryan. "Making It: How Chicago Shaped Obama," *The New Yorker*, July 21, 2008.

Lord, C. G., Ross, L., & Lepper, M. R. 1979. "Biased assimilation and attitude polarization: The effects of prior theories on subsequently considered evidence." *Journal of Personality and Social Psychology, 37*, 2098–2109.

Lukacs, John. 1984, 2004. *A New Republic: A History of the United States in the Twentieth Century*. New Haven: Yale University Press.

Mace, Ruth. 2000. "Evolutionary ecology of human life history." *Animal Behaviour, 59*: 1–10.

Macedo, Stephen and others. 2006. *Democracy at Risk: How Political Choices Undermine Citizen Participation, and What We Can Do About it*. Washington, D.C.: The Brookings Institution.

Mackie, Gerry. 2003. *Democracy Defended*. Cambridge: Cambridge University

Press.

Madison, James. 1787. *The Constitutional Convention – A Narrative History from the Notes of James Madison.* New York: The Modern Library.

Marcus, Gary. 2008. *Kluge: The Haphazard Construction of the Human Mind.* New York: Houghton Mifflin.

Marcus, George E. 2003. *The Sentimental Citizen: Emotion in Democratic Politics.* University Park, PA: University of Pennsylvania Press.

Marcus, George E. with W. Russell Neuman and Michael Mackuen. 2000. *Affective Intelligence and Political Judgment.* Chicago, Ill: University of Chicago Press.

Matsusaka, John G. 2005. "Direct Democracy Works." *The Journal of Economic Perspectives.* Vol. 19, No. 2, p. 185–206.

McCarty, Nolan with Keith T. Poole and Howard Rosenthal. 2006. *Polarized America: The Dance of Ideology and Unequal Riches.* Cambridge, MA: The MIT Press.

Medearis, John. 2001. *Joseph Schumpter's Two Theories of Democracy.* Cambridge: Harvard University Press.

Milbank, Dana. 2008. *Homo Politicus. The Strange and Scary Tribes That Run Our Government.* New York: Doubleday.

Milgram, Stanley. 1974. *Obedience to Authority.* New York: Harper & Row.

Miller, Alan S. and Satoshi Kanazawa. 2007. *Why Beautiful People Have More Daughters: From Dating, Shopping, and Praying to Going to War and Becoming a Billionaire – Two Evolutionary Psychologists Explain Why We Do What We Do.* New York: Penguin Group.

Montanye, James A. 2006. "The Apotheosis of American Democracy." *The Independent Review.* Vol. 11, No. 1, pp. 5–17.

Norris, Pippa. 2000. *Political Communications in Postindustrial Societies.* Cambridge, UK: Cambridge University Press.

O'Donnell, Erin. 2006. "Twigs Bent Left or Right: Understanding How Liberals and Conservatives Differ, From Conception On." *Harvard Magazine:* January–February, 2006, p. 34–39.

O'Leary, Kevin. 2006. *Saving Democracy: A Plan for Real Representation in America.* Stanford, CA: Stanford Law and Politics.

Osler, William. 1903. *The Principles and Practice of Medicine.* New York: D. Appleton and Company.

Packer, George. 2008. "Campaign Coverage." *The New Yorker,* January 28, 2008, p. 30.

Palast, Greg. 2003. *The Best Democracy Money Can Buy: The Truth About Corporate Cons, Globalization and High-Finance Fraudsters.* New York: Penguin Books.

Peirce, Neal R. and Lawrence D. Longley. 1968, 1981. *The People's President: The Electoral College in American History and the Direct Vote Alternative.* New Haven:

Yale University Press.

Pinter, Brad and Anthony Greenwald. 2002. "Exploring Implicit Partisanship: Enigmatic But Genuine Group Attraction and Identification."

Popkin, Samuel L. 1991. *The Reasoning Voter: Communication and Persuasion in Presidential Campaigns.* Chicago, Ill: University of Chicago Press.

Prisching, Manfred. 1995. "The Limited Rationality of Democracy: Schumpeter as the Founder of Irrational Choice Theory." *Critical Review,* Vol. 9, No. 3, pp. 301–324.

Revil, Jo. 2007. "'Sham' Juries Face Controls." *The Observer,* September 30, 2007.

Ridley, Matt. 2003. *Nature via Nurture: Genes, Experience and What Makes us Human.* New York: HarperCollins.

Rubin, Paul H. 2002. *Darwinian Politics: The Evolutionary Origins of Freedom.* Piscataway: Rutgers University Press.

Rush, Mark and Richard L. Engstrom. 2001. *Fair And Effective Represenation? Debating Electoral Reform and Minority Rights.* Lanham, MD: Rowman & Littlefield Publishers.

Rushton, J. Philippe. 2005. "Ethnic nationalism, evolutionary psychology, and Genetic Similarity Theory." *Nations and Nationalism* 11 (4), p. 489–507.

Sanders, Arthur. 2007. *Losing Control: Presidential Elections and the Decline of Democracy.* New York: Peter Lang.

Sapolsky, Robert. 2005. "Are the Desert People Winning?" *Discover* magazine.

Schattschneider, E.E. 1960. *The Semi-Sovereign People: A Realist's View of Democracy in America.* New York: Holt, Rinehart and Winston.

Schumpeter, Joseph A. 1942, 1947. *Capitalism, Socialism and Democracy.* New York: HarperPerennial.

Sears, David O., and Funk, Carolyn. 1999. "Evidence of the Long-Term Persistence of Political Predispositions." *The Journal of Politics,* Vol. 61, No. 1 (Feb., 1999), pp. 1–28

Shermer, Michael. 2004. *The Science of Good & Evil: Why People Cheat, Gossip, Care, Share and Follow the Golden Rule.* New York: Henry Holt & Company.

Shepsle, Kenneth A. and Mark S. Bonchek. 1997. *Analyzing Politics: Rationality, Behavior and Institutions.* New York: W.W. Norton.

Shweder, Richard A. 1991. *Thinking Through Cultures: Expeditions in Cultural Psychology.* Cambridge, MA: Harvard University Press.

Sinclair, Barbara. 2006. *Party Wars: Polarization and the Politics of National Policy Making.* Norman, OK: University of Oklahoma Press.

Slovic, Paul, Melissa L. Finucane, Ellen Peters and Donald MacGregor. 2002. "Risk as Analysis and Risk as Feelings: Some Thoughts About Affect, Reason, Risk and Rationality." Eugene, OR: Decision Research. www.decisionresearch.org.

Smith, David L. 2004. *Why We Lie: The Evolutionary Roots of Deception and the Unconscious Mind.* New York: St. Martin's Press.

Somit, Albert and Petersen, Steven A. 1999. "Rational Choice and Biopolitics: A (Darwinian) Tale of Two Theories." *Political Science,* March 1999, p. 39–44.

Soon, Chun Siong, Marcel Brass, Hands-Jochen Heinze and John-Dylan Haynes. 2008. "Unconscious determinants of free decisions in the human brain." *Nature Neuroscience* 11, 543–545.

Stout, Martha. 2007. *The Paranoia Switch.* New York: Farrar Strauss & Giroux.

Sweet, Frank M. "Features of Today's One-Drop Rule," (2005). "http://backintyme.com/essays/?p=14" http://backintyme.com/essays/?p=14 Last accessed Jan. 12, 2009..

Surowiecki, James. 2004, 2005. *The Wisdom of Crowds.* New York: Anchor Books.

Sutherland, Stuart. 1992. *Irrationality: Why We Don't Think Straight.* Brunswick, NJ: Rutgers University Press.

Tavris, Carol and Elliot Aronson. 2007. *Mistakes Were Made: Why We Justify Foolish Beliefs, Bad Decisions, and Hurtful Acts.* Orlando: Harcourt Inc.

Tetlock, Philip. 2007. *Expert Political Judgment.* Princeton, NJ: Princeton University Press.

Thaler, Richard H., and Cass R. Sunstein. 2008. *Nudge: Improving Decisions About Health, Wealth, and Happiness.* New Haven: Yale University Press.

Thorisdottir, Hulda and John T. Jost, Ido Liviatan, and Patrick E. Shrout. 2007. "Psychological Needs and Values Underlying Left-Right Orientation: Cross-National Evidence from Eastern and Western Europe." *Public Opinion Quarterly:* Vol. 71, No. 2.

Trivers, R.L. 1971. "The Evolution of Reciprocal Altruism." *Quarterly Review of Biology,* Vol 46: 35–57.

—. 1972. "Parental Investment and Sexual Selection." In B. Campbell, ed. *Sexual Selections and the Descent of Man.* Chicago: Aldine-Atherton, pp. 136–179.

Waldman, Paul. 2006. *Being Right is Not Enough: What Progressives Must Learn from Conservative Success.* Hoboken, NJ: John Wiley & Sons.

Westen, Drew. 2007. *The Political Brain: The Role of Emotion in Deciding the Fate of the Nation.* New York: Public Affairs Press.

Wilson, David Sloan. 2007. *Evolution for Everyone: How Darwin's Theory Can Change the Way We Think About Our Lives.* New York: Random House.

Wilson, James Q. 1973. *Political Organizations.* New York: Basic Books, Inc.

—. 2006. "How Divided are We?" *Commentary,* February 2006.

Wolin, Sheldon. 1993. "Democracy: Electoral and Athenian." *Political Science and Politics.* Vol. 26, No. 3, pp. 475–477.

Wood, Nicholas. 2007. "To Reinvigorate Public Interest, Bulgaria Invites 255 for a Day of Intense Democracy." *New York Times*, May 7, 2007.

Wrangham, Richard and Dale Peterson. 1996. *Demonic Males: Apes and the Origins of Human Violence.* New York: Houghton Mifflin.

Wright, Robert. 1994. *The Moral Animal: Why We Are The Way We Are: The New Science of Evolutionary Psychology.* New York: Pantheon Books.

Wright, William. 1998. *Born That Way: Genes, Behavior, Personality.* New York: Routledge.

Zeigler, Harmon. 1993. *Political Parties in Industrial Democracies.* Itasca, IL: F.E. Peacock Publishers.

INDEX

ABOUT THE AUTHOR

Guillermo C. Jiménez, J.D., is a writer and educator living and working in New York. He became acquainted with bi-cultural perspectives at an early age — his mother was a French-Canadian from Boston, his father a Mexican from Mexico City, and Jimenez grew up in Mexico City, Austin, Texas and Los Angeles, California. Studies in evolutionary biology at Harvard awakened a life-long interest in the evolutionary well-springs of human behavior. His legal studies at the University of California–Berkeley, focused on international law. He spent a dozen years working in France, most of it as an international policy specialist for the International Chamber of Commerce, based in Paris. He has lectured in over 35 countries, and addressed such international organizations as UN–ESCAP, the European Commission and UNCITRAL. As an educator, one of his principal interests is exploring the biological and cultural sources of conflict in group situations. He is a recipient of the SUNY Chancellor's Award for Teaching Excellence and is a former Policy Fellow of the Hispanic Association of Colleges and Universities (HACU). After many years of applying insights from evolutionary psychology to international management and legal disputes, he began to do the same for political disputes. *Red Genes, Blue Genes* is the result; it is his fourth book. He blogs at www.redgenesbluegenes.com.